"Fittingly described by the author as 'a diary of a constitutional scholar,' this book offers an important critical account about key constitutional and political developments that shaped the emergence of 'illiberal democracy' in Hungary in 2010–2011. The analysis reflects an impressive breadth of knowledge coupled with deep commitment to the principles of liberal democracy. The book should be of great interest to scholars, students, and policy-makers interested in the future of democratic government in post-Cold War Europe."

Zsuzsa Csergö, Queen's University, Canada

"Pap's fascinating and timely *Democratic Decline* shows how defensible laws and democratic processes can be used to construct illiberalism. Most interesting is how the Hungarian 'System of National Cooperation,' an ideology that puts the national above the political community and has parallels with other European populisms, impacts an incredible range of policies that serve to privilege Christian, middle-class families and protect the state against individual rights claims."

Stephen Deets, Babson College, USA

"As one of the first and most corrosive expressions of the antiliberal Zeitgeist proliferating across today's world, Viktor Orbán's 'illiberal democracy' should be of concern to every politically responsible citizen in every struggling Western democracy. To understand what is at stake, no English-language work is more timely and more illuminating that András Pap's original and biting analysis of Hungary's plunge into constitutional antiliberalism."

Stephen Holmes, New York University School of Law, USA

AF695535

Democratic Decline in Hungary

This book shows the rise and morphology of a self-identified "illiberal democracy," the first twenty-first-century illiberal political regime arising in the European Union. Since 2010, Viktor Orbán's governments in Hungary have convincingly offered an anti-modernist and anti-cosmopolitan/anti-European Unionist rhetoric, discourse, and constitutional identity to challenge neo-liberal democracy. The Hungarian case provides unique observation points for students of transitology, especially those who are interested in states that are to abandon pathways of liberal democracy.

The author demonstrates how illiberalism is present both in "how" and "what" is being done: the style, format and procedure of legislation as well as the substance: the dismantling of institutional rule-of-law guarantees and the weakening of checks and balances. This book also discusses the ideological commitments and constitutionally framed and cemented value preferences, and a reconstituted and reconceptualized relationship between the state and its citizens, which is not evidently supported by Hungarians' value system and lifestyle choices.

András L. Pap is Research Chair and Head of Department for the Study of Constitutionalism and the Rule of Law, Hungarian Academy of Sciences Centre for Social Sciences, Institute for Legal Studies; he is SASPRO-Marie Skłodowska-Curie Fellow, Institute of Sociology, Slovak Academy of Sciences, Bratislava, Slovakia; Professor of Law, Law Enforcement Faculty, National University of Public Service, Recurrent Visiting (Adjunct) Professor, Nationalism Studies Program, Central European University, and currently on leave from Eötvös University Faculty of Humanities, Institute of Philosophy, Budapest, Hungary.

Comparative Constitutional Change
Series editors:

Xenophon Contiades is Professor of Public Law, School of Social and Political Sciences, University of Peloponnese and Director of the Centre for European Constitutional Law-Themistocles and Dimitris Tsatsos Foundation, Athens, Greece.

Thomas Fleiner is Emeritus Professor of Law at the University of Fribourg, Switzerland. He teaches and researches in the areas of Federalism, Rule of Law, Multicultural State; Comparative Administrative and Constitutional Law; Political Theory and Philosophy; Swiss Constitutional and Administrative Law and Legislative Drafting. He has published widely in these and related areas.

Alkmene Fotiadou is Research Associate at the Centre for European Constitutional Law, Athens.

Richard Albert is a tenured Associate Professor and Dean's Research Scholar at Boston College Law School, USA. He is currently a Visiting Associate Professor of Law and the Canadian Bicentennial Visiting Associate Professor of Political Science at Yale University.

Comparative Constitutional Change has developed into a distinct field of constitutional law. It encompasses the study of constitutions through the way they change and covers a wide scope of topics and methodologies. Books in this series include work on developments in the functions of the constitution, the organization of powers and the protection of rights, as well as research that focuses on formal amendment rules and the relation between constituent and constituted power. The series includes comparative approaches along with books that focus on single jurisdictions and brings together research monographs and edited collections that allow the expression of different schools of thought. While the focus is primarily on law, where relevant the series may also include political science, historical, philosophical, and empirical approaches that explore constitutional change.

Also in the series:

Participatory Constitutional Change
The People as Amenders of the Constitution
Edited by Xenophon Contiades and Alkmene Fotiadou

Democratic Decline in Hungary

Law and Society in an Illiberal Democracy

András L. Pap

Routledge
Taylor & Francis Group
LONDON AND NEW YORK

First published 2018 by Routledge

2 Park Square, Milton Park, Abingdon, Oxfordshire OX14 4RN
52 Vanderbilt Avenue, New York, NY 10017

Routledge is an imprint of the Taylor & Francis Group, an informa business

First issued in paperback 2019

Copyright © 2018 András L. Pap

The right of András L. Pap to be identified as author of this work has been asserted by him in accordance with sections 77 and 78 of the Copyright, Designs and Patents Act 1988.

All rights reserved. No part of this book may be reprinted or reproduced or utilised in any form or by any electronic, mechanical, or other means, now known or hereafter invented, including photocopying and recording, or in any information storage or retrieval system, without permission in writing from the publishers.

Notice:
Product or corporate names may be trademarks or registered trademarks, and are used only for identification and explanation without intent to infringe.

British Library Cataloguing-in-Publication Data
A catalogue record for this book is available from the British Library

Library of Congress Cataloging-in-Publication Data
A catalog record for this book has been requested

ISBN: 978-1-138-05212-3 (hbk)
ISBN: 978-0-367-31297-8 (pbk)

Typeset in Galliard
by codeMantra

For Olivia

Contents

Acknowledgments

I want to begin by acknowledging those people who helped me in publishing this constitutional diary.

First on this list is Lídia Balogh, partner and colleague, whose steadfast encouragement, ever-critical perspective, insightful guidance and tireless assistance in reading multiple drafts of various chapters, never tiring of the revision process, made the completion of the book possible.

I have to express my profound appreciation for the support of the academic institutions I have been affiliated with throughout the research and writing process: The Institute for Legal Studies of the Centre for Social Sciences of the Hungarian Academy of Sciences, the Nationalism Studies Program of Central European University, the Faculty of Law Enforcement of the National University of Public Service and the Faculty of Humanities of Eötvös University (ELTE) in Hungary, as well as the Institute for Sociology of the Slovak Academy of Sciences.

The work was partly financed by the SASPRO Programme of the Slovak Academy of Sciences. The research received funding from the People Programme (Marie Curie Actions) European Union's Seventh Framework Programme under REA grant agreement No. 609427.

In particular, I am grateful for the personal and professional support, as well as comments and advice – large and small – at various stages of this process by Michael L. Miller, Maria Kovacs, Michael Stewart, Szabolcs Pogonyi, and Luca Váradi from CEU, Klára Kerezsi from NUPS, István Bodnár from ELTE, as well as Silvia Mihalikova and Zuzana Kusa from SAS.

I consider myself exceptionally privileged to have become part of the inspiring, challenging and also comforting community of the scholars of CSC HAS, where I am particularly indebted to András Jakab, Gábor Kecskés, Zoltán Szente and Balázs Vizi for their support and friendship.

Being part of the Working Group Against Hate Crimes in Hungary has also been a singular source of intellectual and personal invigoration; special thanks to Borbála Ivány, Eszter Jovánovics, Eszter Kirs and Tamás Dombos.

This project could not have been accomplished without the hospitality and support of scholars and friends, including Mátyás Bódig (University of Aberdeen), Zsuzsa Csergő (Queen's University), Susan Gal (University of Chicago), Lynne

Haney (New York University), Elspeth Guild (Queen Mary University of London), Olga Sezneva (University of Amsterdam), Katalin Szelényi (University of Massachusetts Boston) and Matthew Waxman (Columbia University), as well as Géza Finszter and László Korinek from the Hungarian Academy of Sciences.

The generosity of the many other people who have commented on my project helped me immensely and contributed to it in many ways. Special thanks go to Csaba Madarász (Üvegfalu.hu), Anna Sledzinska-Simon (University of Wroczlaw), Eva Sobotka (EU Fundamental Rights Agency) and Iván Szelényi (Yale and NYU).

The book could never have been written without the invaluable editorial and copy-editing contribution of Faith Bailey, Gábor Győri, Carse Ramos, Jacob Verhagen and Illés Szurovecz.

Many of former students made important contributions and provided immeasurable inspiration.

Over the period of writing the book, I presented various earlier draft versions of chapters to audience at conferences and lectures, besides my home institutions, at the University of Aberdeen, University of Amsterdam, University of Barcelona, Cambridge University, University of Chicago, University College London, Erasmus University Rotterdam, Loyola University Chicago School of Law, University of Massachusetts Boston, University of Iceland, New York University, University of Oslo, Queen Mary University of London, University of Toronto and Vrije Universiteit Brussel – I want to thank everyone who invited me, and who attended these meetings, for their curiosity and valuable feedback.

I cannot close without acknowledging the inestimable support of my family, especially in the arduous period of my personal life during which the book was written. The nurturance of my friends, most of all, Anita Bozóki and Judit Horgas helped me more than they could possibly know. All supported this book in different ways.

I also want to thank Palgrave and L'Harmattan for allowing me to adopt, in some cases reprint, ideas presented in previously published material.

I also want to express gratitude for my outstanding editors at Routledge, who believed in this book.

Thanks to all of you!

Any errors in fact or judgement are entirely my own, of course.

Introduction

Meanwhile in Hungary… For an academic publication, this book follows a somewhat untraditional format. It is the diary of a constitutional scholar on select recent political and constitutional developments in Hungary. Some chapters are connected with subjective contextualizing notes. Limiting its focus to the political and constitutional developments of the first two formative and highly intense years in Viktor Orbán's Hungary, the goal is to flesh out and highlight some aspects of a saddening but remarkable story of constitutional law and history in a language accessible for readers outside Central-Eastern Europe. The manuscript was finalized in November 2016. These are dim, worrisome times and feel like the "beginning of the end." More and more voices are heard officially announcing the end of multiculturalism: the refugee crisis paralyzing Europe (and beyond, of course); in Austria, presidential elections are over in a few days, the far-right candidate having lost by less than one percentage point the election that is now scheduled to be repeated (BBC, 2016); in the US, Donald Trump has just been elected 45th president, and we have only recently witnessed a referendum in Britain on leaving the European Union – and possibly ending both historical projects: the EU and Great Britain, maybe even the United Kingdom. A new form of populism is on the rise, which is difficult to ascertain within the conceptual framework of traditional, rational democracy. It is not only Trump's populism and extremism that baffles a Central European observer, but also the way millions of American voters – usually considered rational with a considerable degree of recognition for self-interest – easily disregarded the fact that the presidential candidate failed to demonstrate a minimum degree of competence in actually running a country and administration. Likewise, it is difficult to comprehend why not a single voice from the British royal family was heard before the referendum that could potentially start an avalanche that ends the United Kingdom and Great Britain – as following Brexit, Scotland, is likely to reconsider leaving as well. Also, one wonders if empires and grand historical projects such as the European Union or Great Britain should end so disgracefully, by a shortsighted political bluff of a prime minister, calling for a referendum, then losing popularity anyway and having to campaign against it…

Of course, by the time book gets published, or reaches its, hopefully numerous, readers, these events will be history. The aim of the book, however, will still be timely and relevant to understand the rise and morphology of a self-identified illiberal democracy, the first twenty-first-century illiberal political regime arising from this "new populism" in the European Union. The relevance of the case of Hungary is thus, obviously, beyond the fate of an economically and politically globally insignificant Central-East European state of 10 million inhabitants, a 0.831 Human Development Index, which ranked it 37th in the world in 2014 (UNDP, n.d.), with a purchasing power parity GDP of $196.6 billion, ranking 57th in the world; a 0.2 percent GDP real growth rate, making it the 193rd and a 17.1 percent GDP gross national saving, ranking 97th in world comparison. It is, nevertheless a laboratory for illiberal democracy and a documentary, a learning tool for a variety of students and stakeholders.

The context of the book is that "new populism" centers on the concept, ideology and "Zeitgeist" of disenchantment: questioning the validity and sustainability of the post-WWII (liberal) consensus on human rights centered on political language and even certain sacred democratic institutions and neoliberal policies. The term offers multiple successful political operationalizing strategies for neo-conservative movements as an anti-modernist and fundamentalist answer to the neoliberal consensus, similarly, for example, to the ways in which "(anti) gender ideology" is used. As some scholars convincingly argue, "gender" has been identified as the common ground, a label amidst diverse political cultures, different party structures and a variety of mobilizing tactics, compressing different fears and values and used against diverse causes (Kováts, Põim and Tánczos, 2015; Kováts and Põim, 2015). Disenchantment-driven illiberalism is also very similar to how Hobsbawm (1992) saw nationalism in the twenty-first century – as a substitute, a placebo for disorientation and a surrogate for integration in a disintegrating society; when society fails, the nation appears as an ultimate guarantee (and in post-communist societies as a device to distinguish between the innocent and the guilty). In the Hungarian case, the strategy worked for Viktor Orbán, a liberal-turned missionary and Messiah for illiberalism. Here, the government successfully built a state-funded (pseudo) NGO sector and this, alongside racist and nationalist movements, convincingly offered anti-modernism and anti-cosmopolitanism/Europeanism as a viable alternative to neo-liberal democracy and the market economy.

The new and defining feature of disenchantment-based new populism is that no well-articulated, precisely spelled out re-enchantment strategies are needed, no new grand narratives such as those Marxism, Socialism, Communism, Fascism or Nazism were accompanied by. Hence, despite all the superficial analogies with the 1930s concerning Anti-Semitism, nationalism and the like, new populist illiberal regimes are actually quite different. For example, Anti-Semitism does not, cannot possibly, include the political, economic and legal project of discrimination, exclusion deportation and annihilation. Hungarian nationalism is equally hollow in the sense that the discourse of restoring pre-WWI borders remains at the symbolic level of rhetoric, and actual revisionist policies are nowhere to be seen or called for. In other words, new populism is hollow in the sense that there are no positive, alternative grand narrative constructions. Playing on the criticism and rejection of the current discourses, political and policy regimes seem to suffice. This shallowness and emptiness are the unique and engaging features of the (potentially exportable) Hungarian model of illiberal democracy and, as I argue, of new populism. Apparently, no new re-enchanting ideology is needed for this new populism to gain support: the rejection of a fatigued human rights discourse and social equality can easily be overridden by essentialism and religious fundamentalism – even without the need to revitalize and modernize these mobilizing strategies and ideologies that seem to have lost ground.

The Hungarian case is worthy of attention for three distinct reasons. First, it provides an opportunity to observe the techniques and procedures for building an illiberal democracy, a project that may seem appealing to many politicians. Second, it may also provide an interesting observation point for students of transitology, not only for scholars of post-communist societies but also for those who are interested in democratic U-turn patterns, that is, in states that decide to abandon pathways to liberal democracy. [The term U-turn was introduced by Harvard Emeritus Professor János Kornai (2015a, 2015b)]. Third, the Hungarian case provides valuable points of discussion on multilevel constitutionalism and constitutional identity – especially if the problematic issues are institutionalized at a constitutional level. The latter point refers to the inefficiency of international organizations in protecting the rule of law and constitutionalism. This may be of particular interest in the case of the EU, an organization often criticized for both applying double standards between applicant and Member States, and being unprepared for Member States' illiberal U-turns.

We can identify three dimensions of the EU's inability to address illiberal U-turns. The first can be characterized as an *institutional inability*, meaning that unlike the Council of Europe or the OSCE, the EU was not created as a human rights or a rule of law watchdog organization—its primary goal was to foster economic cooperation and integration, and for a very long time, democratic institutions were only relevant as far they were necessary to secure the EU's primary goals. (It should be added that a notable human rights area in which the EU actually raised the standards for protection is the field of anti-discrimination law, but this, too, was not triggered by human rights or anti-racist considerations, but by the fact that the equal treatment of workers, and the free movement of services, goods and capital were the fundamentals of the union aiming for a single market.) Procedural options to sanction a democratic backlash are extremely limited.[1]

1 Under Article 7. of the Treaty on European Union, on a reasoned proposal by one-third of the Member States, by the European Parliament or by the European Commission, the Council, acting by a majority of four-fifths of its members after obtaining the consent of the European Parliament, may determine that there is a clear risk of a serious breach by a Member State of the values referred to in Article 2. The European Council, acting by unanimity on a proposal by one-third of the Member States or by the Commission and after obtaining the consent of the European Parliament, may determine the existence of such a serious and persistent breach. Thereafter, the Council, acting by a qualified majority, may decide to suspend certain rights deriving from the

The second inability can be called *institutional-philosophical*. According to the precedence principle,[2] enshrined by the Court of Justice of the European Union (CJEU), European law is superior to the national laws of Member States, and this also applies to national constitutions (in a sense that national judges should not apply provisions of a constitution that contradict European law). However, the slow, organic and cautious development of the European project, being very wary of using any language that would create the impression of real federalism (consider, for example, the renaming of the 2003 Draft Treaty establishing a Constitution for Europe for a Charter of Fundamental Rights of the European Union (2007)) explicitly recognizes Member States' constitutional identity as sacrosanct. According to Article 4.2 of the Treaty on European Union (1994):

> The Union shall respect the equality of Member States before the Treaties as well as their national identities, inherent in their fundamental structures, political and constitutional, inclusive of regional and local self-government.

The third item concerns an *inability to decipher legislative cynicism*. This can be demonstrated by how the Hungarian legislative practice of instituting a "worst practice constitutionalism" was temporarily able to survive international organizations' scrutiny. "Worst practice" legislation builds legal regimes from elements that in most cases are not suspicious: no eminent breach of international human rights standards, or solutions that would be unprecedented in well-functioning constitutional democracies. Yet the grand picture generated by these mosaic pieces portrays a constitutional design in which institutional guarantees for government power are dismantled, the protection of fundamental rights is severely weakened and political freedom is curtailed. However, because of the impeccable nature of the building blocks, international monitoring bodies face a considerable difficulty in discovering the destructive features of the regime, let alone being able raise specific, reasoned criticism. The Hungarian government's arguments relying on comparative law actually succeeded for a while in hiding what Princeton Professor Kim Lane Scheppele calls a *Frankenstate*:

> The Fidesz constitutional "reform" has spawned a Frankenstate, a form of government created by stitching together perfectly normal rules from the laws of various EU members into a monstrous new whole. The component

application of the Treaties to the Member State in question, including the voting rights of the representative of the government of that Member State in the Council. The Commission may also bring the matter before the Court of Justice of the European Union.

2 The CJEU enshrined the precedence principle in the 1664 Costa versus Enel case (Case 6–64), declaring that the laws issued by European institutions are to be integrated into the legal systems of Member States, who are obliged to comply with them. European law therefore has precedence over national laws. Therefore, if a national rule is contrary to a European provision, Member States' authorities must apply the European provision. National law is neither rescinded nor repealed, but its binding force is suspended (see Precedence of European Law, n.d).

> pieces of the Hungarian Frankenstate might have operated perfectly well in their original contexts, but combined in a new constitutional system, these once-normal rules produce abnormal results. As government spokespeople have said every time there is criticism of a particular aspect of the new constitutional order: that rule exists in Greece. Or Germany. Or the United Kingdom. It's normal. End of story. But nowhere do all those rules exist together, except in the Hungarian Frankenstate.
>
> (Scheppele, 2013)

Scheppele brings the example of combining Germany's much-criticized rules for drawing electoral districts with Britain's highly disproportionate first-past-the-post rules for constituency elections and topping it off with the widely used d'Hondt system for deriving proportional representation from party-list votes, a system that marginalizes small parties (Scheppele, 2013).

The book is structured in the following way: the first part outlines the chronology and possible causes of recent developments of democratic decline in Hungary.

The *first chapter* shows how the illiberal turn was orchestrated in Hungary by redesigning the constitutional landscape. The goal is not only to outline the process but also to show the substance of illiberalism: defying rule of law principles, dismantling core institutional guarantees for government control and adopting an ideologically biased constitution that cements these developments. The analysis and criticism focuses on the style, format and procedure of legislation, as well as its substance.

The *second chapter* discusses possible explanations to understand the evolution and success of Orbán's constitutional capture: values and political culture, the rhetoric and politics of the "dark side", the rhetoric of finishing the transition suspended in 1989, the rhetoric of "governance by the people instead of useless debates" and "we will not be a colony!", constitutional deadlocks, economic hardship and, finally, a note on the political charisma of Viktor Orbán.

The second part of the book turns to the analysis of the microfabric of the Hungarian illiberal democracy.

The *third chapter* consists of a thought experiment: modelling and conceptually positioning the new political community and the political (theoretical) and constitutional construct Prime Minister Orbán claims to have created and institutionalized through the new constitution. The methodology is to follow statements and declarations by legal, most of all constitutional, documents and the grand architect Mr Orbán: thus, the self-assessment of the "design" and the designers. Two sets of questions are in the center of analysis: the contours, organizational foundations and defining features of the self-proclaimed new political community and the morphology and consequences of the illiberal nature of the newly established regime.

I argue that although Orbán's regime in several fields made a significant departure from the constitutional standards generally held in liberal democracies, neither its creators argued convincingly, nor could an academic analysis support the claim that this would indeed constitute a new, coherent, sui generis illiberal democracy model from the constitutional legal or the political theoretical point of view. Hungarian illiberalism, thus, is a tool to channel, define and dominate general political discourse and to provide a discursive framework for political identification and ideologically biased, yet divergent and ad hoc, legislation. "Illiberal democracy" and "illiberalism" in Hungary are actually forms of constitutional identity, guiding the discursive framework of this new political community.

The remainder of the book aims to outline the morphology and operation of the Hungarian model of illiberal democracy through three select issues.

In showing how the new constitutional regime is ideologically biased, the *fourth chapter* relies on the concept of "intimate citizenship" as an analytical tool to assess the new constitution and the political regime from the aspect of privacy and intimacy/sexuality. The concept of "intimate citizenship" refers to the phenomenon that certain groups (who are formally equal-status citizens) actually face inequality and marginalization based on their status, choices and preferences in private life. Some of their economic, political, social and cultural rights are restricted due to the constitutional and political preferences of the state. It will be shown that illiberalism goes beyond the democratic backlash that surfaces first and foremost in the dismantling of institutional rule-of-law guarantees and the weakening of checks and balances. Illiberalism also manifests in how the new constitution fails to recognize individual autonomy and ideological commitments and that constitutionally enshrined value preferences can authorize future legislation that may restrict autonomy and freedom in all sorts of ways – possibly even leading to the systematic abuse of fundamental rights and individual freedoms. The chapter shows how the new constitution and adjacent legislation set forth several normatively formulated value preferences, which can be defined as illiberal in the sense that they either suggest the denial or at least the disregard of individual autonomy and liberty, and that project a paternalistic, patriarchal and heteronormative concept of society and the political community. I will also explain how the constitutionally framed value preferences are actually not evidently supported by Hungarians' values and lifestyle choices.

The remaining chapters' scope expand the focus beyond the "new political transition of 2010" and the U-turn per se and, dwelling on the force of path dependence, highlight two important features of contemporary Hungarian society and political life.

The *fifth chapter* focuses on two developments in post-2010 Hungary's illiberal multiculturalism: the adoption of a new citizenship law, opening the door for all ethnic kin and providing nonresident voting rights and the renaming of the Roma as a nationality (national minority), following the path of the misleading and deceptive multiculturalist legislation and rhetoric. The chapter shows that the hypocritical model for multiculturalism, which was originally designed to foster minority-friendly legislation for ethnic Hungarians in neighbouring states, was modified in a way to allow for electoral gerrymandering, and a legal framework that allows for abusing minority rights and large-scale ethno-corruption. The marginalized, abandoned, sole-ethnic minority, the Roma, will continue to be disfavoured. Not only were the Roma most severely affected by the economic consequences of the political transition, but the newly emerging political structures and legal regimes were also inadequate for challenges they have been facing. As for the broader relevance of the Hungarian case, the chapter shows that confusing terminology (in the case of ethnic and national minorities and nationalities) reflects and reveals confused conceptualization and the lack of clearly defined political and policy objectives.

The *sixth chapter's* analysis focuses on the relationship between the individual and the state, in particular, the ethno-cultural majority. The chapter investigates how the Fundamental Law and subsequent recent legislation conceptualizes and operationalizes personhood and constitutionally recognized groups. The chapter shows how in Hungary the recognition of individual dignity is conditional on membership in the (most often majority) community (defined by the aforementioned constitutionally cemented value preferences). Also, it is the dignity of communities – not exclusively but including that of the ethnic majority community – that is protected by the new constitution. Besides dignity, the other core concept this chapter concerns is privacy. As it is shown, in Hungarian illiberalism, privacy is used as a tool to obstruct transparency and political accountability. Furthermore, a peculiar and cynical approach to data protection can even be used to discriminate and further marginalize certain communities. Just as in the case of the ill-conceived model of multiculturalism, it will be the only ethnic minority, the Roma, who will be the victims: through both under- and over-policing, insufficient prosecutions of racially motivated hate crimes and inadequate monitoring of ethnic profiling.

András L. Pap

SASPRO-Marie Skłodowska-Curie Fellow at the Institute of Sociology of the Slovak Academy of Sciences in Bratislava. Research Chair and Head of Department for the Study of Constitutionalism and the Rule of Law at the Hungarian Academy of Sciences Institute Centre for Social Sciences Institute for Legal Studies. Professor of Constitutional Law at the Law Enforcement Faculty of the National Public Administration University. Recurrent Visiting (Adjunct) Professor at Central European University's Nationalism Studies Program. Currently on leave from Eötvös University (ELTE) Faculty of Humanities, Institute of Philosophy, in Hungary.

Bibliography

BBC. (2016). Austria presidential poll result overturned. [online] Available at: http://www.bbc.com/news/world-europe-36681475 [Accessed 31 Dec. 2016].

Charter of Fundamental Rights of the European Union. (2007). *Official Journal of the European Union*, C303, pp. 1–16.

Draft Treaty Establishing a Constitution for Europe. (2003). *Official Journal of the European Union*, C169, pp. 1–105.

Hobsbawm, E.J. (1992). *Nations and nationalism since 1780.* 1st ed. Cambridge Cambridge University Press, pp. 163–192.

Kornai, J. (2015a). Hungary's U-Turn. *Capitalism and Society*, 10(1).

Kornai, J. (2015b). Hungary's U-Turn. *Society and Economy*, 37(3), pp. 279–329.

Kováts, E. and Põim, M. ed., (2015). *Gender as symbolic glue: The position and role of conservative and far right parties anti-gender mobilizations in Europe.* 1st ed. Brussels: FEPS-FES.

Kováts, E., Põim, M. and Tánczos, J. (2015). *Beyond gender? Anti-gender mobilization and the lessons for progressives*, FEPS-FES Policy Brief, pp. 4–5.

Precedence of European Law. [online] Available at: http://eur-lex.europa.eu/legal-content/BG/ALL/?uri=URISERV:l14548 [Accessed 31 Dec. 2016].

Scheppele, K.L. (2013). The rule of law and the Frankenstate: Why governance checklists do not work. *Governance*, 26(4), pp. 559–562.

Treaty on European Union. (1994). *Official Journal of the European Communities*, C191, pp. 1–112.

UNDP, United Nations Development Programme. (n.d.). UN Human Development Indicators: Hungary. [online] Available at: http://hdr.undp.org/en/countries/profiles/hun [Accessed 31 Dec. 2016].

Part I

Chronology and explanations

What happened in Hungary in 2010–2012

1 Democratic U-turn, the chronology of building an illiberal democracy

This chapter will show how the illiberal turn was orchestrated in Hungary. Instead of aiming to provide a structured, full picture, or a comprehensive description of what has happened in the past six years in Hungary, this chapter's assessment is limited to the first two years of Prime Minister Orbán's government, which began in 2010. The goal is not only to outline the process but also to show the substance of illiberalism: institutionalizing the tyranny of the majority; a clientelist decision-making regime that defies rule-of-law principles; dismantling core institutional guarantees for government control; passing laws that curtail individual liberties and do not meet international standards for human rights and constitutionalism and lack appropriate prior public debate and deliberation; and adopting an ideologically biased constitution that cements the above-described developments and initiatives.

The starting point of this chapter is the 2010 Spring elections, where a coalition of the Fidesz Party and the Christian Democratic Party, two self-identified right wing, conservative parties led by Fidesz-president Viktor Orbán, received the support of 41.5 percent of all people entitled to vote and 53.1 percent of the actual votes cast, which translated to 68 percent of the mandates in Parliament (Kornai, 2015, p. 12), giving the winners a two-thirds majority[1] that allowed

1 Hungary's electoral law combined three systems to elect the 386-member parliament: voting for single candidates from single-mandate district (SMD) contests (176 seats), voting for party lists in larger territorial districts using proportional rules to award seats (152 seats) and proportionally allocated compensation seats from national compensation lists (58 seats). The first two levels each required a ballot, while the national compensation list used 'surplus' votes not counted at the primary levels. In each SMD, candidates competed directly, and each voter chose her most preferred candidate on the ballot. If no candidate were to obtain more than half of the votes in a first round of voting, a run-off election was held two weeks later. The top three candidates and any candidate with more than 15 percent of the vote were to compete in the run-off election, in which the top vote-getter won the seat. In order to qualify as a candidate in any one of the 176 SMDs, the candidate must have collected the so-called nomination slips from a minimum of 750 voters, each one signed by the voter personally. A party's success in qualifying individual candidates also affected its eligibility in the proportional list races of the territorial districts. For a party to be eligible to register a list of candidates for the territorial districts, the party must have had a certain minimum number (usually one quarter of the total individual seats in that district) of qualified SMDs (IRI, n.d.).

them to amend the constitution and organic laws. These laws were defined and enumerated by the constitution. Orbán's victory did not come as a surprise. In September 2006, Hungarian state radio broadcasted a secret recording of a speech given by Socialist Prime Minister Ferenc Gyurcsány at a closed-door meeting with fellow Socialist MPs following their 2006 election victory. On the tape, in quite profane language, Gyurcsány admitted that the government "fucked it up and lied for the last year-and-a-half, two years," and that they've "done nothing for four years." The speech set off a scandal, triggered riots and continuous demonstrations initiated and supported by right-wing opposition parties and led to a long and steady decline in popular support for the Socialist Party, which had received 48 percent of the vote in the 2006 parliamentary elections but sank to the mid-teens by the next (IRI, n.d.). Fidesz's popularity was steadily increasing, yet the 2010 campaign did not mention either the adoption of a new constitution or transformative changes in the political and constitutional structure.

As we will see, developments in Hungarian political life have triggered significant political, academic and media attention in the past years. Numerous political decisions were made by various fora and organs of the Council of Europe, the European Union, the UN and international NGOs like Amnesty International, Freedom House and Transparency International, and even judgements from the EU's European Court of Justice and the Council of Europe's European Court of Human Rights.

Instead of collecting and systematically reviewing documents condemning, or even documenting the entire process of how illiberal democracy evolved in Hungary in the past six years, this chapter will provide an overview of only the first two formative and highly intensive years' political and constitutional developments. This is not to suggest or imply that the process ended by 2012, as Viktor Orbán's regime continues to solidify, proliferate and flourish week by week – and this obviously involves both political and legal measures. The new constitution adopted in 2011 was, for example, amended for the sixth time in June 2016. This book, however, is limited to outlining developments in 2010–2012, approximately two years, by when architectural sketches of the new regime are finalized, and residents have already moved and settled in. In order to put these developments into an international perspective, let me highlight some (subjectively chosen) events that took place in these months. The chosen news items are used to contextualize the Hungarian developments, by roughly sketching what was happening in the world at the time in politics, society and culture.

In 2010, the FIFA World Cup takes place in South Africa, with Spain championing. China launches its second moon probe, Chang'e 2. The earthquake in Haiti kills 230,000 people and destroys most of the capital Port-au-Prince. Ethiopian Airlines Flight 409 crashes into the Mediterranean Sea shortly after take-off from Beirut Rafic Hariri International Airport, killing all 90 people on board. An explosion in the Icelandic Eyjafjallajokull volcano results in a volcanic ash plume over northern and central Europe, halting air travel for several days, causing the cancellation of several thousand flights and disrupting the travel plans of millions of people. A stampede in the entrance tunnel of the "Love Parade" techno music festival in Duisburg, Germany, kills 21 and injures over 500. Pope Benedict XVI expresses limited support for condom use to prevent AIDS. WikiLeaks begins disclosing a cache of over 250,000 private cables written by U.S. diplomats. Its founder, Julian Assange, is arrested in England on a Swedish warrant for sexual assault. The longest solar eclipse of the third millennium occurs. Apple debuts the iPad, its first tablet computer – a device category between a smartphone and laptop computer. In Thailand, peaceful protests disintegrate into violence. British Prime Minister Gordon Brown resigns and is succeeded by the Conservative David Cameron. The Irish government requests a $100 billion bailout package from the European Union and IMF to help save its flailing economy. The eurozone and the International Monetary Fund agree to a €110 billion bailout package for Greece in exchange for sharp austerity measures. Polish President Lech Kaczyński dies in a plane crash. The U.S. Department of Health and Human Services, Centers for Disease Control and Prevention removed HIV infection from its list of communicable diseases of public health significance. Conan O'Brian screens the Tonight Show's last episode. An explosion on a BP oil drilling rig off the coast of Louisiana kills 11 people, injures 17 and leaks 5 million barrels of oil into the Gulf Coast, making it the world's largest oil spill. In Citizens United v. FEC, the U.S. Supreme Court rules that the government cannot restrict the spending of corporations for political campaigns. President Obama announces, and later in the year signs into law, Obamacare, the massive health-care reform bill. Supreme Court Justice John Paul Stevens announces retirement after serving on the court for 35 years. Solicitor General Elena Kagan becomes his successor, the fourth woman to ever hold this position and the third female member of the current bench. Arizona Governor Jan Brewer signs a new immigration bill into law, designed to identify and deport illegal immigrants, which several federal courts find unconstitutional. In McDonald v. Chicago, the U.S. Supreme Court rules that the right to bear arms applies to local and state gun control laws. Congress approves a financial regulation bill, increasing the number of companies that will be regulated by government oversight, a panel watching for risks in the financial system and a consumer protection agency. Goldman Sachs agrees to a $550 million settlement with the federal government after being accused of misleading investors during the subprime mortgage crisis and housing market collapse. A federal judge strikes down the voter-approved gay marriage ban in California, calling the law unconstitutional. President Obama announces the end of Operation Iraqi Freedom with a withdrawal of combat troops. A federal judge orders the government to stop the enforcement of the "Don't Ask, Don't Tell Law," which forbids gays and lesbians from

(*Continued*)

openly serving in the U.S. military. Senate approves respective legislation, which the President signs. Tom Delay, the former House Majority Leader from Texas, is convicted of money laundering involving corporate campaign contributions. Movies *Toy Story 3* and *Harry Potter and the Deathly Hallows Part 1* are released. Sixteen-year-old Justin Bieber receives four American Music Awards. After 25 seasons and more than 5,000 episodes, "The Oprah Winfrey Show" airs its last original episode.

In 2011, a reactor at the Fukushima Daiichi Nuclear Power Plant explodes. "Game of Thrones," based on the fantasy novels by George R. R. Martin premieres on HBO. Fidel Castro resigns from the Communist Party of Cuba's central committee after 45 years of holding the title. Apple CEO Steve Jobs resigns and in a few months, dies. CERN scientists announce their discovery of neutrinos breaking the speed of light. Spaceport America – the world's first purpose-built commercial spaceport – is opened, offering suborbital spaceflights to the paying public. The Arab Spring movement begins in Tunisia when demonstrators take to the streets to protest chronic unemployment and police brutality. After 23 years of authoritarian rule, President Ben Ali flees the country. Similar protests break out in Egypt, President Hosni Mubarak announces resignation and hands power of the country over to the military. Kate Middleton marries Prince William in a lavish royal wedding at Westminster Abbey in London. U.S. troops and CIA operatives shoot and kill Osama bin Laden in Abbottabad, Pakistan. Fatah and Hamas, rival Palestinian parties, sign a reconciliation accord. Dominique Strauss-Kahn, head of the International Monetary Fund, is arrested for sexually assaulting a maid at a Manhattan hotel. Former Bosnian Serb general Ratko Mladic, who was responsible for the massacre of over 8,000 Muslims at Srebrenica in 1995, is found and arrested in Lazarevo, a farming town north of Belgrade, Serbia. After more than 50 years of struggle, South Sudan declares independence and becomes Africa's 54th state. *News of the World*, a British newspaper owned by Rupert Murdoch, closes after several allegations of having hacked into voicemail accounts. Norway is hit with consecutive terrorist attacks: a bomb explodes in Oslo's government quarter and Anders Breivik, a gunman disguised as a policeman, opens fire at a camp for young political activists on the island of Utoya, killing 68. Award-winning Amy Winehouse is found dead in her apartment in London. King Abdullah of Saudi Arabia grants women the right to vote and run for office in future elections. Libya's interim government announces that Colonel Muammar el-Qaddafi has been killed by rebel troops. Silvio Berlusconi steps down as prime minister of Italy. International and local monitors condemn parliamentary elections in Russia as fraudulent. Kenya, Ethiopia, Djibouti, Somalia and parts of South Sudan have been rocked by the worst drought there in 60 years. Surgeons in Sweden carry out the world's first synthetic organ transplant, a major breakthrough in regenerative medicine. In October 2011, the global population reaches 7 billion. China's Three Gorges Dam, the largest power plant ever built, is fully operational. Arizona Representative Gabrielle Giffords is among 17 shot by a gunman. The Obama Administration determines that the Defense of Marriage Act is unconstitutional. New York passes a law to allow the same-sex marriage. For the first time in history, the US has its credit rating lowered from AAA to AA+ by credit agency Standard & Poor's, removing it from its list of risk-free borrowers. Hurricane Irene kills 44 people in 13 American states. Evacuations are ordered for about 2.3 million people. Damage is estimated at $7 billion. Occupy Wall Street, an organized protest against corporate greed, social inequality and the disproportion between the rich and poor in New York's financial district, expands to other cities across the US. The movie *Twilight Saga: Breaking Dawn Part 1*, the songs "Born This Way" by Lady Gaga and "Under the Mistletoe" by Justin Bieber are released. Books *The Hunger Games* by Suzanne Collins and *The Girl with the Dragon Tattoo* by Stieg Larsson are published.

***

1. Meanwhile in Hungary: An illiberal democracy in the making

This chapter will provide an overview of the process of redesigning the constitutional landscape in Hungary. As it will be shown, illiberalism is present both in "how" and "what" is being done: just as much the style, format and procedure of legislation as its substance. The adoption of the new constitution is an important part of the process and can even be seen as a landmark, but in many cases, it only cemented earlier achievements and innovations of a legislative juggernaut. Let us follow the process of the illiberal U-turn!

2. The legislative juggernaut

As Kornai (2015, p. 24) points out, between 2010 and 2014, altogether 859 laws were passed: nearly twice as many (399 more) as during Orbán's first government between 1998 and 2002 and almost 150 percent (274 laws) more than in the 2006–2010 cycle. The first set of criticism pertains to the style and quality of the legislative process. Orbán's supermajority basically eliminated Parliament from the political process as an autonomous instrument for democratic deliberation and a tool to control government. As will be discussed in the next chapter, "illiberal democracies" rely on the democratic legitimacy of unleashed political power to institutionalize illiberal legislation. This is what happened in Hungary as well. Reforms, enacted by parliamentary legislation, have been extremely swift: in its first 20 months in office, the government pushed through 365 laws. This included 49 cardinal laws, which require a two-thirds majority, but there was no adequate consultation with opposition parties and civil society. In this time,

12 amendments were made to the (old) constitution that together changed more than 50 individual constitutional provisions (Halmai and Scheppele, 2012, p. 7). Most legislation was introduced to Parliament as individual members' bills. Since the government is formally not involved in these bills, these do not require a detailed debate, consultation, impact assessment and traditional venues for negotiation with the civil sector.

As Scheppele points out, in the first few transformative months, very few government-sponsored laws were introduced to Parliament. Ten out of twelve (!) constitutional amendments and even the new constitution were private members' bills which, originally inteded as being tools for the parliamentary minority, became instruments to entrench the government's super-majority:

> Under the rules of parliamentary procedure in Hungary, private member's bills can use a streamlined procedure. No committee review. No multiple readings. No mandatory consultation with opposition parties or interested groups. With a private member's bill, the Fidesz government could take a constitutional amendment from first proposal into full legal effect in 10 days or less. No other country uses private member's bills for the most important bills that a parliament will enact. In other countries, private member's bills are used for personal causes of individual MPs, not for government programs.
>
> (Scheppele, 2012)

Kornai (2015, p. 24) lists 13 laws that were passed in less than a day. To be safe and legally solid, the Fidesz majority-led Parliament passed a change to the rules of parliamentary procedure, which requires only a two-thirds majority (as opposed to the formerly required four-fifths) to approve an extradited procedure allowing a bill to go from first proposal to final vote without debate and consultation. Even for those bills that were submitted by the government, deadlines set by Ministries for public debate and commenting were very tight, sometimes only a few days. For example, the bill on petty offenses (2012), which had a deadline of six working days, was sent out for commenting on the 95-page-long text, while for the 29- and 97-page-long draft bills on the legal status of prosecutors (2011) and the Prosecution Service (2011), the respective Ministry provided no more than one day for comments by professional chambers, civil society, etc.

Laws have often been amended substantially after the parliamentary debate through the use of a special measure aimed at eliminating technical and incoherent provisions. Several pieces of legislation were specifically tailored to accommodate particular acts of favoritism, such as lowering age requirements for ambassadors to enable the appointment of a government loyalist or changing incompatibility regulations to enable former military service members to run for elected office. Kornai (2015, p. 27–29) lists eight documented cases in which laws were amended in order to make certain candidates eligible. These laws were even given nicknames in common language: "Lex X" (X stands for the names of the people in whose interest the laws were passed. For example, Lex Baranyai pared down incompatibility regulations for the president of the Hungarian Development Bank, Lex Vida, eliminating the requirements of university degrees and five years of administrative practice for the president of the tax authority, or Lex Mocsai, deleting the requirement of a PhD for university presidents).

The same strategy was used to remove non-government appointees from office. For example, shortly before the European Parliament elections, the tenure of the members of the National Election Committee, the independent supervisory body of the legality of the elections, was terminated under the auspices of the reorganization of the institution. A similar strategy led to the dismissal of the National Radio and Television Body, the Data Protection Commissioner (ombudsman) and even the President of the Supreme Court. Government clientelism cementing loyalists into power even for the future when the government loses its two-thirds majority was achieved by passing legislation that infinitely extends the mandates for public offices if Parliament fails to elect the successor – often by a supermajority. Such offices include the prosecutor general, constitutional court judges, etc.

The political-legislative strategy of "over-constitutionalisation," that is, amending the Constitution/Fundamental Law in order to legitimize unconstitutional legislation, has also been applied on numerous occasions. In the first few months, before the Constitutional Court was castrated and deprived of many of its competences, several acts of Parliament were struck down. In order to remedy these obstacles to the supermajority's legislative efforts, the constitution would promptly be amended, respectively (the Constitutional Court may not review the constitutionality of constitutional amendments). For example, amendments of the Code of Criminal Procedure adopted in July 2011 authorized prosecutors to select and cherry-pick the courts in which they press charges, upon the decision of the prosecutor general, a former Fidesz parliamentary candidate. The Constitutional Court found this unconstitutional (166/2011). As a reaction, Parliament included this procedure in the Transitory Provisions of the new constitution, the Fundamental Law on 23 December 2011.

Parliament also implemented retroactive taxation (a special 98 percent tax on certain revenues for public sector employees above a 2 million HUF/month [7200 USD, 6600 EUR] threshold) and a retroactive withdrawal of pensions – again, reauthorized by a constitutional amendment after a Constitutional Court decision striking it down (184/2010).

Parliament also passed a bill of attainder legislation, directly engaging in modifying court decisions. Shortly after the elections, a parliamentary subcommittee was established to investigate responsibility for occasional use of force against anti-government demonstrators and rioters before the elections when Fidesz was in opposition. The subcommittee subpoenaed judges and called for the review of judgements. This practice was held to be a violation of judicial independence by the President of the Supreme Court and the National Council of Justice. On 7 March 2011, Parliament adopted the so-called Nullification Act, annulling and condemning court decisions. Constitutional lawyers were divided on the question of whether the parliamentary subcommittee in charge of the assessment of events occurring five years earlier should be authorized to subpoena judges. Twenty judges requested for the Constitutional Court to review the law, and it upheld the law in 2013 (24/2013).

Also, the 2012 Act on the National Assembly vested the Speaker of the Parliament with extensive discretionary powers to limit MPs' free expression, including the authority to fine MPs for displaying the EU-flag, which was removed from the Parliament building. Journalists' freedom was also severely limited in terms of moving about in the premises or recording and broadcasting sessions. Monopolies were given to reporters and photographers of the National News Agency, and some reporters were banned entry for months for having "violated the dignity of the Parliament" (Index.hu, 2012).

János Kornai published an article in January 2012, presenting a list of 33 elements illustrating the centralization processes in Hungary. He concluded that:

> There would be no difficulty about adding to the list of thirty-three examples I have given, which purposely ranges from the huge changes involved in winding up the second pillar of the pension system, or the powerful new central office jeopardizing the independence of the judicial system, or the new law on the National Bank, to the slighter ones of amalgamating two galleries or amusement venues, although the second too will bring radical changes for those involved in them. The spread of the examples to include some tiny or even bizarre instances is intended to demonstrate how centralization has turned into a kind of merger mania. [...] Notable ingenuity has gone into this: the legal form of the changes varies from case to case. Sometimes whole institutions are united, sometimes the procedure for appointing heads changes, sometimes executive boards are packed to increase central control, sometimes statutes are altered.

The examples given by Kornai include merging most local state administration services with regional government offices (the directors of which are appointed by the prime minister); seizing the assets of compulsory private insurance companies; merging Budapest's medical spas, street cleaning, and funerals into one holding company, which represents the capital city on the boards of the private and semiprivate utility companies (gas, water, etc.); nationalizing trade in tobacco products (with the number of retail outlets falling from 40,000 to 5000 – and mostly into politically reliable business operators); and transferring ownership of regional hospitals and all primary and secondary schools to the central government. This not only involves the appointment of new chief executives and school directors but also the introduction of a centralized, mandatory, politically biased curriculum. State universities' quasi-autonomy has also been strongly curtailed, rectors and chancellors are picked and appointed by the government, and University bodies have the right to express an opinion but have no veto powers.

Law professor and former member of the Constitutional Court Imre Vörös went as far as to argue that the government is involved in an attempt to overthrow the constitutional order via a legally orchestrated *coup d'etat*, as the parliamentary supermajority is used in an abusive, and consequently unconstitutional manner, institutionalizing a "tyranny of the majority" (Vörös, 2012).

3. Dismantling rule-of-law guarantees

First, the Constitutional Court. The first important institutional action in building the Hungarian illiberal democracy was aimed at dismantling one of the world's most powerful judicial organs authorized to carry out constitutional review: the specialized Constitutional Court. The 1989 roundtable discussions ending Communist rule and opening the constitutional pathway to a liberal democracy produced a consensus on having a very powerful constitutional court authorized to review laws based on *actio popularis* abstract ex post review claims that procedures can be initiated by anyone, with no standing, injury, or ongoing judicial procedure required. Indeed, most of the Court's formative decisions were initiated by *actio popularis* petitions. It was a well-established, well-functioning element of Hungarian political and legal culture, and it contributed to making the Hungarian Constitutional Court a powerful, internationally respected body. As European University Institute professor Gábor Halmai argues,

> Over the past two decades or more, this unique institution has provided not only private individuals, but also non-governmental organizations and advocacy groups with the opportunity to contest in the Constitutional Court, for the public good, legal provisions that they regard as unconstitutional. While other democratic states have of course been able to survive without this institution, it has nevertheless contributed substantially to ensuring a level of protection of fundamental rights which is now diminishing.
>
> (Halmai, 2012)

The reason for opting for this model lay in the unique political power field of the time. The 1989 roundtable talks and the subsequently revised constitution (for more on this, see Chapter 2) prepared a constitutional amendment, making way for the first democratic elections, which would decide the fate of further legislation and constitution making. However, since neither the Communists nor the self-appointed, at the time practically unknown, dissident opposition representatives were in the position to foresee the outcomes of this election, it was in everybody's interest to institute as many control mechanisms as possible, in case of electoral defeat. Thus, a strong Constitutional Court was made. Its first activist and charismatic president and future head of state László Sólyom, who believed in an "invisible constitution," (23/1990) actually made the Court one of the major participants in the constitutional transition and an important political powerhouse as well. The court's seminal decisions included striking down the death penalty (23/1990) carving the path for lustration (11/1992), defining the limits of abortion (64/1991, 48/1998) and the standards of free speech, (95/2008, 96/2008, 46/2007, 18/2004, 14/2000, 13/2000, 2/1999,

30/1992) and even getting involved in direct political issues such as torpedoing austerity measures (43/1995, 56/1995).

The new Constitution and a new law on the Constitutional Court (Act CLI of 2011), as well as constitutional amendments, delivered serious blows to the competences, independence and autonomy of the court. Severe measures such as the elimination of *actio popularis* procedures for ex post review, the abolition of powers to review all budget-related legislation[2] and the repeal of all court decisions made before 1 January 2012 (when the new Constitution entered into force) were introduced to weaken the competences of the Constitutional Court. Thus, precedents of the Court cannot be invoked in new cases based on the new Constitution. Additionally, the number of justices has been raised from 11 to 15, allowing the government to nominate and elect seven judges (out of a body of 15) within a few months; the procedural requirement to try to reach a consensus within Parliament regarding their election was eliminated. Now, all of the judges are government loyalists, including two former members of Orbán's first government, several appointed directly from their positions as (majority) members of Parliament. The new laws allow "infinite membership" for judges, should a new member not be elected by a two-thirds majority by the time the term of office of another justice ends. The new provisions also state that only the government, one-fourth of MPs, and the Commissioner of Human Rights are entitled to request ex post review of any piece of legislation. In the post-2010 constellation, it is almost impossible that one-fourth of the opposition MPs would submit such a motion, as it would require an unlikely coalition of the far right and the Socialists. The possibility of turning to the Constitutional Court became even more difficult as legal representation became mandatory and legal aid is not available for this purpose. At the same time, a procedural fine ranging from 20,000 to 500,000 HUF (from 70 to 1700 EURs) may be imposed on petitioners initiating procedures in an "abusive" way; the sum of the fine is due to the Constitutional Court. The uncertainty of the word "abusive" might deter many from turning to the Constitutional Court (Halmai, 2012, p. 5).

Second, the judiciary. In an attempt to weaken the independence of the judiciary, the six-year-long mandate of the former President of the Supreme Court was prematurely ended after two years, and the mandatory retirement age for all judges was reduced from 70 to 62 years of age, a move that practically removed all court-presidents (chief judges) – with replacements to be chosen by the head of the newly created administrative unit. A new powerful administrative organ for the judiciary titled the National Judicial Office was created with powers to appoint judges. The body is presided over by one of the new constitution's drafters – who is also the wife of a Fidesz member of the European Parliament

2 The right to review financial laws is restricted to review from the perspective of rights (the right to life and human dignity, protection of personal data, freedom of thought, conscience and religion or the right to Hungarian citizenship), which they typically cannot breach. The restriction remains in effect for as long as state debt exceeds half of what is referred to in the Hungarian text as the 'entire domestic product', the content of which is uncertain.

and a long-time friend of the prime minister. Her mandate, similarly to the prosecutor general, a former Fidesz MP candidate, is automatically prolonged if no new president is elected by two-thirds of Parliament. As Halmai argues,

> According to the new act on the judiciary, any judge in the ordinary courts can be elevated or demoted by this single state official, who has the sole power to appoint judges and no other judicial bodies have a decisive role in the process.
>
> (Halmai, 2012)

Another innovation that raises questions about the independence of the judicial process is that despite traditional rules for designating judicial fora, the president of the new National Judicial Office and the prosecutor general have been authorized to appoint courts for hearing individual criminal proceedings. The prosecutor general, whose mandate was extended from 6 to 9 years, is neither responsible to the government nor to the Parliament: he/she has the duty only to report to the Parliament annually, and MPs only have the right to pose questions to him/her; the right to pose interpellations was abolished.[3]

Third, the independent parliamentary ombuds offices. A single Office of the Commissioner for Fundamental Rights was created, which replaced four formerly independent ombuds institutions. The portfolio of the former Ombudsperson for Data Protection and Freedom of Information was transformed into a quasi-governmental office. Since the institutions of the Parliamentary Commissioner for the Rights of National and Ethnic Minorities and the Parliamentary Commissioner for Future Generations, the ombudsperson responsible for environmental issues, were abolished, the mandate of the respective commissioners was also terminated before the end of their term of office.[4] For the new ombuds office, the (parliamentary) Commissioner for Fundamental Rights, Parliament elected a former civil law professor and former Fidesz government commissioner who had no any constitutional or human rights track record.

Fourth, the Central Bank. The centralization of the Central Bank also initiated an infringement procedure against Hungary by the EU concerning provisions of the new Constitution on the Central Bank, which merged it with

3 The Council of Europe's European Commission for Democracy through Law (Venice Commission) issued a special report on the case (2012a). On 17 January 2012, the EC launched an accelerated infringement proceeding against Hungary regarding the independence of the judiciary. In 2016, the Grand Chamber of the European Court of Human Rights held (Baka v. Hungary) that Hungary had been in violation of Article 6 § 1 (right of access to a court) and of Article 10 (freedom of expression).

4 In 2014, the Grand Chamber of the EU's European Court of Justice held in the infringement procedure initiated by the European Commission that, by prematurely bringing to an end the term served by the supervisory authority for the protection of personal data, Hungary has failed to fulfill its obligations under Directive 95/46/EC of the European Parliament and of the Council of 24 October 1995 on the protection of individuals with regard to the processing of personal data and on the free movement of such data (EC v Hungary, 2014).

the Financial Supervisory Authority. The Central Bank's new president, György Matolcsy, a former Fidesz MP and government minister, is one of Orbán's closest advisors.

Fifth, the Fundamental Law also creates a National Budget Council, an unelected body with limited democratic legitimacy, with members chosen by the government, tenured for up to 12 years, who can only be replaced if two-thirds of the Parliament can agree on the successors. The new body can practically veto the budget. According to the new Constitution, if Parliament fails to pass a budget by March 31 of each year, the head of state, elected by a simple majority, with a mandate exceeding that of the Parliament, can dissolve the Parliament and call new elections. Thus, even if Fidesz is outvoted in the next elections, severe constraints burden any future government; for example, Scheppele argues that if Fidesz loyalists can veto the budget by making it miss the deadline, the president (also named by Fidesz) will call new elections. This can be repeated until an acceptable government is voted back into power (Scheppele, 2011).

Sixth, local governments. The government introduced substantial reform concerning self-governments (Act 189 of 2011; eGov Hírlevél, 2012). Besides restructuring local elections, most administrative competences (including health care and secondary education) have been removed from elected local municipalities and given to either central regional administration or newly established administrative entities. The Committee of the Regions (the EU's Assembly of Regional and Local Representatives) expressed serious concern for Hungarian local democracy, pointing to, *inter alia*, the limitations on the autonomy of local authorities. Particular concern was raised over the fact that under the new Constitution, elected municipal councils can be dissolved by the national Parliament on the grounds of a breach of the constitution, without a binding judgement from the Constitutional Court. Moreover, the new constitution's provisions curtail the autonomous management of local authorities' property and provide the possibility to "nationalize" it (COR, 2012).

Seventh, media laws. Rewriting the regulations of the press and electronic media was a highly significant stage of the transformation of the Hungarian constitutional order. Through two new laws, the government not only established such a wide-ranging government control of the print and electronic media unprecedented in constitutional democracies, but it also abolished the safeguards against unilateral political influence. Without these safeguards, the governing majority had the opportunity to create an entirely politically homogenous body, with all members nominated by the governing party, to oversee compliance with the rules. As a result of these measures (Act CIV of 2010; Act CLXXXV of 2010), the freedom of the press, which has a key role in holding those exercising public authority accountable, has been curtailed to an extraordinary degree.

The main criticisms voiced by the Hungarian Constitutional Court (165/2011), alongside academics and human rights NGOs and various European and international organizations (such as the European Newspaper Publishers' Association, the World Association of Newspapers and News Publishers (2010), the International Press Institute (2011), the South East Europe Media Organisation (2011,

2012), the European Federation of Journalists (2012), the Reporters without Borders (2011) and larger international civil organizations, like Amnesty International (2011) and Freedom House (2011) concerned the political dependence of the Hungarian Media and Telecommunication Authority and its overbroad regulatory authority powers; the unreasonable and unconstitutional regulation of the print and online press; the political influence on public service media and the disproportionate and unpredictable sanctions causing chilling effects. In March 2011, the European Parliament passed a resolution condemning the new media laws, calling on the Hungarian authorities to restore the independence of media supervision and to put an end to governmental interference in the freedom of expression and "balanced programming" (EP, 2011c). In February 2011, the OSCE (2011) also prepared a detailed critical analysis of the Hungarian regulation, which was soon followed by a critical analysis of the Human Rights Commissioner of the Council of Europe, released on 25 February 2011. Following negotiations with the European Commission (Hungarian Government, 2010; Kroes, 2011), Parliament amended the regulations in 2011. Still, criticism has not subdued.

And more… Newly adopted rules allowed for the dismissal of civil servants without justification. As a result, thousands of civil servants were fired from public administration positions (HCLU, EKI, HHC, 2010). The law was held to be unconstitutional by the Constitutional Court and was squashed *pro futuro*. Dismissals nevertheless continued. Nominally independent institutions have, of course, been staffed by government loyalists elected by a two-thirds majority. Often the heads (and in some cases the full membership) of certain institutions have been removed and replaced before the official term of their office – mostly through the amendment of the related legal framework (HHC, EKI and HCLU, 2011a). As mentioned above, for example, besides the President of the Supreme Court and the Data Protection Commissioner, members of the National Election Committee and the National Radio and Television Body were removed before the end of their term of office. According to Freedom House (2015), by 2014, all major independent institutions were headed by partisan or personal loyalists who (in Scheppele's words): "will be able to conduct public investigations, intimidate the media, press criminal charges and continue to pack the courts long after the government's current term is over" (2011). Former members of the Fidesz parliamentary group were elected as President of Republic, the Head of the State Audit Office and one member of the Constitutional Court, while the president of the Central Bank and another judge of the Constitutional Court was a member of the previous Fidesz government.

4. And the new constitution…

The new constitution triggered criticism from several aspects. Its contribution to dismantling crucial instruments for separation of powers and rule-of-law guarantees was discussed above. Ideological commitments will be discussed in separate chapters. Here, the focus is limited to the context and process of adoption.

On 28 June 2010, upon the proposal of a Fidesz MP, Parliament repealed Article 24 (5) of the Constitution (Amendment, 2010), which required a four-fifths majority of MPs to adopt the procedural rules of the preparation of a new Constitution. Thus, the governing coalition, having a two-thirds majority, eliminated the provision obliging it to cooperate with opposition parties while preparing the new Constitution. A parliamentary Ad Hoc Committee Preparing the Constitution was established (Parliamentary Resolution 47/2010) on the same day. About 30 out of its 45 were members of the governing coalition. The committee prepared a concept paper, which in the end was only considered to be a working document, and a draft was prepared by Fidesz/Christian Democrat MPs and introduced to Parliament on 14 March 2011. The new Constitution, the so-called Fundamental Law, was adopted with only the votes of the Fidesz/Christian Democrats coalition on 18 April and entered into force on 1 January 2012. It has been the sole product of the governing political party and has been adopted by the governing majority without the support of any other political force. The text, widely criticized by national, European and international NGOs and organizations (Venice Commission, 2011a, 2011b; EP, 2011b; PACE, 2011), was adopted on the basis of a bill submitted after only a 35-day debate and exclusively by the votes of members of the governing coalition.

Also, to create the delusion of popular support, a so-called "national consultation" was launched. The National Consultation Committee sent questionnaires to all 8 million Hungarian citizens entitled to vote, asking them to answer 13 questions concerning the draft. According to the government (as there were no transparent means to verify this), 12 percent of voters returned it (Osvát and Osvát, 2011).

5. Expanding the electorate and gerrymandering

Besides the government taking political control over the Election Commission, electoral reforms introduced a remarkable form of gerrymandering that disproportionately favors the governing parties. In April 2010, both the local election and the parliamentary election law were rewritten (Act CCXXXVIII of 2013, Act XXXVI of 2013, Act CCIII of 2011, Act L of 2010). The overhaul of both laws includes more stringent ballot access requirements and a greater weight for the majoritarian element of the mixed election system. The parliamentary election law also involves a redrawing of single-member district (hereinafter SMD) boundaries with a view towards giving the ruling parties more seats. The new law has roughly halved the number of MPs in Parliament (386 to 199) and has correspondingly reduced the number of SMDs from 176 to 106. In parliamentary elections, the proportion of seats distributed in the majoritarian SMDs rises from 46 percent of all seats to 53 percent. Coupled with the advantages from gerrymandering, this could give the ruling parties a parliamentary majority even if they fall far shy of a popular majority (Karácsony, 2012).

In local elections, previously 60 percent of local council members were elected in SMDs, and now 70 percent, while the proportion of counselors elected on proportional party lists shrank accordingly from 40 to 30 percent. In effect, party preferences as expressed in votes submitted for party lists will have considerably less impact on the distribution of seats in Parliament and local councils.

By amending Act LV. 1993 on Hungarian citizenship (Act XLIV of 2010), Parliament has allowed the possibility of persons who were previously citizens of Hungary, or whose ancestors were citizens of Hungary, or who are of Hungarian descent but are now foreign citizens, to receive Hungarian citizenship. This law is primarily meant to offer citizenship to persons of ethnic Hungarian descent whose Hungarian ancestors were placed outside the Hungarian borders as a consequence of the Paris Peace Treaties following WWI. The new electoral law abolished residency requirements for eligibility to vote but instituted a construction in which nonresidents' votes are worth less than half of those residents: as they do not have SMDs and cannot vote for SMD candidates, their votes are counted only in the national list. Estimates of the size of the ethnic Hungarian communities across the border vary, ranging between 2.5 and 3 million (É. Kiss, 2004; Gyurgyík, 2005; Nol.hu, 2009; Transindex.ro, 2010). It needs to be added that voters are also discriminated against on the basis of residence: Hungarian residents who work or study abroad cannot vote by mail but need to travel to a Hungarian embassy or consulate, whereas nonresident citizens can cast their votes from home.[5]

As Central European University professor and citizenship scholar Szabolcs Pogonyi (2015, p. 85) shows, these nonresident votes actually played a crucial role in the final-mandate allocation of the 2014 April parliamentary elections: 600,000 nonresident Hungarians had acquired citizenship and 193,793 registered to vote, but as a result of the overcomplicated voting procedure, only 128,429 valid mail votes were cast, with Fidesz receiving the overwhelming 95.4 percent of these votes. Fidesz won 133 seats in Parliament exactly the number necessary for the two-thirds majority. Votes from the nonresident constituency secured one seat for Fidesz – and a crucial one.[6]

The new Constitution also changed the rules on the validity of a national referendum: at least half of all eligible voters must cast a valid vote to have a valid referendum result, while the previous Constitution (1949: XX) only required that a quarter of all eligible voters cast a vote on one side of the issue. Most referenda held since the political transition would have failed to meet these criteria, including the referenda on NATO and EU membership (Szigetvári, Tordai and Vető, 2011).

5 Both the European Court of Human Rights (Vámos and others v. Hungary) and the Hungarian Constitutional Court (3086/2016) rejected appeals in this regard, arguing that the equality of votes is not violated, since nonresidents form a different group, as they only have one vote. Ironically, the same rules apply for national referenda, where all voters have only one vote, answering the same questions (Bodnár, 2015; Jakab and Szilágyi, 2015).

6 In 2014, 26.6 percent of eligible voters and 53.1 percent of all voters chose Fidesz, which gained 66.8 percent of parliamentary mandates (Kornai, 2015).

6. Constitutional partnership or cemented clientelism?

Due to the aforementioned peculiarities of the 1989 roundtable discussions, the subsequently revised 1989 Constitution envisioned a constitutional partnership, relying on a broad consensus. The founding fathers institutionalized a qualified two-thirds majority consensus for a wide variety of issues. The Fundamental Law expanded these significantly, covering a wide range of issues beyond political institutions and fundamental rights. A qualified majority is required for regulations concerning family law, the tax and pension systems, cultural, religious, socioeconomic and financial policies, which normally fall within the sphere of competence of the government or are covered by the regular decision-making powers of the legislature.

As the second Venice Commission report pointed out, the wide use of cardinal laws is problematic. The Constitution contains far too many – over 50 – references to cardinal laws, most of which concern issues that should have been left to ordinary legislation and majoritarian politics, such as family legislation and social and taxation policy.

> The more policy issues are transferred beyond the powers of simple majority, the less significance will future elections have and the more possibilities does a two-third majority have of cementing its political preferences and the country's legal order[...] When not only the fundamental principles but also very specific and "detailed rules" on certain issues will be enacted in cardinal laws, the principle of democracy itself is at risk.
>
> (Venice Commission, 2011b, para 22–25)

As mentioned above, the proliferation of cardinal laws was accompanied by the extension of the mandates of several crucial public offices: the public prosecutor (9 years), the head of the state audit office (12 years), the head of the national judicial office (9 years), the head of the media board (9 years) and the head of the budget council (6 years). If a two-thirds consensus is not achieved in future Parliaments, each can be allowed to stay in office even longer.

7. Immediate responses

These developments have triggered significant political, academic[7] and media attention in the past years. Numerous political decisions were passed by various fora and organs of the Council of Europe (2012),[8] the European Union,[9]

7 For critical academic literature, see Chronowski (2012); Chronowski, Drinóczi and Kocsis (2012); Majtényi (2012); Tóth (2012); Blokker (2013); Hajnal and Rosta (2014); Scheppele (2014); Hegedűs and Végh (2015); Chronowski and Varjú (2016).

8 Concerns were also raised about the adoption of a set of laws, introduced by the Hungarian authorities between June and December 2010, affecting media freedom and pluralism. See OHCHR UN (2012); Jagland (2012).

9 Following Oral Questions tabled in the EP (2011a), the EP (2011b) issued a highly critical resolution on the Revised Hungarian Constitution. Also, see EC (2012a, 2013a); EP (2012, 2013).

the UN;[10] experts' bodies such as the Venice Commission of the Council of Europe[11] or, as we will see, international NGOs like Amnesty International, Freedom House, and Transparency International; and even judgements from the EU's European Court of Justice (ECJ)[12] and the Council of Europe's European Court of Human Rights. Thus, international judicial fora ruled repeatedly against Hungary: for example, the European Court of Justice ruled that the abrupt termination of the data protection commissioner's term in 2011 infringed on the authority's independence, and the European Court of Human Rights ruled that the church law violated the European Convention of Human Rights. It declared that the early removal of the former Supreme Court president in 2012 violated his rights and condemned Hungary for violating freedom of expression because the opposition party's MPs were sanctioned. Likewise, the 98 percent retroactive tax was found to be contrary to the Convention.[13]

It is worth noting that when responding to international criticism, the Hungarian government repeatedly sent documents that were not identical to those adopted by the Parliament. As Kim Lane Scheppele points out:

On 17 January 2012, the EC (2012b) launched an urgent 'infringement procedure' against Hungary for violating EU treaties on the independence of its central bank and data protection authorities, as well as over measures affecting the judiciary. On 7 March 2012, the EC (2012c) decided on continuing accelerated infringement procedure on independence of the data protection supervisor and measures affecting the judiciary and asks additional information on central bank's independence. The Commission sent two reasoned opinions – the second stage under EU infringement proceedings after which the matter may be referred to the Court of Justice of the European Union – and two administrative letters. The reasoned opinions concerned the independence of the data protection authority and measures regarding the retirement age of judges – which would lead to the anticipated retirement of 274 judges and public prosecutors. Due to the urgency of the matter (the various laws in question are already in force), the Commission has accelerated the deadline for Hungary to respond to the reasoned opinions and administrative letters to one month instead of the normal two-month period.

10 The UN Special Rapporteurs on Freedom of Opinion and Expression and on Freedom of Religion addressed joint letters to the Hungarian authorities in January 2011, expressing their concerns about the media laws (Nol.hu, 2011). The Special Rapporteur on Freedom of Opinion and Expression carried out a technical mission to Hungary from 3 to 5 April 2011, after which he issued a press statement emphasizing his concern that the media laws still fell short of the required international benchmarks to which Hungary has committed itself (OHCHR UN, 2011). The Special Rapporteur on extreme poverty and human rights jointly with the Special Rapporteur on the right to adequate housing issued a press statement on 15 February expressing concern about recent legislation, which criminalizes homelessness and threatens those living in the streets with prosecution that can lead to heavy fines or prison (OHCHR UN, 2012).

11 In Strasbourg, 19 March 2012, the Venice Commission issued two highly critical opinions on the right to freedom of conscience and religion and the legal status of churches, denominations and religious communities of Hungary (2012b), and on the legal status and remuneration of judges and the organization and administration of courts (2012a). Also see Venice Commission (2011a, 2011b, 2012c, 2012d, 2012e, 2013a, 2013b); Venice Commission and OSCE/ODIHR (2012).

12 EC v. Hungary (2012, 2014); Magyar Keresztény Mennonita Egyház v Hungary (2014); Freehungary.hu (2014); EC (2013b).

13 Baka v. Hungary (2016); József Belegi and Others v. Hungary (2012), Hagyó v. Hungary (2013).

> Hungary has repeatedly produced draft laws for review by European authorities that did not reflect the laws that were actually introduced into the Parliament. Each time, the English-language versions offered to foreign reviewers were substantially more compliant with European law than the laws actually enacted in Hungarian [...] I'll give just two examples. During the one month that the constitution was open for public debate, the Hungarian government sent an English translation to the European Commission [...] But the English translation left out the controversial and inflammatory preamble. [...] And the errors and omissions were not random, but systematically made the constitution look better to European eyes than the Hungarian version would have. When the Hungarian government sent a draft law on the central bank to the European Central Bank in fall 2011, the English version was also misleading. Nonetheless, the ECB was highly critical of the draft. The actual law introduced into the parliament, however, was much worse since it proposed to merge the central bank with the bank regulator to create a new agency with a Fidesz official at its helm, a major institutional change not in the English version. When international bodies discovered the bait-and-switch, the IMF walked out of its negotiations with Hungary and has refused to go back unless the law is change.[14]
>
> (Scheppele, 2012)

It needs to be added that as a result of these critiques, some legislation has been amended. However, the scheme, and most of the substantive part of the legislation, has remained intact.

Bibliography

Act II of 2012 on petty offences, on petty offence procedure and the petty offence registry system.
Act XX of 1949. The Constitution of the Republic of Hungary.
Act XXXVI of 2013 on electoral procedures.
Act XLIV of 2010 on Hungarian citizenship.
Act L of 2010 on local elections.
Act CIV of 2010 on the freedom of the press and the fundamental rules of media content.
Act CLXXXV of 2010 on media services and mass media.
Act CLI of 2011 on the Constitutional Court.
Act CLXIII of 2011 on the prosecution service.
Act CLXIV of 2011 on the legal status of the Chief Public Prosecutor, prosecutors and other prosecution service employees and on prosecutors' career path.
Act CCIII of 2011 on parliamentary election.
Act CCXXXVIII of 2013 on referenda.
Act 189 of 2011 on local governments.
Amendment of the Constitution of 5 July 2010, Article 2. Fundamental Law of Hungary, 25 April 2011.

14 Also see HHC, EKI and HCLU, 2011b.

Amnesty International (2011). La dureté de la loi hongroise sur les médias suscite des protestations. [online] Available at: https://www.amnesty.org/fr/latest/news/2011/01/protests-over-restrictive-hungarian-media-law/ [Accessed 31 Jan. 2016].

Baka v. Hungary (2016) 20261/12 (the Grand Chamber of the European Court of Human Rights).

Blokker, P. (2013). *New democracies in crisis? A comparative constitutional study of the Czech Republic, Hungary, Poland, Romania and Slovakia*. London/New York: Routledge.

Bodnár, E. (2015). A külföldön élő magyarok választójogának egyenlősége. *JTI Blog*. Available at: http://jog.tk.mta.hu/blog/2015/07/a-kulfoldon-elo-magyarok-valasztojoganak [Accessed 31 Dec. 2016].

Chronowski, N. (2012). The new Hungarian Fundamental Law in the light of the European Union's normative values. *Revue Est Europa, (numéro spéciale 1)*, pp. 111–142.

Chronowski, N., Drinóczi, T. and Kocsis, M. (2012). What questions of interpretation may be raised by the New Hungarian Constitution? *Vienna Journal on International Constitutional Law*, 5(1), pp. 41–64.

Chronowski, N. and Varjú, M. (2016). Two eras of Hungarian Constitutionalism: From the Rule of Law to rule. *Hague Journal on the Rule of Law*, 8(2), pp. 271–289.

Constitutional Court Decision 11/1992 (III.5).

Constitutional Court Decision 12/1999 (V.21).

Constitutional Court Decision 13/2000 (V.12).

Constitutional Court Decision 14/2000 (V.12).

Constitutional Court Decision 18/2004 (V.25).

Constitutional Court Decision 23/1990 (X.31).

Constitutional Court Decision 24/2013 (X.4).

Constitutional Court Decision 30/1992 (V.26).

Constitutional Court Decision 43/1995 (VI.30).

Constitutional Court Decision 46/2007 (VI.27).

Constitutional Court Decision 48/1998 (XI.23).

Constitutional Court Decision 56/1995 (IX.15).

Constitutional Court Decision 64/1991 (XII.17).

Constitutional Court Decision 95/2008 (VII.3).

Constitutional Court Decision 96/2008 (VII.3).

Constitutional Court Decision 165/2011 (XII.20).

Constitutional Court Decision 166/2011 (XII.20).

Constitutional Court Decision 184/2010 (X.28).

Constitutional Court Decision 3086/2016 (IV.26).

COR (European Committee of the Regions) (2012). Hungary: Committee of the Regions expresses serious concern for Hungarian local democracy. [online] Available at: http://europa.eu/rapid/pressReleasesAction.do?reference=COR/12/2&format=HTML&aged=0&language=EN&guiLanguage=en [Accessed 31 Dec. 2016].

Council of Europe (2012). Hungary: Legislative changes threaten democracy and human rights. [online] Available at: http://www.coe.int/bg/web/commissioner/-/hungary-legislative-changes-threaten-democracy-and-human-rights?inheritRedirect=true [Accessed 31 Dec. 2016].

É. Kiss, K. (2004). *Anyanyelvünk állapotáról*. Budapest: Osiris Kiadó.

EC (European Commission) (2012a). Statement of the European Commission on the situation in Hungary on 11 January 2012. [online] Available at: http://europa.eu/rapid/press-release_MEMO-12–9_en.htm [Accessed 31 Dec. 2017].

EC (European Commission) (2012b). European Commission launches accelerated infringement proceedings against Hungary over the independence of its central bank and data protection authorities as well as over measures affecting the judiciary. [online] Available at: http://europa.eu/rapid/press-release_IP-12–24_en.htm?locale=fr [Accessed 31 Dec. 2016].

EC (European Commission) (2012c). Hungary – infringements: Commission takes further legal steps on measures affecting the judiciary and the independence of the data protection authority, notes some progress on central bank independence, but further evidence and clarification needed. [online] Available at: http://europa.eu/rapid/press-release_MEMO-12–165_en.htm [Accessed 31 Dec. 2017].

EC (European Commission) (2013a). The European Commission reiterates its serious concerns over the Fourth Amendment to the Constitution of Hungary. [online] Available at: http://europa.eu/rapid/press-release_IP-13–327_en.htm [Accessed 31 Dec. 2016].

EC (European Commission) (2013b). Internal market: the Commission has brought Hungary before the Court of Justice to contest restrictive conditions on the issue of luncheon vouchers and other benefits in kind. [online] Available at: http://europa.eu/rapid/press-release_IP-13–578_en.htm [Accessed 31 Dec. 2017].

EC (European Commission) v. Hungary [2012] C-286/12 (the First Chamber of the European Court of Justice).

EC (European Commission) v. Hungary [2014] 2014/234 (the Grand Chamber of the European Court of Justice).

eGov Hírlevél (2012). Szabó Erika: fő cél az egyablakos ügyintézés. [online] Available at: http://hirlevel.egov.hu/2012/03/08/szabo-erika-fo-cel-az-egyablakos-ugyintezes/ [Accessed 31 Dec. 2016].

EP (European Parliament) (2011a). Debate on the revised Hungarian Constitution, 8 June 2011. [online] Available at: http://www.europarl.europa.eu/sides/getDoc.do?pubRef=-//EP//TEXT+CRE+20110608+ITEM-011+DOC+XML+V0//EN [Accessed 31 Dec. 2016].

EP (European Parliament) (2011b). Resolution on the Revised Hungarian Constitution. 5 July 2011, P7_TA(2011)0315.

EP (European Parliament) (2011c). Resolution on media law in Hungary. 10 March 2011, P7_TA(2011)0094.

EP (European Parliament) (2012). Resolution on the recent political developments in Hungary. 16 February 2012, P7_TA(2012)0053.

EP (European Parliament) (2013). Report on the situation of fundamental rights: Standards and practices in Hungary (pursuant to the European Parliament resolution of 16 February 2012) (2012/2130(INI). 24 June 2013, A7–0229/2013.

European Federation of Journalists (2012). EC Hungary opinion must address press freedom, says EFJ. [online] Available at: http://mediamonitor.ceu.hu/archive/archive-download?id=163112259444796118238581138236752122743 [Accessed 31 Dec. 2016].

Freedom House (2011). Freedom of the Press: 2011. [online] Available at: https://freedomhouse.org/report/freedom-press/2011/hungary [Accessed 31 Dec. 2016].

Freedom House (2015). Nations in transit 2015: Hungary. [online] Available at: https://freedomhouse.org/report/nations-transit/2015/hungary [Accessed 31 Dec. 2016].

Freehungary.hu (2014). Commission opens new infringement procedure against Hungary. [online] Available at: http://freehungary.hu/index.php/56-hirek/2832-commission-opens-new-infringement-procedure-against-hungary [Accessed 31 Dec. 2016].

Gyurgyík, L. (2005). Magyar kisebbségek a kutatások tükrében: A határon túli magyarok számának alakulása az 1990-es években. *Magyar Tudomány*, [online] 50(2), pp. 132–144. Available at: http://www.matud.iif.hu/05feb/03.html [Accessed 31 Dec. 2016].

Hagyó v. Hungary [2013] 52624/10 (the Second Section of the European Court of Human Rights). [online] Available at: http://hudoc.echr.coe.int/eng#{"itemid":["001–118647"]} [Accessed 31 Dec. 2016].

Hajnal, G. and Rosta, M. (2014). The illiberal state on the local level: The doctrinal foundations of subnational governance reforms in Hungary (2010–2014). *Working Papers in Political Science*, [online] 5(1). Available at: http://politologia.tk.mta.hu/uploads/files/archived/hajnal_rosta_wpps_2014_1.pdf [Accessed 31 Dec. 2016].

Halmai, G. (2012). Towards an illiberal democracy. *Eurozine.com*. [online] Available at: http://www.eurozine.com/articles/2012–01–25-halmai-en.html [Accessed 31 Dec. 2016].

Halmai, G. and Scheppele, K.L. ed. (2012). Opinion on Hungary's new Constitutional order: Amicus Brief for the Venice Commission on the Transitional Provisions of the Fundamental Law and the Key Cardinal Laws. Princeton, NJ: Princeton University.

HCLU (Hungarian Civil Liberties Union), EKI (Eötvös Károly Institute) and HHC (Hungarian Helsinki Committee) (2010). Assessing the first wave of legislation by Hungary's New Parliament. [online] Available at: http://tasz.hu/node/1486 [Accessed 31 Dec. 2016].

Hegedűs, I. and Végh, Z. (2015). Illiberal democracies: What can the European Union do in case a member state regularly and systematically breaches European values and regulations? [online] *Hungarian Europe Society*. Available at: http://www.europatarsasag.hu/images/2016Sept/Illiberal%20Democracies%20-%20Policy%20paper%20-%20Final%20version.pdf [Accessed 31 Dec. 2016].

HHC (Hungarian Helsinki Committee), EKI (Eötvös Károly Institute) and HCLU's (Hungarian Civil Liberties Union) letter to Viviane Reding (2011a). [online] Available at: http://helsinki.hu/wp-content/uploads/Letter-to-Viviane-Reding-29–12–11.pdf [Accessed 31 Dec. 2016].

HHC (Hungarian Helsinki Committee), EKI (Eötvös Károly Institute) and HCLU (Hungarian Civil Liberties Union) (2011b). Full list of mistakes and omissions of the English version of the Hungarian draft Constitution. [online] Available at: http://tasz.hu/files/tasz/imce/list_of_all_the_omissions_and_mistranslations.pdf [Accessed 31 Dec. 2016].

Hungarian Government (2010). Hungarian Government's reply to the EC [online] Available at: http://www.europarl.europa.eu/meetdocs/2009_2014/documents/libe/dv/navracsics_kroes_humedialaw_291210/navracsics_kroes_humedialaw_291210en.pdf

Index.hu (2012). Visszamehet az Index a Parlamentbe. *Index.hu* [online] Available at: http://index.hu/belfold/2012/02/08/na/ [Accessed 31 Dec. 2016].

International Press Institute (2011). Hungarian Media Law: International Mission condemns chilling effect and calls for change. [online] Available at: http://ipi.freemedia.at/newssview/article/hungarian-media-law-international-mission-condemns-chilling-effect-and-calls-for-change.html [Accessed 31 Dec. 2016].

IRI (International Republican Institute) (n.d.). Hungary pre-election watch: April 2010 Parliamentary elections, http://www.iri.org/sites/default/files/Hungary%20Post-Election%20Watch,%20April%202010%20Parliamentary%20Elections.pdf [Accessed 31 Dec. 2016].

Jagland, Thorbjorn's letter to János Martonyi (2012). [online] Available at: https://rm.coe.int/CoERMPublicCommonSearchServices/DisplayDCTMContent?documentId=0900001680089065 [Accessed 31 Dec. 2016].

Jakab, A. and Szilágyi, E. (2015). Sarkalatos törvények a magyar jogrendben. *MTA Law Working Papers*, [online] 2(32). Available at: http://jog.tk.mta.hu/uploads/files/mtalwp/2015_32_Jakab.pdf [Accessed 31 Dec. 2016].

József Belegi and Others v. Hungary [2012] 45438/12 (the Second Section of the European Court of Human Rights). [online] Available at: http://hudoc.echr.coe.int/eng#{"itemid":["001–142352"]} [Accessed 31 Dec. 2016].

Karácsony, G. (2012). Választási matematika haladóknak. *Karacsonygergely.blog.hu*. Available at: http://karacsonygergely.blog.hu/2012/02/27/valasztasi_matematika_haladoknak [Accessed 31 Dec. 2016].

Kornai, J. (2012). Centralization and the capitalist market economy. *Nol.hu*. [online] Available at: http://nol.hu/belfold/centralization_and_the_capitalist_market_economy-1297262 [Accessed 31 Dec. 2016].

Kornai, J. (2015). Hungary's U-Turn. *Capitalism and Society*, 10(1), [no pagination].

Kroes, Neelie (2011). Letter to the government [online] Available at: http://nol.hu/media/file/attach/61/10/00/000001061–1855.pdf. [Accessed 31 Dec. 2016].

Magyar Keresztény Mennonita Egyház v. Hungary [2014] 70945/11, 23611/12, 26998/12, 41150/12, 41155/12, 41463/12, 41553/12, 54977/12 and 56581/12 (the Second Section of the European Court of Human Rights).

Majtényi, B. (2012). Legislative stupidities in the New Hungarian Constitution. *1 Peace Human Rights*, 1(9), pp. 105–110.

Nol.hu (2009). Már csak emlék a 15 milliós magyarság. Nol.hu, 23 May [online] Available at: http://nol.hu/kulfold/20090523-letszamjelentes_a_kisebbsegi_magyarsagrol-334091 [Accessed 31 Dec. 2016].

Nol.hu (2011). Az ENSZ kőkemény véleménye a médiatörvényről. *Nol.hu*, 4 April [online]. Available at: http://nol.hu/belfold/az_ensz_kritikus_velemenye_a_mediatorveny-rol_-1031471 [Accessed 31 Dec. 2016].

OHCHR UN (Office of the High Commissioner for Human Rights, United Nations) (2011). Statement delivered by the UN Special Rapporteur on the promotion and protection of the right to freedom of opinion and expression, Mr. Frank La Rue, after the conclusion of his visit to Hungary. [online] Available at: http://newsarchive.ohchr.org/en/NewsEvents/Pages/DisplayNews.aspx?NewsID=10915&LangID=E [Accessed 31 Dec. 2016].

OHCHR UN (Office of the High Commissioner for Human Rights, United Nations) (2012). Hungary's homeless need roofs, not handcuffs - UN experts on poverty and housing. [online] Available at: http://newsarchive.ohchr.org/en/NewsEvents/Pages/DisplayNews.aspx?NewsID=11829&LangID=E [Accessed 31 Dec. 2016].

OSCE (Organization for Security and Co-operation in Europe) (2011). Legal Analysis of Hungarian Media Legislation. [online] Available at: http://www.osce.org/fom/75990 [Accessed 31 Dec. 2016].

Osvát, K. and Osvát, S. (2011). Hungary's 2011 Constitution: Key features and political background. *ANU Centre for European Studies Briefing Paper Series*, [online] 2(2). Available at: http://politicsir.cass.anu.edu.au/sites/politicsir.anu.edu.au/files/documents/2011–2_Hungarian-Constitution-Osvat-and-Osvat.pdf [Accessed 31 Dec. 2016].

PACE (Parliamentary Assembly of the Council of Europe) (2011). Motion for resolution on serious setbacks in the fields of the rule of law and human rights in Hungary (No 12490). 25 January 2011.

Parliamentary Resolution 47/2010. (VI. 29.) on Parliamentary Ad Hoc Committee Preparing the Constitution.

Pogonyi, S. (2015). Transborder kin-minority as symbolic resource in Hungary. *Journal on Ethnopolitics and Minority Issues in Europe*, 4(3), pp. 73–98.

ReporterswithoutBorders,(2011).Hungary'smedialawisunacceptabledespiteamendments. [online] Available at: https://rsf.org/en/news/hungarys-media-law-unacceptable-despite-amendments [Accessed 31 Dec. 2016].

Scheppele, K.L. (2011). Hungary's Constitutional revolution. *The New York Times.* [online] Available at: http://krugman.blogs.nytimes.com/2011/12/19/hungarys-constitutional-revolution/ [Accessed 31 Dec. 2016].

Scheppele, K.L. (2012). Hungary, misunderstood? *The New York Times.* [online] Available at: http://krugman.blogs.nytimes.com/2012/01/21/hungary-misunderstood/ [Accessed 31 Dec. 2016].

Scheppele, K.L. (2014). Hungary and the end of politics. *The Nation.* [online] Available at: https://www.thenation.com/article/hungary-and-end-politics/ [Accessed 31 Dec. 2016].

South East Europe Media Organisation (2011). Press freedom 2011: International Mission condemns chilling effect and calls for change. [online] Available at: http://www.seemo.org/activities/pressfreedom/11/press1185.html [Accessed 31 Dec. 2016].

South East Europe Media Organisation (2012). Press freedom 2012: SEEMO reminds European institutions that Hungary's public broadcasters violate European principles. [online] Available at: http://www.seemo.org/activities/pressfreedom/12/press1206.html [Accessed 31 Dec. 2016].

Szigetvári, V., Tordai, Cs. and Vető, B. (2011). Beyond democracy - The model of the new Hungarian parliamentary electoral system (Part 2). Haza és Haladás Közpolitikai Alapítvány. [online] Available at: http://lapa.princeton.edu/hosteddocs/hungary/Beyond%20democracy%20-%2027%20Nov%202011.pdf [Accessed 31 Dec. 2016].

Tóth, G.A. ed. (2012). *Constitution for a disunited nation Hungary's New Fundamental Law.* Budapest: Central European University Press.

Transindex.ro, (2010). Negyedmillióval csökkent tíz év alatt a magyarok száma a Kárpát-medencében. *Transindex.ro.* [online] Available at: http://itthon.transindex.ro/?cikk=13124 [Accessed 31 Dec. 2016].

Vámos and others v. Hungary [19 March 2015] 48145/14 (European Court of Human Rights).

Venice Commission (2011a). Opinion on three legal questions arising out of the process of drafting the new constitution of Hungary. 28 March 2011, 614/2011.

Venice Commission (2011b). Opinion on the new constitution of Hungary. 20 June 2011, 621/2011.

Venice Commission (2012a). Opinion on Act CLXII of 2011 on the legal status and remuneration of judges and Act CLXI of 2011 on the organisation and administration of courts of Hungary. 19 March 2012, 663/2012.

Venice Commission (2012b). Opinion on Act CCVI of 2011 on the right to freedom of conscience and religion and the legal status of churches, denominations and religious communities of Hungary. 19 March 2012, 664/2012.

Venice Commission (2012c). Opinion on the cardinal acts on the judiciary that were amended following the adoption of opinion CDL-AD (2012)001 on Hungary. 15 October 2012, 683/2012.

Venice Commission (2012d). Opinion on Act CLXIII of 2011 on the Prosecution Service and Act CLXIV of 2011 on the Status of the Prosecutor General, Prosecutors and

other Prosecution Employees and the Prosecution Career of Hungary. 19 June 2012, 668/2012.
Venice Commission (2012e). Opinion on Act CLI of 2011 on the Constitutional Court of Hungary. 19 June 2012, 665/2012.
Venice Commission (2013a). Comments of the government of Hungary on the draft opinion on the Fourth Amendment to the Fundamental Law of Hungary. 14 June 2013, 720/2013.
Venice Commission (2013b). Opinion on the Fourth Amendment to the Fundamental Law of Hungary. 17 June 2013, 720/2013.
Venice Commission and OSCE/ODIHR (Organization for Security and Co-operation in Europe, Office for Democratic Institutions and Human Rights) (2012). Joint opinion on the Act on the elections of Members of Parliament of Hungary. 18 June 2012, 662/2012.
Vörös, I. (2012). Államcsínytevők? *HVG*. [online] Available at: http://hvg.hu/velemeny/20120308_allmcsinytevok_voros_imre [Accessed 31 Dec. 2016].
World Association of Newspapers and News Publishers (2010). Hungarian Media Law fuels international concern. [online] Available at: http://www.wan-ifra.org/articles/2010/12/13/hungarian-media-law-fuels-international-concern [Accessed 31 Dec. 2016].

2 Causes and explanations

1. Values and political culture[1]

According to a recent analysis, in no other country in Europe do populist parties have stronger support than in Hungary (Boros and Kadlót, 2016). Value surveys portray Hungarians as passive, uninterested in politics, isolated and distrustful, with an especially low trust in democracy, market economy and transparent, merit-based structures. In 2012, only 40 percent of Hungarian youth (mostly college and university students) accepted democracy as a legitimate system of government, and roughly one-third did not see a difference between dictatorship and democracy (Szabó, 2013). According to another survey, only about 20 percent of respondents were interested in politics (Szabó, 2013, p. 22). While in 1991, 74 percent of Hungarians approved of the change from a one-party system to a multiparty system, by 2009 only 56 percent favoured the change and 77 percent were dissatisfied with the way democracy was working in Hungary, which was the highest percentage of dissatisfied respondents in the region. While 89 percent held that politicians have benefited a great deal from the changes since 1989, only 17 percent believed ordinary people have similarly profited. About 76 percent said that corrupt political leaders are a very big problem (Wike, 2010). Only 38 percent believed that voting is a mechanism for affecting politics, and 91 percent thought the country is on the wrong track (Pew Research Center, 2009).

Hungary is a closed, introverted society that is frustrated with the European Union and the development of capitalism, but it also has a high tolerance for corruption and an attraction to charismatic leaders. Regarding values, Hungary is in the vicinity of Orthodox cultures and far from its neighbouring countries with similar levels of economic development; Hungary is closer culturally to Bulgaria and Moldova than to Slovenia.[2] In a comparative analysis, Hungary was ranked the very last of all European countries, including the former socialist states, in its levels of trust in institutions. Hungarians were found to have especially low

1 This and the next chapter are based on an earlier writing: Pap, A.L. (2016). Constitutional identity? The Hungarian model of illiberal democracy. In: M. Fish, G. Gill and M. Petrovic, ed., *A quarter century of post-communism assessed*, 1st ed. Palgrave Macmillan, pp. 161–186.

2 See Keller (2010); Szabó (2013); Wike (2010); Pew Research Center (2009).

levels of trust towards politicians, bankers and journalists (Hungarian Spectrum, 2009). Hungarians also live in social isolation: 81 percent reported difficulty in finding friends, and according to 85 percent, relationships often become increasingly unstable. About 58 percent expressed little interest in politics, and 41 percent reported no interest in solving social problems (Van Til, 2015).

It is apparent then that the new political regime resonates with the expectations of a disillusioned, frustrated, inward-looking, closed Hungarian society that has lost its comparative advantage enjoyed during the time of relative freedom and economic prosperity created by the "Goulash communism" of the pre-transition 1980s. The term "Goulash communism" evokes images of a community-style dish cooked in the open air to symbolize a communist regime with a relatively pleasant overall atmosphere. This term characterizes the mixing of certain elements of the free market with a planned economy that allowed Hungary to have had slightly higher living standards than its Iron Curtain neighbours and be among the rare countries in the Eastern Bloc that did not have a shortage of food (Wike, 2010). Paradoxically, Hungarian society retains a sense of superiority, especially towards its neighbours with a significant ethnic Hungarian Diaspora traditionally looked down upon by the dominant (self-referenced) "Magyars." Still, Hungarians have severely lacked feelings of success in the two decades since the political transition.

It should be added that conservative political ideology still centers around 1920, when in the post-WWI treaty Hungary lost two-thirds of its territory and corresponding population. Ever since, the aspiration to reunite the old glory and territorial integrity, or at least a responsibility for ethnic kin in the neighbouring countries, has been a cornerstone of conservative domestic politics and after the political transition in 1989, a constitutional responsibility and foreign policy priority as well. The 1920 Treaty of Trianon through which Hungary lost vast land and people (most of which were not ethnic Hungarian but homogenous Hungarian cities and territories) is a symbol of Hungarians' victimization and mistreatment by the international community.[3] The narratives of victimhood allow for the culture of frustration, refusing to take responsibility for one's own fate and allowing others to be blamed for failures and the lack of success.

Another important feature of Hungarian political culture is what András Bozóki (2015) describes as "partocracy," in which political parties assume civic duties and dominate public life. Such practices may be, for example, establishing public benefit foundations, professional groups and club-like community fora called "civic circles" *(polgári kör)*; delegating curators to committees; employing their own journalists and political and market analysts and self-administering most of the media outlets and think tanks. Similar to other post-communist states, Hungarian civil society is usually characterized as weak and resource dependent. Additionally, the pervasiveness of party loyalist government-organized

3 Shortly after the elections, in 2010, Parliament passed a law declaring June 4, the 90th anniversary of the Trianon Peace Treaty, a national day of remembrance (Act XLV of 2010).

non-governmental organizations (GONGOs) masquerading as independent NGOs is remarkable (Kövér, 2015). According to Jarábik (2015), although loyalty to political sides and parties is not a Hungarian specialty, nowhere else was the emerging civil society and the media captured by the political parties to such a degree as in Hungary.

2. Orbán and his strategy: The rhetoric and politics of the "dark side"

A contradictory feature of Hungarian politics lies in the fact that despite a significant proportion of the population is in a state of political apathy and disinterest in public affairs, society is nonetheless highly politicized. Polarizing strategies aimed at demonizing and delegitimizing political opponents, initiated and utilized mostly by the right and foremost by Orbán and his party, have set the tone in political debates for over a decade. As Krasztev (2015) shows, private political preferences were transformed to identity issues, widely represented by a variety of commonly displayed symbols of self-definition against those with different political views. As a consequence, families, friendly circles and communities at work were split because of this sophisticated power trick (Rupnik, 2012).

Thus, it is a defining feature of the Orbán regime that, as political analyst and liberal-turned conservative, later Fidesz MP Péter Tölgyessy argues, instead of attempting to form and change society and culture, as Adenauer and Thatcher did, Orbán deliberately builds on the dark side of Hungarians' values and orientation: populism, pessimism and conspiracy theories that blame all of the nation's problems on the hostile cooperation of foreign interests and a general disenchantment with democracy and the free market (Lambert, 2015; Jarábik, 2015). Hegedűs (2014)[4] demonstrates the irreconcilable polarization of Hungarian political life and culture through the example of Orbán's strategy for maintaining influence after losing the 2002 election. After this loss, Orbán initiated a political discourse centered on the phrase "*the nation cannot be in opposition*," and in doing so he relativized the outcome of the democratic elections. His expropriation of the phenomenon of the "nation" established a political environment that excluded any further compromise or cooperation with the governing socialists and liberals, even in important strategic issues. This created a political cold war and after 2008 a permanent crisis of governance. According to Rupnik (2012), Orbán actively deepened political and cultural divides and transformed transitology to traumatology by not only breaking with the communist past, but also reconnecting with pre-communism by reopening old divides between cosmopolitan modernizers and traditionalist conservatives, "urbanists and populists" (*Völkisch*). He positions Western liberal democracy counter to the rural lifestyle, which he poses as the source of true national values and authentic democracy.

4 For official data see Knoema (n.d.) and Eurostat (2015, 2016).

2.1. The rhetoric of finishing the political transition suspended in 1990

Although it was never part of the 2010 electoral campaign, as demonstrated in the next chapter, the cornerstone of the rhetoric of Orbán's regime is that the new Constitution finally finishes the political transition and completes the de-communization process that was suspended in 1990 (Wiktorek Sarlo and Otarashvili, 2013). In Jenne and Mudde's (2012) words, Fidesz has argued that their proposed transformations represent the realization of the promises of 1989, which went unfulfilled by the communists and dissidents who signed the pacted transitions. Hungary certainly followed a unique path in post-communist transitions: unlike the process in other states, the first wave of democratization of the "pacted" or "post-sovereign" Constitution making, the adoption of an interim constitution, which was designed as the first of a two-step process, was never followed by the adoption of a final constitution after the first democratic elections (Halmai, 2013).

As mentioned above, the 1989 Constitution, to be replaced by the 2011 Fundamental Law, consisted of a vast amendment (involving over 100 provisions) of the communist constitution, originally adopted in 1949 and passed by the communist legislature in 1989 following peaceful negotiations between the representatives of the authoritarian regime and their democratic opposition, in particular by its umbrella organization, the Opposition Round Table (Halmai, 2013, pp. 69–70). The amendment, promulgated on the 33rd anniversary of the 1956 revolution, just two weeks before the fall of the Berlin Wall, practically created a new constitution – essentially only one provision remained from the original Stalinist document: the provision that declared Budapest the state capitol. The old-new document, alongside a correction passed instantly by the first democratically elected Parliament in 1990, met most of the criteria liberal constitutional democracies require: a representative government, a parliamentary system, an elaborate system of checks and balances, an independent judiciary, an ombudsmen to guard fundamental rights and, as shown above, probably the world's most powerful Constitutional Court (Kovács and Tóth, 2011).

The unique feature of the Hungarian velvet revolution, the term referring to a peaceful, negotiated transition, thus lies in the fact that as the amended constitution was suitable for liberal democracy and a capitalist market economy, there was no political and legal-technical or constitutional pressure to write a new constitution, and the constitutional moment passed.

As János Kis (2012) points out, however, this symbolic defect had to pay a price. He claims that the very weakness of the substantially workable constitution lies in the fact that while it was democratic in nature, the 1989 amendment lacked democratic confirmation, and the unfulfilled (and substantially moot) reference in the preamble of the 1989 amendment, which stated that a new constitution would be adopted after the first free elections, created the impression that the new Hungarian post-communist society was still unfit to constitute a political community. Thus the old-new constitution could not serve as the symbolic glue for the Hungarian Republic, and subsequently, it was too weak to withstand most of the shocks of the political transition Kis identifies: the shocks of the dark side of fundamental rights (i.e., hate speech, due process provided for even the guilty and claims by minority communities – such as the LGBTQ community, for example, which is seen as controversial by the conservative majority); shocks brought by the market economy; the shock of weak institutions that were unable to withstand corruption and the shock of globalization. The constitution could not stop the erosion of social solidarity, it could not build trust in the political class, it was incapable of combating skepticism towards market economy and democracy, it could not sustain anti-establishment sentiments and most of all, although built to foster a constitutional partnership, it could not withstand a polarizing and obstructive powerful political party. In sum, the constitution became an easy target and a useful scapegoat (Kis, 2012; Arato, 2012).

It is noteworthy that despite the fact that Orbán's party played a crucial role in the 1989 negotiations, in 2010 his rhetoric played on the lack of legitimacy of the roundtable talks and the constitution.

2.2. *The rhetoric of stability and governance by the people instead of debates*

As Csillag and Szelényi (2015) argue,

> "liberalism" for Orbán means the excessive emphasis of individual interest over "national" interest (p. 23), In one of his most widely cited speeches, Orbán envisions that in the next 15–20 years Hungary should be dominated by a single, massive right-wing political party that would rule the whole political field without "unnecessary" debates (Rácz, 2015). Bánkuti et al. (2012) quotes Orbán in 2009, even before the victorious elections visioning a [...] real chance that politics in Hungary will no longer be tied by a dualist power space [...] Instead, a large governing party will emerge in the center of the political stage (that) will be able to formulate national policy, not through constant debates but through a natural representation of interests.

As Tölgyessy (Lambert, 2015) states, this also relies on the assumption that the rule-of-law state built in 1989 never belonged to the people. It was an elite project, manifested in the activism of the Constitutional Court, that brought legalism instead of justice, wealth and prosperity for former communist elites, and the ordinary people were left behind and neglected. Halmai points out that his rhetoric also reinforces that there was no real transition in 1989–90, only the communist nomenclature converting its lost political power to an economic one; Orbán exemplified this with the example that the last socialist prime ministers in office before his takeover in 2010 both became rich after the transition through to the privatization process (Lambert, 2015).

2.3. *"We will not be a colony!"*

It needs to be emphasized that Orbán's regime utilizes a new, precisely tailored, well-targeted and highly effective political rhetoric. Hegedűs (2014, pp. 28–29) cites Orbán's speech delivered at the Summer Open University of Bálványos in July 2014, stating that:

> The political and intellectual program of 1848 proclaimed: we will not be a colony! The program and the desire of Hungarians in 2012 is: we will not be a colony! Hungary could not have stood against the pressure and dictats from abroad in the winter of 2011–2012 [referring to government supported pro-government mass demonstrations, ALP] non-if it were not for those hundreds of thousands of people who stood up to show everyone that Hungarians will not live as foreigners dictate, will not give up their independence or their freedom, therefore they will not give up their constitution either, which they finally managed to draft after twenty years. Thank you all!

2.4. *A note on Orbán...*

Last but not least, Viktor Orbán's personal and political charisma needs to be mentioned among the potential causes for his success. This charisma appears to be incomparable to that of his contemporaries, and it certainly makes him the most influential politician in post-transition Hungary.

3. A little help from the constitutional structure...

As mentioned above, the institutional structure set forth by the 1989 Constitution envisioned a constitutional partnership, relying on a broad consensus that could not withstand the political cold war Fidesz instrumentalized (Kis, 2012, p. 19). The founding fathers institutionalized the qualified two-thirds majority consensus for a wide variety of issues, and this enabled the opposition to obstruct structural reforms for decades. Following the German chancellor-type model, the prime minister, on the other hand, could have only been removed by a constructive vote of non-confidence, which in turn created a strong government with limited responsibility to the strong opposition. This in practice meant that no incumbent government was ever removed. As Bozóki (2015, p. 5) argues, the illusion of stability brought a plethora of informal practices as modus operandi: tax evasion and party finance stalling democratic institution building.

4. Economic hardship

According to a 2009 poll, a half a year before Orbán's takeover, 72 percent of Hungarians actually felt they were worse off economically than they had been under communism. About 94 percent described the country's economy as bad, and 42 percent disapproved of the move from a state-controlled economy to a market economy (Pew Research Center, 2009; Wike, 2010), even though in 1991, 80 percent answered just the opposite to the same question (Wike, 2010). Not only have Hungarians felt that they were the losers in the political transition to free market democracy, but also, as Hegedűs (2014) points out, though Hungary carried out widely recognized economic reforms during the late state socialist era and was the first post-socialist state to pave the way for liberal economic reforms in East Central Europe during the 1990s, in the 2000s its competitiveness continuously decreased. The country's external debts and economic imbalances soared during the first decade of the new millennium.[5] In 2010, Hungary's GDP was further from Austria's (the former sibling-state apropos the Austro-Hungarian Monarchy, dismantled in the post-WWI treaties) than it was in 1990, by the time of the political transition (Lambert, 2015). Since 2002, the gross debt in GDP percentage has grown by approximately 3 percent annually, from a level of 55.9 percent in 2002 to 58.6 percent in 2003, 65.9 percent in 2006, 73 percent in 2008 and finally 82.2 percent in 2010 (World Bank, n.d.; Hegedűs, 2014). In the years 2002 to 2008, the budget deficit varied between 5 percent and 9 percent annually, and all initiatives to create structural reforms and restore the balance of public spending remained unsuccessful. This was partly due to the then-opposition Fidesz torpedoing education and healthcare reforms with a "social referendum" in 2009, which pressed the government to suspend the system of individual financial contributions to healthcare and higher education. Thus, by the time the economic crisis hit, Hungary was greatly in debt in both the public and private sectors and was without feasible crisis management strategies (Hegedűs, 2014, pp. 4–5). Additionally, the lack of appropriate structural reforms led Hungary to lose earlier competitive advantages over other countries in the region (Hegedűs, 2014, Bozóki, 2015). Being in public and private debt, as well as in a structural economic and competitiveness crisis, Hungary was hit hard by the global economic crisis and was endangered both by the collapse of the national currency, the forint, and in 2009 by state insolvency (World Bank, 2016). Before Orbán's takeover, his predecessors focused mainly on spending cuts and the securing of the IMF–EU–IBRD loan package amounting to approximately 20 billion euros for 2008 (IMF, 2008; Hegedűs, 2014).

In conclusion, this chapter argued that in order to understand the evolution and success of Orbán's constitutional capture, two features of post-transition Hungarian political life need to be highlighted: the domination of political parties in public affairs and the prevalence of Orbán's long-held political strategy to demonize and delegitimize political opponents and polarize politics to its extremes.

5 For official data see Knoema (n.d.) and Eurostat (2015, 2016).

Bibliography

Act XLV of 2010 on the testimony for national cohesion.

Arato, A. (2012). Regime change, revolution and legitimacy. In: G. Tóth, ed., *Constitution for a disunited nation: On Hungary's 2011 Fundamental Law*, 1st ed. Budapest: Central European University Press, pp. 35–58.

Bánkuti, M., Halmai, G. and Scheppele, K.L. (2012). Hungary's illiberal turn: Disabling the Constitution. In: G. Tóth, ed., *Constitution for a disunited nation: On Hungary's 2011 Fundamental Law*, 1st ed. Budapest: Central European University Press, pp. 237–268.

Boros, T. and Kadlót, T. (2016). *A populizmus helyzete az Európai Unióban. Populista trendek és témák 2016-ban.* 1st ed. Policy Solutions – Friedrich-Ebert-Stiftung.

Bozóki, A. (2015). Broken democracy, predatory state, and nationalist populism. In: P. Krasztev and J. Van Til, ed., *The Hungarian patient. Social opposition to an illiberal democracy*, 1st ed. Budapest: Central European University Press, pp. 3–36.

Csillag, T. and Szelényi, I. (2015). Drifting from liberal democracy: Traditionalist/neo-conservative ideology of managed illiberal democratic capitalism in post-communist Europe. Intersections. *East European Journal of Society and Politics*, 1(1), pp. 18–48.

Eurostat. (2015). General government gross debt-annual data [online] Available at: http://ec.europa.eu/eurostat/tgm/table.do?tab=table&init=1&language=en&pcode=teina225&plugin=1 [Accessed 31 Dec. 2016].

Eurostat. (2016). Real GDP growth rate. [online] Available at: http://ec.europa.eu/eurostat/web/products-datasets/-/tec00115 [Accessed 31 Dec. 2016].

Halmai, G. (2013). The rise and fall of Hungarian constitutionalism. In: *The democratic disconnect citizenship and accountability in the transatlantic community*, 1st ed. Washington, DC: Transatlantic Academy, pp. 67–76.

Hegedűs, D. (2014). From front-runner's 'EUphoria' to backmarker's 'pragmatic adhocism'? Hungary's ten years within the European Union in a Visegrad comparison. *DGAPanalyse.* [online] Available at: https://dgap.org/en/think-tank/publications/dgapanalysis/front-runners-euphoria-backmarkers-pragmatic-adhocism [Accessed 31 Dec. 2016].

Hungarian Spectrum, (2009). Value structure of Hungarian society, 2009. [online] Available at: http://hungarianspectrum.org/2009/10/13/value-structure-of-hungarian-society-2009/ [Accessed 31 Dec. 2016].

IMF (International Monetary Fund), (2008). IMF survey: IMF, EU, and World Bank line up $25 billion for Hungary. [online] Available at: https://www.imf.org/external/pubs/ft/survey/so/2008/car102808b.htm [Accessed 31 Dec. 2016].

Jarábik, B. (2015). From Belarus to Hungary: Lessons from a traditionalist revolution. In: P. Krasztev and J. Van Til, ed., *The Hungarian patient. Social opposition to an illiberal democracy*, 1st ed. Budapest: Central European University Press, pp. 319–324.

K. Jenne, E. and Mudde, C. (2012). Hungary's illiberal turn: Can outsiders help? *Journal of Democracy*, 23(3), pp. 147–155.

Keller, T. (2010). Hungary on the world values map. *Review of Sociology*, 20(1), pp. 27–51.

Kis, J. (2012). Introduction: From the 1989 Constitution to the 2011 Fundamental Law. In: G. Tóth, ed., *Constitution for a disunited nation: On Hungary's 2011 Fundamental Law*, 1st ed. Budapest: Central European University Press, pp. 1–22.

Knoema. (n.d.). Hungary GDP, 1980–2016. [online] Available at: https://knoema.com/atlas/hungary/gdp [Accessed 31 Dec. 2016].

Kovács, K. and Tóth, G. (2011). Hungary's constitutional transformation. *European Constitutional Law Review*, 7(2), pp. 183–203.

Kövér, Á. (2015). Captured by state and church: Civil society in democratic Hungary populism. In: P. Krasztev and J. Van Til, ed., *The Hungarian patient. Social opposition to an illiberal democracy*, 1st ed. Budapest: Central European University Press, pp. 81–90.

Krasztev, P. (2015). Social responses to the "hybridization" of the political system: The case of Hungary in the Central and Eastern European context. In: P. Krasztev and J. Van Til, ed., *The Hungarian patient. Social opposition to an illiberal democracy*, 1st ed. Budapest: Central European University Press, pp. 167–180.

Lambert, G. (2015). Azután egyszer csak beütött a mennykő – interjú Tölgyessy Péterrel. *Figyelő Online*. [online] Available at: http://figyelo.hu/cikkek/427454-azutan-egyszer-csak-beutott-a-mennyko---interju-tolgyessy-peterrel [Accessed 31 Dec. 2016].

Orbán, V. (2014). A munkaalapú állam korszaka következik. Speech at the Summer Open University of Bálványos. [online] Available at: http://www.kormany.hu/hu/a-miniszterelnok/beszedek-publikaciok-interjuk/a-munkaalapu-allam-korszaka-kovetkezik [Accessed 31 Dec. 2016].

Pap, A.L. (2016). Constitutional identity? The Hungarian model of illiberal democracy. In: M. Fish, G. Gill and M. Petrovic, ed., *A quarter century of post-communism assessed*, 1st ed. Palgrave Macmillan, pp. 161–186.

Pew Research Center (2009). End of Communism cheered but now with more reservations. [online] Available at: http://www.pewglobal.org/2009/11/02/end-of-communism-cheered-but-now-with-more-reservations/ [Accessed 31 Dec. 2016].

Rácz, A. (2015). Multi-vectorialism failing? The Russia-policy of the Orbán-government. *Russkii vopros*, [online] 15(1). Available at: http://www.russkiivopros.com/?pag=one&id=619&kat=7&csl=69 [Accessed 31 Dec. 2016].

Rupnik, J. (2012). How things went wrong. *Journal of Democracy*, 23(3), pp. 132–137.

Szabó, A. ed. (2013). *Political orientations, values and activities of Hungarian University and college students, active youth in Hungary research group*. 1st ed. Prague: Heinrich-Böll-Stiftung.

Van Til, J. (2015). Democratic resurgence in Hungary: Challenges to oppositional movement (an open-ended conclusion). In: P. Krasztev and J. Van Til, ed., *The Hungarian patient. Social opposition to an illiberal democracy*, 1st ed. Budapest: Central European University Press, pp. 367–384.

Wike, R. (2010). Hungary dissatisfied with democracy, but not its ideals. *Pewglobal.org*. [online] Available at: http://www.pewglobal.org/2010/04/07/hungary-dissatisfied-with-democracy-but-not-its-ideals/ [Accessed 31 Dec. 2016].

Wiktorek Sarlo, A. and Otarashvili, M. (2013). Can the EU rescue democracy in Hungary? *Foreign Policy Research Institute: E-notes*. [online] Available at: https://www.files.ethz.ch/isn/167427/Wiktorek_Otarashvili_-_EU_and_Democracy_in_Hungary.pdf [Accessed 31 Dec. 2016].

World Bank (n.d.). Hungary: Data. [online] Available at: http://data.worldbank.org/country/hungary [Accessed 31 Dec. 2016].

World Bank (2016). Resolving insolvency in Hungary. [online] Available at: http://www.doingbusiness.org/data/exploreeconomies/hungary/resolving-insolvency/ [Accessed 31 Dec. 2016].

Part II

The microfabric of the Hungarian illiberal democracy

3 Illiberalism as constitutional identity

This chapter consists of a thought experiment: modelling and conceptually positioning the new political community and the political (theoretical) and constitutional construct, Prime Minister Orbán claims to have created and institutionalized through a new Constitution. The methodology is to follow statements and declarations by legal, most of all constitutional, documents and the grand architect Mr. Orbán: thus, the self-assessment of the 'design' and the designers. Two concepts will be in the center of analysis: the contours, organizational foundations and defining features of the self-proclaimed new political community and the morphology and consequences of the illiberal nature of the newly established regime. In most cases, constitutional and political regimes do not self-identify as illiberal (or even as liberal) – analysts and academics do this job. In our case, in a quite unique declaration, Prime Minister Orbán has done us the favour of actually doing so. We will, on the other hand, find no authentic, first-hand definitions for the details and precise circumcision of what the specificities of the newly emerged political community and source of legitimacy are or what the nature and role of illiberalism are. These are the questions that this thought experiment will try to answer.

It needs to be noted that there is a multilayered intellectual and ethical dilemma within this process, and I have certainly been struggling with it. First, there is the classic problem of analyzing legal (and constitutional) documents: these texts are almost always outcomes of political compromises (rather than consensus), and rarely is there a fully coherent philosophical or conceptual framework behind legislative solutions. Ironically, academics and courts, especially those engaged in constitutional review, are bound to interpret these texts as doctrinally sound wholes and work with the presupposition that there is a coherent and compact theoretical framework behind them.

Even more troubling is when we have reason to believe that ad hocism or sheer and empty political PR is behind the statements and declarations that serve as building blocks for modelling. As I will show, both core concepts scrutinized within this chapter, "illiberal democracy" and the emergence of a new political community (labelled as the "System of National Cooperation") appear to be marketing products. As an analysis of official government and Fidesz communications shows, the concept of illiberal democracy as a new path for Hungary, introduced by Prime Minister Orbán in a seminal speech that placed him on international media headlines, was completely abandoned and never mentioned again after the first wave of publicity and media discourse-setting subdued. The concept of the "System of National Cooperation" had a similar fate. It was identified as the epiphany of the new political community legitimizing a new constitutional regime, which was solemnly declared in the form of a parliamentary resolution. It was the rhetorical center of the government program, and a government order even made it mandatory to be displayed in all government facilities in Hungary. However, after October 2012, not a single reference has been made to it in government sources, politicians' speeches or documents. This makes one skeptical of intellectual endeavours involving grand theoretical designs. My former doctoral advisor, András Sajó, now a judge at the European Court of Human Rights, told me during one of our consultations (and this always echoes in my head): it is a mistake to put ideas and improvisations of East European politicians up for serious and unreflected scientific scrutiny and comparative analysis. On a further note, scholars need to be aware of the fact that academic recognition of certain phenomena may contribute to their political legitimacy simply by making them subjects of analysis.

***

1. Terminology and conceptualization

In his seminal essay in which he argues that liberalism, either as a conception of political liberty or as a doctrine about economic policy, does not necessarily coincide with democracy, Fareed Zakaria (1997) defines liberal democracy as a political system marked not only by free and fair elections but also by rule of law, separation of powers and the protections of basic liberties of speech, assembly, religion and property. Scholarly discussion on definitions has burgeoned in the past years. As Rupnik and Zielonka (2013) and Collier and Levitsky (1997) argue, authors often qualify the term democracy by adding adjectives such as liberal (or illiberal), deliberative, representative, participatory, delegative, façade, direct (or indirect), electoral, hybrid, Western, Islamic, managed (Anderson, 2007), etc. Others refer to electoral or competitive autocracies (Shevtsova, 2000; Levitsky and Way, 2010). Following Huntington (1991) in his recent analysis, which serves as a starting point for this assessment, Csillag and Szelényi (2015, p. 22) define liberalism and democracy as two distinct dimensions of good governance, identifying "liberalism" with separation of powers and the security of private property rights and "democracy" as majoritarian rule. They do not explicitly define illiberal democracy but describe the features of the "emergent illiberal post-communist systems" in political terms and claim that as long as democratic institutions operate and leaders are elected to office, the ruling elites of these "illiberal democracies need a legitimating ideology which can appeal to a broader electorate." In their genealogy of what they call "post-communist managed illiberal democracy," where property relations shift from private property and market capitalism to neo-patrimonial and eventually neo-prebendal property relations, they argue that the core distinguishing feature is this ideology, which they call post-communist traditionalist or neo-conservative. As Gábor Halmai argues, under the standard political science definition for liberal democracy, the three independent but interconnected elements of democracy, human rights and the rule of law need to be simultaneously present. An illiberal regime in contrast is one in which formal electoral democracy prevails but either or both of the other elements are missing, for example, as in the case of theocratic (such as Iran or Saudi Arabia) or communitarian (such as the South Korean or the Taiwanese) constitutions, which nevertheless retain a certain minimum level of constitutionalism. These, he argues, must be distinguished from autocratic regimes (such as Putin's Russia), where there are opposition parties and an independent press, and these allow for the pretense of electoral competition, though in reality the opposition has no chance of winning an election, and dictatorships (such as the Soviet Union and the former communist countries or contemporary China, Vietnam, Cuba and Belarus), in which there is neither an opposition nor an independent press, and which cannot be considered constitutional regimes, even if they happen to have written constitutions (Halmai, 2014).

To avoid further entanglement in a conceptual and terminological labyrinth, throughout this volume "illiberal" should be understood as a privative prefix, referring to a constitutional and political condition that creates a middle ground between a constitutional democracy and an autocracy. This reading is not unique in the literature. Csillag and Szelényi (2015, p. 27) claim that the road from democracy to autocracy is paved with the "stones" of illiberalism, and while "illiberalism does not necessarily eliminate democracy, it creates conditions (given the weakness of Constitutional Courts and the legislative branch) for particularly powerful political leaders to flirt with abandoning democratic procedures if they may sense their electoral support eroded and they may not win the next elections." Bozóki (2011) argues that the "System of National Cooperation," introduced by Prime Minister Viktor Orbán, which I will analyze in detail below in order to make the claim that it is one of the manifestations of the "Hungarian illiberal democracy," has emerged as an alternative to liberal democracy. In developing this interpretation, it will be argued that illiberalism in Hungary is a form of constitutional identity, a political discourse that creates the rhetorical and political framework for the newly constructed political community.

A note on populism is needed here. I accept Ádám and Bozóki's (2016) assessment[1] according to which populism is an anti-elitist, anti-institutional

1 And the synthesis of Canovan (1999), Canovan, Ionescu and Gellner (1969), Finchelstein (2014). Kriesi and Pappas (2015), Laclau (1987), Mudde (2015), Shils (1956, p. 97), and Urbinati (2014).

political behaviour that identifies with "the people" and enhances their "direct" participation in the political process as opposed to representative government. Modern democratic populism in the post-WWII era can be interpreted as the substitute of totalitarian politics in the hegemony of democratic representation. Populism has an ideological character but in itself does not have a particular ideological content. It can be nationalistic, xenophobic, anti-feminist, anti-LGBT, anti-liberal, anti-Western or, anti-Semitic, anti-Muslim or, even neoliberal. The main idea is that governing is based on popular participation with limited public contest for power. Thus, populism is truly 'democratic' even if it openly rejects the constitutional norms of liberal democracy; the only criterion is that populist political entrepreneurs perform top-down mass mobilization. In populist governance, power is personalized, and its execution is organized along personal relations. Formal political and administrative institutions need to be sufficiently fluid to allow for mass participation in politics, as "simplification and polarization produce verticalization of political consent, which inaugurates a deeper unification of the masses under an organic narrative and a charismatic or Caesarist leader personating it" (Ádám and Bozóki, 2016, p. 100). I agree with Zoltán and Bozóki's argument that "populism should be seen as the political manifestation of illiberalism, especially in (semi-) peripheries such as Latin America and Eastern Europe," (Ádám and Bozóki, 2016, pp. 115–116) and that in the Hungarian case, "Fidesz managed to combine anti-elitism, nationalism and an anti-EU stance with a pragmatist approach in most policy areas, presenting a charismatic leadership, allegedly defending the national interest and those of ordinary people" (Ádám and Bozóki, 2016, p. 100).

2. Illiberalism and the emergence of a new political community: The System of National Cooperation

Orbán's regime claims to have created a new a political community. A key reflection is the changing of the official name of the state from "Magyar Köztársaság" to "Magyarország." The former, although commonly referred to in English as the "Republic of Hungary", was actually "Hungarian Republic," with the adjective "Hungarian" (*magyar*). Magyarország (*Magyarstan*) means "Hungarian Country," grammatically a morpheme, a complex word derived from the agglutination of the words "Hungarian" (*magyar* can be either a noun or an adjective) and "country" (*ország*) (for a monograph on this, see Takács, 2015). Border signage, passport cover pages and identity cards have all been changed, and courts deliver judgments in the new name.

The new political community was officially founded using a formally non-binding, unique pre-constitutional document, a political declaration on "National Cooperation," adopted on 16 June, 2010. This document foresees and legitimizes a total break with the preexisting political community and declares the emergence of a new political community, the System of National Cooperation (hereinafter SNC), which originates retroactively from a "voting booth revolution," a term used to describe the election that created the parliamentary supermajority of the governing coalition (Fidesz and the Hungarian Christian Democratic Party, the two parties that ran jointly). Retroactivity refers to the fact that the idea of creating a new political community (or even the adoption of a new constitution) was not part of the political campaign in the elections; needless to say, the principles of this new regime were not up for political deliberation either.

The Declaration (1140/2010), adopted shortly after the new government took office, was to be displayed in all government facilities in Hungary per a government order, which even specified the size, colour, fonts, and details of framing. The president, the speaker of the Parliament, the presidents of the Constitutional Court and the Supreme Court, the Central Bank, mayors, ombudspersons, chief prosecutors and judges were requested to follow suit in the form of a government resolution. Most state institutions, such as hospitals or universities, complied. Opposition parties and human rights NGOs considered this duty to display an oath of allegiance an intrusion to the separation of powers and the independence of crucial institutions. The statement issued by the Socialist Party argued that "This ordinance is Viktor Orbán's letter of resignation from western civilization" and "the first symbolic step toward building a totalitarian regime that doesn't tolerate differences of opinion" (Hungarian Spectrum, 2010). Even the far-right party Jobbik (Jobbik Magyarországért Mozgalom Párt – Movement for a Better Hungary Party) stated that this recalled the days when "one had to put up similar documents next to the pictures of Lenin, Stalin, Rákosi, and Kádár" (Hungarian Spectrum, 2010). Socialist MPs even submitted a satirical bill mocking the Declaration and, *inter alia*, declaring Orbán's birthday a national holiday (Krekó, 2010).

The political credo of the new regime and the new political community reads as follows:

> At the end of the first decade of the 21st century, after forty-six years of occupation and dictatorship and two turbulent decades of transition Hungary has regained the right and ability of self-determination[...] In the spring of 2010 the Hungarian nation once again summoned its vitality and brought about another revolution in the voting booths. [...] The National Assembly declares that a new social contract was laid down in the April general elections through which the Hungarians decided to create a new system: the National Cooperation System. [...] We, members of the National Assembly declare that we shall elevate the new political and economic system emerging on the basis of the popular democratic will [...] that connect the members of our diverse Hungarian society. Work, home, family, health and order – these will be the pillars of our common future[...] The National Cooperation System is[...] an opportunity for, as well as a requirement of, everybody who lives, works or has an undertaking in Hungary. We firmly believe that we will be able to change Hungary's future through the solidarity represented by the National Cooperation System and build a strong and successful

> country. This solidarity that releases tremendous energies and gives great hope to every Hungarian [...] and [...] after decades gives a chance to the Hungarians to fulfil their own goals at last.[2]

The term and concept of the SNC were used to form a central theme in the government program, submitted to Parliament on 22 May 2010.[3] In fact, the 80 pages long program, which contains a subchapter on the "New Social Contract" and in which the government consistently refers to itself as "The Government of National Affairs," is titled "The Programme of National Cooperation" and has three chapters: The Declaration of National Cooperation, the (description of) the System of National Cooperation and Issues of National Importance, and a joint declaration with the Hungarian Chamber of Commerce and Industry. Let us see some of the highlights of the government program:

> Hungarians want deep-seated and fundamental change in every area of life. They have authorized more than mere adjustment or change; they have authorized us, through the strength of national cooperation, to establish a new political, economic, and social system built on new rules in every area of life. They expect me with all my strength and ability to help the Hungarian community dispose of the old system and create, consolidate, and operate a new one. By adopting the Declaration of National Cooperation the new National Assembly has acknowledged the inception of a new social contract in the elections held in April whereby Hungarians decided on the foundation of a new system, the System of National Cooperation. Through this declaration we acknowledge the will of the people, and make it the compass of the future.

The government program contains important statements and points of references for constitutional identity:

> In April 2010 the long period of transition rife with struggles, divisiveness, and crises came to an end. The era was brought to an end by the act of the revolution which took place in the polling booths. In spring 2010 for the first time in Hungary since the system change a single political force was granted democratic authority of constituent import. This act imposes historical responsibility on the newly formed parliament. The new parliament is more than Hungary's sixth freely elected parliament. The new Assembly is in fact a constituent national assembly and system-founding parliament. With the two-thirds mandate voters entrusted the new Assembly and the new government using democratic means to carry out revolutionary changes in national issues of the greatest importance. By doing so the country's

2 Official government translation.

3 http://www.parlament.hu/irom39/00047/00047_e.pd, official translation.

> citizens regained their ability of self-determination and the opportunity by joining forces, instead of pacts and forced compromises, to turn the country in the interest of the common good in a new direction.

The idea that the new government program is actually a new social contract is made explicit:

> The social contract is the foundation which ensures that the country, in spite of the cyclical nature of the political-economic rotation, develops along a stable path in the direction specified by the people. For lack of a social contract Hungary during the era of transition was controlled by elite agreements and invisible pacts; fruitless debates hampered the country's progress. On account of this the country in recent years was smothered in the battle of private and partial interests; our common national causes were obscured. The current Constitution – as its first sentence reveals – is a temporary, transitional constitution. Its authors intended it as temporary precisely because there was no underlying and valid social contract. The new social contract has now been concluded in the 2010 parliamentary elections. Legislators have been entrusted over the next four years with the creation of the country's new constitution. The essence of constitutional democracies is that power is exercised by the people. Accordingly, in April 2010 Hungarian voters availed of their right to exercise power and made a firm and clear decision: they gave their blessing, in place of the era of transition and in the spirit of the new social contract, to a new system founded on national cooperation. In constitutional democracies representatives elected by the people exercise power. As during the transition no social contract was born expressing national unity, it was possible in the past eight years for the government to openly turn against the common will, and without consequence to abuse the power vested in it. The new social contract was created by national unity revolutionary in its power which expresses the common will of the Hungarian nation. The common will of the nation may not be overridden by any visible or invisible political pact or challenged by any partial interest. This fact compels the country's leaders to do their job, to perform their work in this spirit. With overwhelming force Hungarians ousted the politics which for years went against their will. For this reason, it is the duty of the new National Assembly among its first measures to declare that the united will of the people is the main source of power in Hungary. The responsibility of the first government of the new era is to enforce the new social contract, namely to erect the System of National Cooperation. The System of National Cooperation will be the foundation of the country's reconstruction and of the creation of a strong Hungary. Today Hungary is weak, undergoing times of economic, social, and spiritual crisis. However, the social contracts of Western Europe also emerged in situations of crisis. These ambitious agreements also sought solutions for deepening crises of political confidence, as well as for severe economic problems and social ills.

Having identified the agents of the new constitutional identity, the government program sets forth the framework of the modus operandi and administration of the new political community:

> The new social contract calls for cooperation instead of divisiveness, service of the public good instead of the advocacy of private interests, and the strong and effective representation of common national causes. A government for whom the sole benchmark is the nation and the advancement of its members. A government for whom the interests of the individual and the community are not at odds, but rather complement each other. The System of National Cooperation is built instead of ostracism on unity, instead of political irresponsibility on political responsibility, instead of tolerance of extremes on the rejection and elimination of such, instead of the limitation of citizens' self-determination on the proliferation of such, and on the restoration of balance between rights and obligations. [...] the policy of the new government does not have to change the cultural attitudes of Hungarian society – this must stem from other, non-political motives – but it has to change politics and government in order to free up the energies of individual ambition in a way that is beneficial in terms of community building. The public thinking and public sentiment of the era of transition were explicitly/implicitly built on the assumption that individual interests could only be enforced at each other's expense, by weakening each other. In reality, however, individual interests can reinforce each other if this is a conscious part of our efforts [...] The System of National Cooperation calls for deep-seated and fundamental change in every important area of government. In the future, instead of private aims and interests, politics must serve common aims and interests. A government and governance is needed which once again turns towards people and their everyday problems, and which is based on the representation of our common national causes. A government is needed, therefore, which pays attention to people, listens to them, respects their diversity, and understands their concerns. Therefore it represents and enforces those interests which are important to everyone, and thus unites, not separates us. Politics are necessary, therefore, which build and develop these common values, and strive to make these accessible to everyone. [...]Hungarians are now experiencing that freedom without order breeds chaos and fear. Where order is lacking bars, locks, latches, barriers, cordons, and surveillance cameras are soon to follow. Thus work, home, family, health, and order are the solid pillars of the System of National Cooperation. In the years to come the Government of National Affairs shall enforce the social contract based on our common values, namely it shall establish the primacy of public good over private interests, the primacy of order over lawlessness, the primacy of safety over unpredictability and governmental chaos, and the primacy of economic advancement over debt and vulnerability.

The government program, thus, declares a supreme source of political legitimacy, which actually created a new constitutional community, embodied by the government (majority in Parliament) and expressed a messianic determination for transformative changes in political and spiritual life:

> The national unity which came about in the elections compels the new government to carry out its electoral program. We are going to fulfil this commitment. [...] Hungarians expressed the will that henceforth common aims and issues of national importance must be served in the System of National Cooperation which unite Hungarians in all their diversity, because they embody those core values which are important to all of us for prosperity and a respectable life: work, home, family, health, and order.[4]

It is illuminating to look at how the concept and the very term were used in subsequent government communication. I conducted a comprehensive survey of press releases and other entries in the archives of the national news agency, Magyar Távirati Iroda (MTI), which supposedly contains all relevant entries. The SNC was mentioned for the first time on the night of the elections in Orbán's speech announcing victory. The next time it was mentioned, again by Orbán, was during the first meeting of Fidesz's parliamentary group and a few days later in the opening session of the Parliament. He again talked about the SNC at two campaign rallies in May and later in June 2010 when signing an agreement with a leader of Hungarians living in Serbia (where he declared that the System of National Cooperation includes Hungarians living outside Hungary). In Parliament, on his 56th (!) day of office (reflecting on the revolution of 1956), the prime minister stated that the new political community, which he referred to as the "national center," was a community of rationality, and his efforts were focused on transforming the two thirds parliamentary majority into a political community of a "central force field," the System of National Cooperation. In a somewhat contradictory fashion, he also said that the reason to govern is the creation of this "political center," and the way to achieve it is the SNC. In September 2011, on his 100th day of his government in office, Orbán reported to Parliament on the development of the four distinct "national cooperations" of politics, economy, administration and morality – the latter to be elaborated within and by the new Constitution. According to my research, the last time he ever mentioned the SNC was on 23 October 2012 when giving out awards on the national holiday. In addition to the Orbán speeches, the term was mentioned only four times by politicians: once by the spokesman for the prime minister, by the deputy spokesman for Fidesz in political rebuttals, by an undersecretary and by an MP in connection with the new law on churches, expressing the importance of including traditional churches in the SNC. That is

4 Official government translation.

all. After October 2012, not once was this term and concept, so central to the new political community that it was required to be displayed in state buildings, mentioned by government sources. After the adoption of the new Constitution, the displayed copies of the Declaration of National Cooperation in government offices were mostly replaced by the Preamble of the new Constitution, the National Avowal of Faith.[5]

3. Illiberalism and the System of National Cooperation

Another term and concept that is corollary to understanding Orbán's Hungary is self-proclaimed illiberalism and the identification of his regime as an illiberal democracy. No normative legal document, formal political manifesto or official government communication ever provided a coherent description of the nature, design or constitutional philosophy of the Hungarian illiberal democracy model. It is therefore the task and challenge of academic analyses to decipher its normative and analytic content. I will argue that Hungarian illiberal democracy manifests itself in the SNC – a vaguely defined, yet even normatively presented political construct in which majority rule may operate unbounded by the rule of law, separation of powers and other constraints of liberal democracies. The SNC, which was never actually defined or explained in a normative document or even a political manifesto, is arguably both the conceptualization and a metaphor of the political community. Although it is not a formalized set of political institutions, it is the conceptualization of the illiberal democratic decision-making process, which makes traditional constitutionalism obsolete.

It needs to be added that illiberalism was not part of the first marketing package of the SNC. On the contrary, the aforementioned 2010 government program of "National Cooperation" contained several commitments to liberal democracy and even a quote from Abraham Lincoln:

> The Government of National Affairs intends to pursue a policy that ensures everyone the greatest possible freedom [...] Overall, given our aims, we can avow the words of Abraham Lincoln as applicable to us: 'It is rather for us to [ensure] [...] that this nation, under God, shall have a new birth of freedom – and that government of the people, by the people, for the people, shall not perish from the earth.'
>
> (The Programme of National Cooperation, 2010, p. 16)

Part 5.1 contains important references to Fidesz's self-proclaimed identity. It starts by stating: "We will remain loyal to the ideas of democracy and the rule of law," as "Fidesz was formed in 1988 [...] so that Hungarians can live in real democracy enjoying the same freedom and wealth as Western-European states."

5 Curiously, while the initial display was ordered by law, in the form of a government order, I could not locate a source of law for the replacement, only a communiqué on the Fidesz website (2011).

It continues by holding that "Fidesz – Hungarian Civic Union has for 20 years consistently represented politics which rests on unconditional respect for solidarity, freedom, civil rights and human dignity, as well as legal certainty."

The reader is ensured of the party's commitment to freedom and the rule of law:

> True wealth is inconceivable without freedom. The most important guarantee of freedom is, in turn, law and order, and therefore the principal task of the current Government is to defend the property of its citizens, legal certainty and legality. At the core of it is the imperative that the State itself respects the law. Compliance with the norm is not only an obligation binding on the citizen, but is a fundamental requirement the possessors of power must fulfil themselves. Within the frame of the rule of law it is unacceptable for the Government, in possession of parliamentary majority, to pass unconstitutional laws and thus expose its citizens to uncertainty, also jeopardising the principle of legal certainty.

4. Illiberal democracy as constitutional identity

Illiberalism as a chosen feature of the new regime was introduced by Orbán, at a speech delivered at the Summer Open University of Bálványos in July 2014 (Orbán, 2014); it immediately went viral and was reported widely in international media. Here, Orbán identified his regime as illiberal in the following manner:

> [...]while breaking with the dogmas and ideologies that have been adopted by the West and keeping ourselves independent from them, we are trying to find the form of community organisation, the new Hungarian state, which is capable of making our community competitive in the great global race for decades to come. [...] a democracy does not necessarily have to be liberal. Just because a state is not liberal, it can still be a democracy. [...] until now we have known three forms of state organisation: the nation state, the liberal state and the welfare state. And the question is, what's next? The Hungarian answer to this question is that the era of the work-based state is approaching. We want to organise a work-based society that, as I have just mentioned, undertakes the odium of stating that it is not liberal in character. [...] we must break with liberal principles and methods of social organisation, and in general with the liberal understanding of society. [...] and forge a new method of Hungarian state organisation [...], following [in the sense of bypassing[...], ALP] the liberal state and the era of liberal democracy [...] we suggest, and are attempting to construct Hungarian state life around this idea, that (liberalism) should not be the principle on which society is built. [...] the Hungarian nation is not simply a group of individuals but a community that must be organised, reinforced and in fact constructed. And [...] the new state that we are constructing in Hungary is an illiberal state, a non-liberal state. [...]we want to organise our national state to replace the liberal state,

> construct a new state built on illiberal and national foundations within the European Union. […] the Government has come to a decision according to which within this new state concept, this illiberal state concept, the reorganisation of the Hungarian state is underway, in contrast to the liberal state organisation logic of the previous twenty years.[6]

As Csillag and Szelényi (2015, p. 23) argue, "liberalism" for Orbán means the excessive emphasis of individual interest over "national" interest. In one of his most widely cited speeches, Orbán envisions that in the next 15–20 years, Hungary should be dominated by a single, massive right-wing political party that would rule the whole political field without "unnecessary" debates (Rácz, 2015). Bánkuti et al. (2012, p. 145.) quote Orbán in 2009, even before the victorious elections visioning a

> […] real chance that politics in Hungary will no longer be tied by a dualist power space […] Instead, a large governing party will emerge in the center of the political stage (that) will be able to formulate national policy, not through constant debates but through a natural representation of interests.

Although the populist rhetoric (of the SNC) aims at targeting and attracting both moderate and far-right voters, the SNC is not inherently and intrinsically racist, misogynist, anti-Semitic or homophobic. It does, however, neglect and deny the discursive recognition of and questions the importance, relevance and legitimacy of liberal values and fails to adopt an individual freedom and human rights approach that would, for example, endorse Roma inclusion, feminism and multiculturalism, post-nationalism, individualism or a particular vision of modernism – ideals and commitments Hungarian liberal public intellectuals would advocate.[7] In other words, the discourse is not inherently anti-liberal, only "a-liberal."

We need to note here that Orbán, the omnipotent charismatic leader, and his party were "liberal" before a sharp turn to the right in 1993, which a former mentor and political ally Miklós Haraszti (2002) calls a purely political maneuver. Fidesz was "the ultimate anarcho-liberal, a pupil and an embodiment of the Democratic Opposition's underground culture. […] He has led himself and his Fidesz party from radical anti-authoritarians to radical Christian-Conservatives.

6 Speaking in an interview with Bloomberg, Orbán said the following: "Hungarians welcomed illiberal democracy. The fact that in English it means something else is not my problem. In the Hungarian context, the word liberal has become negative. Liberal democracy has no or very little support in Hungary. What I want to say is that it's not true that a democracy can only be liberal" (Simon, 2014).

7 This is not to argue that liberalism is necessarily multicultural, or that any form of collectivistic constitutionalism would be inherently liberal, only that these would be the most characteristic and typical commitments by Hungarian liberal public intellectuals (who, in the absence of a visible liberal party, can be identified as relevant 'liberal' voices.)

He took pride in 1990 in making Fidesz a member of the Liberal International one step earlier than SZDSZ (the Alliance of Free Democrats)," the leading opposition party in 1990–94 and Fidesz's political and ideological role model before and during the roundtable talks and the transition. Michael Shafir calls this the crowning of the party's "transfiguration," when it left the Liberal International and joined the conservative European People's Party in 2010 (Shafir, 2004).

Thus, allegiance to illiberalism is also a quasi-Freudian reiteration of Orbán's conservative turn in 1993 and the formal and overt rejection of his party's initial liberal commitments to values and principles such as human rights, inclusive intimate citizenship, cosmopolitanism, modernism, political correctness and multiculturalism: commitments endorsed by liberal politicians and intellectuals in Hungary. Illiberal democracy as per Orbán is a manifesto against the now mostly imagined, but habitually demonized, arch-enemy, a once-envied powerful and popular father party advocating the above liberal values and commitment.

Again, let us return to the seminal Orbán speech:

> The Hungarian nation is not simply a group of individuals but a community that must be organised, reinforced and in fact constructed. And [...] the new state that we are constructing in Hungary is an illiberal state, a non-liberal state. It does not reject the fundamental principles of liberalism such as freedom, and I could list a few more, but it does not make this ideology the central element of state organisation, but instead includes a different, special, national approach.

As he points out, "This cannot be entered into law, we are talking about an intellectual starting point now." Thus, illiberalism in Hungary goes beyond political and legal action. It is a form of ideology and a discursive construct. Even though self-identified "unorthodox" legal and political institutions are instrumental in the establishment, solidification and cementing of the Orbán regime, they are only by-products. The real product is the (conceptual framework of the) newly established political community. Illiberal democracy and the SNC serve as tools of constitutional identity and an ideological framework for institutionalizing the well-documented process of anti-democratic backlash in Hungary.

It would, therefore, be a mistake to identify the Hungarian illiberal democracy model with these constitutional and legal developments. Instead, an alternative, not institution-focused, analysis is offered. "Hungarian illiberal democracy" is neither a construct of constitutional philosophy nor a principle of constitutional design. It cannot be properly described by the evisceration of classic democratic institutions, and it is not characteristically illiberal within the interpretative framework of political theory. It would equally not qualify as a sui generis un-republican,[8] un-participatory (Bouza Garcia, 2015), un-agonistic (Wenman,

8 See for example: Niederberger and Schink (2013); Pettit (2013).

2013) or un-deliberative model.[9] Despite the political mantra used by Orbán's party of the legitimating force of a parliamentary supermajority being based on a single event of popular vote, the Hungarian model of illiberal democracy cannot be equated with the unfettered freedom of a parliamentary majority to do as it pleases. Rather, it is a tool to channel, define and dominate general political discourse and to provide a discursive framework for political identification and ideologically biased yet divergent and ad hoc legislation.

I argue that "illiberal democracy" and "illiberalism" in Hungary are actually forms of constitutional identity guiding the discursive framework of this new political community. Illiberalism is thus the culmination of government discourse along with the discursive framework of the new political community, which in turn reframes politics in terms of nationhood. It is the form and means to construe and express the new and novel (constitutional) identity, which emphasizes cultural particularism and values such as fidelity, faith and charity as opposed to universal values of equality, human rights and social inclusion. This creates official historical narratives but disregards individual autonomy and projects a paternalistic conception of society in which value preferences are not centered on liberty and autonomy. Orbán's illiberal democracy instrumentalizes a special form of nationalism built on the uniqueness of the Hungarian "people," where illiberalism is a form of ethno-symbolism. According to the concept of ethno-symbolism, nations are based on ethnic groups, where cultural cohesion is built on myths and symbols.[10] Here, the myth of the election of the new political community via the SNC is constituted through independence from modernist universalist values, which only brought failure and frustration. This framework for constitutional identity politics centers on the rejection of the liberal political ideology, which places individual freedom front and center.

As argued briefly above, and as will be shown in the upcoming chapters, the morphosis of this Hungarian model for illiberal democracy manifests itself normatively through value preferences expressed in the new Constitution, the Fundamental Law, as well as in a quasi-normative political declaration that serves as a manifesto for not only Orbán's new political regime but also the new political community he and his regime envisages. It is important to highlight that, contrary to what it claims to be, the SNC is not an actual institutionalized modus operandi for the Hungarian illiberal democracy, nor is it a form of political institutional design. It is rather the manifesto of illiberal democracy: the political and quasi-normative declaration of the Orbán regime's discursive framework. The quintessential feature of the Hungarian illiberal democracy is that it is the discursive framework through which the Orbán government constructed a new national and constitutional identity. It is a form of constitutional

9 See for example Gutman and Thompson (2002).

10 Anthony D. Smith (1996; 1999; 2009) explains how myths are highly significant factors in nation building. Also consider John Armstrong (1982) arguing that "A most significant effect of the myth recital is to arouse an intense awareness among the group members of their 'common fate'".

commoditization intended to sell a political regime in which a significant emphasis is put on authenticity and difference. Thus, illiberalism is not so much a constitutional term describing and legitimizing an overall backlash in democratic control mechanisms and the protection of human rights as it is a discursive framework constructed to describe and market (see Comaroff and Comaroff, 2009) the new imagined community of the SNC-Hungarian nation and to narrate its shared common belonging.[11] To paraphrase Thierry Balzacq's (2010) securitization theory, one may argue that the Hungarian illiberalization process is a perlocutionary constitutional speech act (for the original theory, see Austin (1962)), in which consequential effects or sequels aim to evoke the feelings, beliefs, thoughts or actions of the target audience.[12] "Illiberalism" is a mobilizing tactic utilized to question the validity and sustainability of post the WWII (liberal) consensus on human rights-centered political language, disenchantment, certain sacred democratic institutions and neoliberal policies. The term (which is not a coherent concept) can be operationalized by neoconservative movements as an anti-modernist and fundamentalist (Vidra, Horváth and Fox, 2012) answer to the neoliberal consensus, similarly, for example, to the ways in which "(anti) gender ideology" is used. As Kováts et al. argue, "gender" has been identified as the common ground, a label amidst diverse political cultures, different party structures and a variety of mobilizing tactics, compressing different fears and values and used against diverse causes (Kováts, Põim and Tánczos, 2015; Kováts and Põim, 2015). Orbán's illiberalism is also very similar to Hobsbawm's (1992) view of nationalism in the 21st century – as a substitute, a placebo for disorientation and a surrogate for integration in a disintegrating society; when society fails, the nation appears as an ultimate guarantee (and in post-communist societies, as a device to distinguish between the innocent and the guilty). In the Hungarian case, the strategy worked. As Pető and Vasali (2014) point out, the government successfully built a state-funded (pseudo) NGO sector and this, alongside racist and nationalist movements,[13] convincingly offered anti-modernism and anti-cosmopolitanism/Europeanism (Melegh, 2006) as viable alternatives to neoliberal democracy and market economy.

Similarly to the grand vision of the National System of Cooperation, the concept of (announcing and defining) Hungary as an illiberal democracy, in contrast to its corollary status, does not appear to be something government communication would utilize for the long term. In fact, it creates the impression of a short-term marketing slogan, a tool to control public discussion and media attention. According to the aforementioned media analysis I carried out, using

11 For scholarly assessments on the role of discursive action in the process of identity formation see Cohen (1985); Fox and Miller-Idriss (2008); and Wodak (2009).

12 Balzacq (2010) argues that three different aspects should be considered when analyzing perlocutionary speech acts: (i) the centrality of the audience; (ii) the co-dependency of agency and context; (iii) the dispositive and structuring force of practices.

13 For more see for example Feischmidt and Hervik (2015); Vidra and Fox (2014); Wodak, KhosraviNik and Mral (2013).

the database of the national news agency, which is mandated to document all relevant government and public communication, the term and concept were used only seven times. Five times by Orbán: following the seminal speech, once in a debate in the Hungarian, once in the European Parliament and once during a press conference following a meeting with German Chancellor Angela Merkel, who specifically mentioned her concerns in regard to this statement, as well as in an interview in the German economic weekly, *Wirtschaftswoche*. The two other substantive references were made by Orbán's spokesperson and by one of his cabinet members (Kovács, Horváth and Vidra, 2011).

To sum up the findings of the thought experiment built on the presumption that there is a substantive theoretical construction behind legislative and political developments, and it can be and is worthy of being deciphered, this chapter made the following arguments: first, the Orbán government's self-proclaimed revolutionary regime claims to have reconstituted and reconceptualized the relationship between the state and its citizens, in both institutional and normative terms. For example, the Republic of Hungary was renamed Hungary. Second, the new regime in several fields of life made a significant departure from the constitutional standards generally held in liberal democracies. However, neither its creators argued convincingly nor could an academic analysis support the claim that this would indeed constitute a new, coherent, sui generis illiberal democracy model from the constitutional legal or political-theoretical point of view. Third, this self-identified illiberal regime, however, sets forth a political discourse and discursive framework that also materializes in the form of legal, constitutional documents that reject ideological and policy commitments towards human rights and an autonomy-centered (and in this sense liberal) concept of personhood.

Bibliography

Anderson, P. (2007). Russia's managed democracy. *London Review of Books*, 29(2), pp. 3–12.

Armstrong, J. (1982). *Nations before nationalism*. 1st ed. Chapel Hill, NC: University of North Carolina Press.

Austin, J. (1962). *How to do things with words*. 1st ed. Oxford: Clarendon Press.

Balzacq, T. (2010). *Securitization theory: How security problems emerge and dissolve*. 1st ed. Milton Park, Abingdon, Oxon: Routledge.

Bouza Garcia, L. (2015). *Participatory democracy and civil society in the EU: Agenda-setting and institutionalisation*. 1st ed. Basingstoke and New York: Palgrave Macmillan.

Bozóki, A. (2011). Occupy the state: The Orbán regime in Hungary. *Journal of Contemporary Central and Eastern Europe*, 19(3), pp. 649–663.

Bozóki, A. and Ádám, Z. (2016). State and faith: Right-wing populism and nationalized religion in Hungary. *East European Journal of Society and Politics*, 2(1), pp. 98–122.

Canovan, M. (1999). Trust the people! Populism and the two faces of democracy. *Political Studies*, 47(1), pp. 2–16.

Cohen, A. (1985). *Symbolic construction of community*. 1st ed. London: Routledge.

Collier, D. and Levitsky, S. (1997). Democracy with adjectives: Conceptual innovation in comparative research. *World Politics*, 49(3), pp. 430–451.

Comaroff, J. L. and Comaroff, J. (2009). *Ethnicity, Inc.* 1st ed. Chicago: University of Chicago Press.

Csillag, T. and Szelényi, I. (2015). Drifting from liberal democracy: Traditionalist/neo-conservative ideology of managed illiberal democratic capitalism in post-communist Europe. *East European Journal of Society and Politics*, 1(1), pp. 18–48.

Feischmidt, M. and Hervik, P. (2015). Mainstreaming the extreme: Intersecting challenges from the far right in Europe, intersections, *East European Journal of Society and Politics.*

Fidesz (2011). A Nemzeti Hitvallás szövege. [online] Available at: http://www.fidesz.hu/hirek/2011-04-18/a-nemzeti-hitvallas-szovege/ [Accessed 31 Dec. 2016].

Finchelstein, F. (2014). Returning populism to history. *Constellations*, 21(4), pp. 467–482.

Fox, J. and Miller-Idriss, C. (2008). Everyday nationhood. *Ethnicities*, 8(4), pp. 536–563.

Government Declaration 1140/2010. (VII. 2.)

Gutmann, A. and Thompson, D. (2002). *Why deliberative democracy?* Princeton, NJ: Princeton University Press.

Halmai, G. (2017). Az illiberális demokrácián is túl? [Moving even beyond illiberal democracy?]. *Élet és Irodalom*, 58(36).

Haraszti, M. (2002). The "real" Viktor Orbán. *Open Democracy.* [online] Available at: https://www.opendemocracy.net/democracy-newright/article_358.jsp [Accessed 31 Dec. 2016].

Hobsbawm, E.J. (1992). *Nations and nationalism since 1780.* 1st ed. Cambridge: Cambridge University Press, pp. 163–192.

Hungarian Spectrum (2010). Orbán's proclamation of national cooperation on every wall [online] Available at: https://hungarianspectrum.wordpress.com/2010/07/03/orbans-proclamation-of-national-cooperation-on-every-wall/ [Accessed 31 Dec. 2016].

Huntington, S. P. (1991). *The third wave: Democratization in the late twentieth century.* 1st ed. Norman, OK: University of Oklahoma Press.

Ionescu, G. and Gellner, E. ed. (1969). *Populism: Its meaning and national characteristics.* 1st ed. New York: Macmillan.

Kovács, A., Horváth, A. and Vidra, Zs. (2011). The ferry-country between East and West: Debates on modernity and Europe in Hungary. In: A. Ichijo, ed., *Europe, nations and modernity*, 1st ed. Basingstoke: Palgrave Macmillan, pp. 158–182.

Kováts, E. and Põim, M. ed. (2015). *Gender as symbolic glue: The position and role of conservative and far right parties anti-gender mobilizations in Europe.* 1st ed. Brussels: FEPS-FES.

Kováts, E., Põim, M. and Tánczos, J. (2015). *Beyond gender? Anti-gender mobilization and the lessons for progressives*, FEPS-FES Policy Brief, pp. 4–5.

Krekó, P. (2010). Fidesz & hubrisz. *The Budapest Times.* [online] Available at: http://budapesttimes.hu/2010/07/12/fidesz-hubrisz/ [Accessed 31 Dec. 2016].

Kriesi, H. and Pappas, T. (2015). Populism in Europe during crisis: An introduction. In: H. Kriesi and T. Pappas, ed., *European Populism in the Shadow of Great Recession.*, 1st ed. Colchester: ECPR Press, pp. 1–22.

Laclau, E. (1987). Peronism in historical and comparative perspective. In: E. Archetti, P. Cammack and B. Roberts, ed., *Sociology of the 'developing countries': Latin America*, 1st ed. New York, London: Monthly Review Press, pp. 137–147.

Levitsky, S. and Way, L. A. (2010). *Competitive authoritarianism.* 1st ed. Cambridge: Cambridge University Press.

Melegh, A. (2006). *On the East/West Slope: Globalization, nationalism, racism and discourses on Eastern Europe.* 1st ed. New York: Central European University Press.

Mudde, C. (2015). Is Hungary run by the radical right? *The Washington Post.* [online] Available at: https://www.washingtonpost.com/blogs/monkey-cage/wp/2015/08/10/is-hungary-run-by-the-radical-right/ [Accessed 31 Dec. 2016].

Niederberger, A. and Schink, P. ed. (2013). *Republican democracy: Liberty, law and politics.* 1st ed. Edinburgh: Edinburgh University Press.

Orbán, V. (2014). A munkaalapú állam korszaka következik. Speech at the Summer Open University of Bálványos. [online] Available at: http://www.kormany.hu/hu/a-miniszterelnok/beszedek-publikaciok-interjuk/a-munkaalapu-allam-korszaka-kovetkezik [Accessed 31 Dec. 2016].

Pető, A. and Vasali, Z. (2014). The 'laboratory' called Hungary: A challenge for understanding protest movements. *Open Democracy.* [online] Available at: https://www.opendemocracy.net/can-europe-make-it/andrea-pet%C5%91-zolt%C3%A1n-vasali/%E2%80%98laboratory%E2%80%99-called-hungary-challenge-for-understanding [Accessed 31 Dec. 2016].

Pettit, P. (2013). *On the people's terms: A Republican theory and model of democracy.* 1st ed. Cambridge: Cambridge University Press.

Political Declaration 1 of 2010 (16 June) of the Hungarian Parliament on national cooperation.

Rácz, A. (2015). Multi-vectorialism failing? The Russia-policy of the Orbán-government. *Russkii vopros,* [online] 15(1). Available at: http://www.russkiivopros.com/?pag=one&id=619&kat=7&csl=69 [Accessed 31 Dec. 2016].

Rupnik, J. and Zielonka, J. (2013). Introduction: The state of democracy 20 Years on. Domestic and external factors. *East European Politics and Societies,* 27(1), pp. 3–25.

Shafir, M. (2004). The politics of public space and the legacy of the holocaust in postcommunist Hungary, Part 3. Viktor Orban's 'transfiguration' or the making of a radical conservative. *East European Perspectives,* 6(12).

Shevtsova, L. (2000). Can electoral autocracy survive? *Journal of Democracy,* 11(3), pp. 36–38.

Shils, E. (1956). *The torment of secrecy: The background and consequences of American security policies.* 1st ed. Chicago: Ivan R. Dee.

Simon, Z. (2014). Hungary on path to shed junk grade and shield Forint, Orban Says. *Bloomberg.* [online] Available at: https://www.bloomberg.com/news/articles/2014-12-15/hungary-on-path-to-shed-junk-grade-and-shield-forint-orban-says [Accessed 31 Dec. 2016].

Smith, A.D. (1996). Culture, community and territory: The politics of ethnicity and nationalism. *International Affairs,* 72(3), pp. 445–458.

Smith, A.D. (1999). Ethnic election and national destiny: Some religious origins of nationalist ideals. *Nations and Nationalism,* 5(3), pp. 331–355.

Smith, A.D. (2009). *Ethno-symbolism and nationalism: A cultural approach.* 1st ed. London, New York: Routledge.

Takács, P. (2015). *A rózsa neve: Magyar Köztársaság – Az államok nevéről és a magyar állam átnevezéséről.* 1st ed. Budapest: Gondolat.

The Programme of National Cooperation (2010). Office of the National Assembly. Document Number: H/47. [online] Available at: http://www-archiv.parlament.hu/irom39/00047/00047_e.pdf [Accessed 31 Dec. 2016].

Urbinati, N. (2014). *Democracy disfigured: Opinion, truth, and the people.* 1st ed. Cambridge: Harvard University Press.

Vidra, Zs. and Fox, J. (2014). Mainstreaming of racist anti-Roma discourses in the media in Hungary. *Journal of Immigrant and Refugee Studies,* 12(4), pp. 437–455.

Vidra, Zs., Horváth, A. and Fox, J. (2012). Tolerance and cultural diversity discourses in Hungary. In: R. Zapata-Barrero and A. Triandafyllidou, ed., *Addressing tolerance and diversity discourses in Europe: Comparative overview of 16 European countries*, 1st ed. Barcelona: Barcelona Centre for International Affairs, pp. 317–343.

Wenman, M. (2013). *Agonistic democracy: Constituent power in the era of globalisation.* 1st ed. Cambridge: Cambridge University Press.

Wodak, R., KhosraviNik, M. and Mral, B. ed. (2013). *Right-wing populism in Europe: Politics and discourse.* 1st ed. London: Bloomsbury Academic.

Zakaria, F. (1997). The rise of illiberal democracy. *Foreign Affairs*, 76(6), pp. 22–43.

4 Intimate citizenship and value preferences in the new Constitution

The remainder of the book will provide case studies to demonstrate how illiberalism manifests in the post-2010 Hungarian legal and political regime. Illiberalism takes the form of ideological commitments and biases in legal and constitutional documents, as well as in patterns of judicial and political practices. It will be shown that in many cases it is only the formal legal and constitutional declaration of these illiberal commitments and biases that is new (and shocking or controversial) but often it has been present in judicial or government practices. Illiberalism, and in particular the Orbán regime, is most often portrayed as the democratic backlash that surfaces first and foremost in the dismantling of institutional rule-of-law guarantees, the weakening of checks and balances, but it needs to be added that the systematic abuse of fundamental rights and individual freedoms is not part of the package (as yet). This is true, but two important features that relate to individual freedom also characterize the SNC: the new Constitution fails to recognize individual autonomy as a constitutional principle, and its ideological commitments and constitutionally enshrined value preferences may authorize future legislation that may restrict autonomy and freedom in all sorts of ways.

Currently, debates that dominate Hungarian constitutional scholarship still center on the legitimacy and "constitutionality" of the new constitutional regime and how its language and paradigm is compatible with international standards. It is for the future to assess whether initial concerns will actually prove well founded by the practical application and interpretation of the Fundamental Law and subsequent legislation. For example, the new Constitution authorizes legislation restricting abortion or even prohibiting in vitro fertilization, but no such initiatives have been floored so far. It will also be interesting to investigate whether the new Constitution will be capable of creating a new constitutional identity. This analysis is limited to exploring whether biases and ideological commitments can be supported by current identities, preferences and lifestyle choices of the political community.

In showing how the new constitutional regime is ideologically biased, I will rely on the concept of 'intimate citizenship' as an analytical tool to assess the Fundamental Law from the aspect of privacy and intimacy/sexuality. The concept of 'intimate citizenship' refers to the fact that certain groups (of formally equal-status citizens) within the political community face inequality and marginalization based on their status, choices and preferences in private life because their access to certain economic, political, social and cultural rights is restricted by constitutional and political preferences.[1]

In the case of the SNC's Hungary, not only is freedom to make autonomous choices in private matters not declared or recognized in the Constitution as an explicitly endorsed value, the declaration of the principle of non-discrimination in regard to certain specific freedoms implied by intimate citizenship is also absent. Furthermore, I will illuminate[2] how the new Constitution and adjacent legislation set forth several normatively formulated value preferences, which can be defined as illiberal in the sense that they suggest either the denial or at least the disregard of individual autonomy and liberty and that project a paternalistic, patriarchal and heteronormative concept of society and the political community. As this and the subsequent chapters will show, the new political community reflects an image of ethnically Hungarian individuals who belong to the middle class; are active in the labor market; are not unemployed; are practicing Christians – or at least belong to a denomination that is recognized by the state – are heterosexuals, married and living with their spouses; are sexually monogamous and are able to conceive naturally. At most, it allows for some expansion to include members of indigenous national minorities, but (the recognition of) individual dignity is conditional on belonging to a community based on the features described above. Also, as we will see, the dignity of communities – including that of the ethnic majority community – is protected (in ways unknown in liberal democracies) by civil and criminal law and even against various minorities (be they ethnic, ideological or lifestyle) if need be.

When pointing to particular constitutional biases and preferences, I will try to assess whether the founding fathers (who, as we will see, actually were overwhelmingly male) could have had empirical data supporting the presupposition that these values, preferences and lifestyle choices are actually shared and supported by the majority of the political community. This is not to imply that popular support for illiberal or oppressive political commitments would make them automatically legitimate – this is the very argument that makes populist illiberal democracy problematic for liberal democracies – but if these preferences are not

1 See, for example, Plummer (2003); Walby (1994).

2 For the author's earlier writings on this, see Pap, A.L. (2015a). Who are "We, the people"? Biases and preferences in the Hungarian Fundamental Law. In: Z. Fejes, F. Mandák and Z. Szente, ed., *Challenges and pitfalls in the Recent Hungarian Constitutional Development – Discussing the New Fundamental Law of Hungary,* 1st ed. Paris: L'Harmattan, pp. 53–75; Pap, A.L. (2014). Személyiségkép és alkotmányos identitás a Nemzeti Együttműködés Rendszerében. I. rész (Personhood and constitutional identity under the new constitution. Part I). *Közjogi Szemle,* 7(4), pp. 1–11; Pap, A.L. (2015b). Személyiségkép és alkotmányos identitás a Nemzeti Együttműködés Rendszerében. II. rész (Personhood and constitutional identity under the new constitution. Part II). *Közjogi Szemle,* 8(1), pp. 1–11; Pap, A.L. (2015c). Személyiségkép és alkotmányos identitás a Nemzeti Együttműködés Rendszerében. III. rész (Personhood and constitutional identity under the new constitution. Part III). *Közjogi Szemle,* 8(2), pp. 1–8.

even shared by the majority, as this chapter will argue in part, the conceptual basis of the regime is even more scrupulous. Let us remember, the adoption of a new Constitution was never part of Orbán's political campaign in 2010, nor was there a widespread, thorough, inclusive political debate on the new Constitution. The ideological declarations in the new Constitution create the impression that these values were actually expressed in the "voting-booth revolution." This retroactive argument logically cannot hold water, due to the very fact that the campaign did not include it. Furthermore, as this chapter will show, people's actual choices concerning marriage or church attendance, for example, do not support the claim that Hungarians would actually live under these "intimate citizenship principles."

Arguments in this chapter and the book overall are not weakened by the fact that Orbán was reelected in 2014 by a convincing majority, which provides a political ex post (and pro futuro) legitimization of the SNC.

***

The following pages[3] will provide examples for the bias and value preferences in the new Hungarian Constitution. The concept of "intimate citizenship,"[4] used as an analytic category, will provide the framework for this scrutiny. As mentioned before, the Fundamental Law defines the nation as a community, the binding fabric of which is "intellectual and spiritual": not political, but cultural. Arguably the normative, often binding endorsement of certain cultural elements is antithetical to individual autonomy, privacy and the freedom to make choices concerning private life and constitutes discrimination.

1. The SNC as a workfare state

The idea of the so-called work-based society, mentioned in the prime minister's cited speech delivered at the Summer Open University of Bálványos in July 2014 (Orbán, 2014a) and elsewhere (Nol.hu, 2011; Orbán, 2014b), highlights the SNC's preferences for middle-class people who are active in the labor market and are definitely not homeless. A clearly illiberal notion of the constitution is expressed in Article XII of the Constitution, which declares in one and the same passage a right to choose one's employment and profession freely, *and* the duty to contribute to the welfare of the community by doing work in accordance with

3 A much earlier version of this chapter was published in Pap, A.L. (2015a). Who are "We, the people"? Biases and preferences in the Hungarian Fundamental Law. In: Z. Fejes, F. Mandák and Z. Szente, ed., *Challenges and pitfalls in the Recent Hungarian Constitutional Development – Discussing the New Fundamental Law of Hungary,* 1st ed. Paris: L'Harmattan, pp. 53–75.

4 See, for example, Plummer (2003). For more on the subject matter also see Kuhar (2015); Mosse (1985) and Walby (1994).

one's abilities and opportunities. This is incompatible with a liberal democracy, in which citizens are also free to choose not to work.

The Constitution includes a number of preferences towards middle-class citizens: Article O of the Foundations chapter of the Fundamental Law states that "[e]veryone shall be responsible for him- or herself," which suggests that the individual is not subject to state or social guardianship. This is reinforced by Article V: "Everyone shall have the right to repel any unlawful attack against his or her person or property, or one that poses a direct threat to the same, as provided for by an Act." While this authorizes the wealthy to take even the most drastic measures against the extremely marginalized underclass, it might at the same time also undermine Article C (3), which proclaims the state's legal monopoly on violence.

Article XIX (3) of the chapter on Freedom and Responsibility further holds that "The nature and extent of social measures may be determined in an Act in accordance with the usefulness to the community of the beneficiary's activity." Institut für Ostrecht München scholar Herbert Küpper (2012a) argues that reading this in conjunction with the National Avowal's thesis stating that "[...] the strength of community and the honour of each man are based on labour, an achievement of the human mind," this work ethic displays "some extent of doubt concerning human dignity [...] Such formulations are reminiscent of the 20th century's totalitarian left- and right-wing ideologies, which suggest that the 'value' of humans is not inherent but must be earned by the individual – generally by his/her work."[5]

Following a Constitutional Court decision (38/2012) that struck down the 2012 Act on Petty Offenses that made homelessness an offense, an amendment to the constitution codified the possibility to criminalize homelessness, a subject of forceful criticism by several domestic and international human rights organizations (UN OHCHR, 2012; HHC, EKI and HCLU, 2013). Thus, while the National Avowal proclaims that we Hungarians "hold that we have a general duty to help the vulnerable and the poor," Article XXII (3) states that "In order to protect public order, public security, public health and cultural values, an Act or a local government decree may, with respect to a specific part of public space, provide that staying in public space as a habitual dwelling shall be illegal."

As constitutional scholar Balázs Majtényi (2014, p. 93) points out, it is very unusual to authorize the sanctioning of homelessness within the same constitutional provision that sets forth the right to adequate housing. Also, while restrictions on fundamental rights due to public order, public safety and public health are common, it is peculiar to invoke cultural values to justify them.

2. The SNC as a Christian state

The Preamble of the Constitution characterizes the nation as a Christian community, allowing for an even narrower interpretation concerning membership

5 It is an abbreviated version of Küpper (2012b).

in the political community. Not only was the Fundamental Law adopted by MPs who are "aware of their responsibility before God,"[6] but, according to the National Avowal,

> We, the members of the Hungarian nation, [...] recognize the role of Christianity in preserving nationhood. [...]We hold that the family and the nation constitute the principal framework of our coexistence, and that our fundamental cohesive values are fidelity, faith and love.

The text does not presume an exclusive religious identity, but it does reserve a pre-eminent role for religion, specifically for Christianity. This preference is made explicit by Article 4 of Chapter VII, entitled Freedom and Responsibility, which states that

> [T]he State and religious communities may cooperate to achieve community goals. At the request of a religious community, the National Assembly shall decide on such cooperation. The religious communities participating in such cooperation shall operate as established churches. The State shall provide specific privileges to established churches with regard to their participation in the fulfillment of tasks that serve to achieve community goals.

Section (5) sets forth that

> The common rules relating to religious communities, as well as the conditions of cooperation, the established churches and the detailed rules relating to established churches shall be laid down in a cardinal Act.

Authors of one of the first comprehensive expert opinions on the Fundamental Law (henceforth: Fleck et al., 2011, pp. 7–8) claim that the new Constitution actually characterizes the nation as the subject of the constitution as a Christian community by stating that:

> We recognize the role of Christianity in preserving nationhood, it declares, not as a statement of historical fact, but also with respect to the present. And it expects everyone who wishes to identify with the constitution to also identify with its opening entreaty: God bless the Hungarians!

The SNC further narrows the kind of Christianity it endorses. On 30 December 2011, a new Act on Churches was passed, which made official recognition conditional on prior approval by a two-thirds majority in Parliament. The law distinguished between incorporated churches and other religious

6 See the next to last line in the Fundamental Law.

organizations with certain privileges, such as tax benefits (e.g., tax exempt status) and subsidies – including support for charitable activities, available only for the former. Subsequently, 14 religious organizations became recognized religions and the rest were decertified, making over 350 denominations lose their first-class official status in Hungary – including their tax exemptions and abilities to run state-funded schools. (Fleck et al., 2011, pp. 7–8). Incorporated churches have access to a much broader degree of state funding and financial autonomy, and only they are eligible for one percent of their personal income taxes. Other religious organizations need to compete with all other non-governmental organizations. Only officially recognized churched may be involved in the mandatory one-hour-per-week faith and ethics or ethics-only public education programs, for which they, and only they, are entitled to prepare their own textbooks and determine curricula. (Non-incorporated religious organizations are not entitled to provide religious education as part of the mandatory curricula in public schools, but they may offer extracurricular religious education in public schools if requested by students or parents.) Incorporated churches receive automatic authorization to provide pastoral services in hospitals and in the military, while religious organizations must seek permission. Military personnel may freely access their religion in private and public (US State Department, 2015).

The Bill was submitted to Parliament on 21 December by MPs, instead of the government, and was and adopted nine days later, without a proper parliamentary or public debate. The new requirements for full-fledged recognition include 20 documented years of existence in Hungary (in which case it must have a membership of 0.1 percent of the total population, approximately 10,000 people) or have existed at least 100 years internationally (in which case its foreign affiliation needs to be certified by at least two other churches of "similar doctrine" that are recognized in foreign countries) (US State Department, 2015). None of these criteria bind the Parliament in practice, however, as it can always refuse or "pocket veto" recognition (HHC, EKI, HCLU, 2012; Halmai and Scheppele, 2012).

On a strict reading of the Constitution, Parliament is not bound by the universal human right to religious freedom when deciding on awarding the highest status of recognition, and it is actually authorized to consider the "realization of public objectives" when selecting premium social partners. As authors of an *amicus brief* (Halmai and Scheppele 2013, p. 22) drafted for the Venice Commission (henceforth Venice Commission amicus) argue

> In this respect the state cooperation condition is most problematic from a human rights perspective because the state's willingness to cooperate with a religious organization is not simply a solely discretionary criterion, but also openly invites the state to prefer certain religious organizations or communities above others on the basis of its own views of the helpfulness of specific churches to state goals. This criterion requires the state to abandon its neutral stance towards religious communities. This requirement clearly runs counter to the state's duty of neutrality and impartiality.

The above cited constitutional provision is actually the outcome of an amendment, passed subsequent to constitutional court decisions (6/2013 and 23/2015) that struck down the newly adopted law (Act CCVI of 2011)[7] and a decision by the European Court of Human Rights (Magyar Keresztény Mennonita Egyház v. Hungary, 2016), which found Hungary in violation of the right to freedom of association read in light of the freedom of religion, and the law was amended in part. The number of recognized churches grew, and fierce legal debates surrounded de-and re-recognition. Some minority religious groups reached agreement with the government on their compensations; others requested another Strasbourg decision, which was delivered in 2016, again finding Hungary in violation of the European Convention on Human Rights.[8]

In sum, the Fundamental Law breaks with the tradition of the 1989 constitutor, which remained neutral towards religion, be it a doctrine or an organization. The Fundamental Law includes a direct preference for Christianity and traditional religious ideology. It is worth investigating whether Hungarians' lifestyle choices actually support this newly expressed dedication for religion or if it is unsolicited.

In the following, I will show that census data and other research do not support the SNC's firm and selective commitment to religion. In the 2011 national census, 16.7 percent of the population indicated no religious affiliation, 1.5 percent indicated they were atheists, and 27.2 percent offered no response to the question on religion (US State Department, 2015). The fact that a comparison of 2001 and 2010 census data showed a substantial decline in the number of persons who claim to belong to the major Christian denominations is a significant addendum in evaluating the constitutional construction adopted by the legislature. Over one decade, the number of persons who self-identified as Catholic dropped from 5.5 million to 3.9 million, while the number of those who belong to the Calvinist and Lutheran churches also fell, from 1.6 to 1.15 million and 304,000 to 214,000, respectively. The number of those who did not indicate an affiliation with any organized religious community simultaneously rose to 2.7 million in 2010, up from 1.1 million in 2001 (KSH, 2014a). According to earlier research, the number of those who regularly exercise their religion (at least once a month) dropped by around a third between 1998 and 2008, and now amounts to roughly 13 percent of the total population[9] (Keller, 2010).

7 Also see Venice Commission (2012) and Majtényi (2014).

8 For example, on 19th March the European Commission for Democracy Through Law held that the law "*falls short of international standards*" on some key aspects (Venice Commission, 2012).

9 The 2011 national census included an optional question on religious affiliation. Responses indicated 37.1 percent of the population self-identifies as Roman Catholic, 11.6 percent as Hungarian Reformed (Calvinist) Church, 2.2 percent as Lutheran, 1.8 percent as Greek Catholic and less than 1 percent as Jewish. In the same census, 16.7 percent indicated no religious affiliation, 1.5 percent indicated they were atheists and 27.2 percent offered no response. Religious groups together constituting less than 5 percent of the population include Greek Orthodox, the Faith Congregation (a Pentecostal group), other Orthodox Christian groups, other Christian denominations, Buddhists and Muslims (see US State Department, 2015).

It is worth noting the results of a research study surveying the national and European identities of Hungarians and other nationalities in the region between 1992 and 2014. The project measured the personal construction of national identity through assessing eight constitutive elements of identity. In the survey, respondents were asked to rate the following propositions in accordance with the importance they assign to each in terms of its role in constituting a "real Hungarian": (1) birthplace, (2) citizenship, (3) place of residence (specifically that someone spends most of his or her time in Hungary), (4) knowledge of Hungarian language, (5) Christianity, (6) an acceptance of the democratic set of institutions, (7) self-identity (that is someone considering him- or herself Hungarian) and, in the years 2003 and 2013, (8) Hungarian ancestry (the individual is of Hungarian descent/has Hungarian forebears). Hungarian respondents rated Christianity as the least important factor in defining Hungarianness (Simonovits, 2014).

3. Family in the SNC

The new constitution also expresses clear, normative preferences towards conservative family values. The Preamble, the National Avowal states:

> We hold that the family and the nation constitute the principal framework of our coexistence and that our fundamental cohesive values are fidelity, faith and love (The Fundamental Law of Hungary, 2013). The National Avowal serves as the basis of our legal order [...] shall [also] be an alliance among Hungarians of the past, present and future. It is a living framework which expresses the nation's will and the form in which we want to live.[10]

Curiously, the Preamble is more than a festive declaration, under Article R (3) of the constitution's chapter entitled Foundation, it has somewhat of a normative force, as "[t]he provisions of the Fundamental Law shall be interpreted in accordance with their purposes, the National Avowal and the achievements of our historical constitution." Also, under Article I, paragraph (3) fundamental rights may be restricted in the interest of protecting a constitutional value; this provision could serve as the basis for a restriction of fundamental rights (Fekete, 2011).

The term fidelity may, of course, be interpreted both as applying to marriage and to patriotic loyalty. Article L nevertheless goes on to say: "(1) Hungary shall protect the institution of marriage as the union of a man and a woman established by voluntary decision, and the family as the basis of the survival of the

10 Pursuant to Article R (3) in the constitution's chapter entitled Foundation, "[t]he provisions of the Fundamental Law shall be interpreted in accordance with their purposes, the National Avowal and the achievements of our historical constitution."

nation." It also states that "[f]amily ties shall be based on marriage and/or the relationship between parents and children." This formulation recognizes parent-child relations that have emerged outside of marriages but not the civil law partnership of the parents. This is a clear expression of a moral preference that denies the equal recognition of the plurality (freedom) of forms of life, the neutrality of (and tolerance by) the state and respect for personal autonomy (Halmai and Scheppele, 2013, p. 15).

As the Venice Commission amicus argues,

> The text brings several elements of private life under its regulatory purview in a manner that is not doctrinally neutral, but is based on a Christian-conservative ideology. With this, it prescribes for the members of the community a life model based on the normative preferences that fit in with this ideology in the form of their obligations towards the community (p. 16).

This constitutional language is also an outcome of an amendment to the text adopted in 2011, overruling a 2012 Constitutional Court decision (43/2012) in which the Court ruled that "family life" is a historically changing and evolving concept, a matter of factual rather than legal assessment and that same-sex couples are entitled to the same right of respect for their family life as heterosexual couples. Although this formulation recognizes parent-child relations that have emerged outside of marriage, it does not extend to the mutual relationship between parents who are not married to one another. As Fleck et al. (2011, pp. 17–18) argue, the Fundamental Law's concept of marriage corresponds roughly to the Catholic natural-law interpretation of marriage, which regards fidelity, procreation and the unbreakable sanctity of the relationship between spouses as the most important elements of marriage. With this strict definition of marriage, the Constitution actually rules out the future ability to expand its scope.

On the whole, the opinion argues that the Fundamental Law is essentially old-fashioned and even regresses the old one:

> [t]he 1989 Constitution was based on the equal recognition of individual and communal forms of life and a plurality of views regarding the good life. The Fundamental Law breaks with this tradition by including moral duties among the fundamental rights. It thereby selects those forms of the good life which it regards as morally valuable and worthy of constitutional protection. The Fundamental Law excludes the [...] equal recognition of the plurality (freedom) of forms of life, the neutrality of (and tolerance by) the state and respect for personal autonomy.
>
> (Fleck et al. 2011, p. 15)

All of these breach the autonomy and create potential exposure to being ostracized from the political community for everyone who does not follow the normative life models set forth by the new constitution's value preferences – as the Preamble holds, "the form in which we want to live" (Fleck et al., 2011, p. 19). As Fleck et al. (2011) point out, this notion of family also permeates other fields of law, such as media and education. According to Act CXC of 2011 on public education, it is the task of the teacher to "make students familiar with and respect family values" (Act CLXXXV of 2010).

In 2016, the United Nations Working Group on the issue of discrimination against women in law and in practice pointed out how schoolbooks contain many gender stereotypes, depicting women almost exclusively as mothers and wives, and, in some cases, depicting mothers as less intelligent than fathers (OHCHR UN, 2016). A telling example concerns Act CXC of 2011 on public education, according to which teachers are obliged to show and teach students to "respect family values." The government order on mandatory national curriculum,[11] a binding law of the land, sets forth a class on family life in its specifications in chapter 5 on "Gender – male/female identity – relationships subchapter." It sets forth the following when defining the goals and principles of the framework curriculum, for teaching family life, grades 9–12: The class syllabus

> helps fostering sexual identity that reflects biological sex, the fundamental differences among sexes [...] brain functions, communication[...]), a fertility-conscious attitudes, where children are gifts... it is important that children develop a family-friendly attitude, to prepare for [...] An engaged partnership (marriage) that serves as a basis for mature, responsible, balanced, healthy sexuality [...] through learning about the beauty of conception and fetal development they should learn that human life is a value from conception to natural (sic!) death.[12]

As Fleck et al. (2011, p. 12) point out, the media law includes the aim of public broadcast to 'respect the institution of marriage and family values.'

> Read together with the Fundamental Law's exclusionary definition of family, these provisions might result in limiting freedom of expression with regard to LGBT people in the media, as well as encouraging ignorant and often discriminatory views on same-sex and other not marriage-based relationships in school curricula.

Looking at this through intimate citizenship lenses, it has cisheterosexual and essentialist biases in refusing to recognize citizens' autonomy and freedom, especially by expressing normative preferences towards relationships and partnerships exclusively among a man and a woman, excluding transgender, childless citizens, and those who would choose euthanasia.

11 Government decree 110/2012 (VI. 4.) Article 62.

12 Translation by the author.

A resolution of the European Parliament, adopted on 5 July 2011, concludes that the new Hungarian Fundamental Law,

> through the values it enshrines and its unclear wording when defining basic notions such as 'family' and the right to life from the moment of conception, creates the risk of discrimination against certain groups in society, namely ethnic, religious and sexual minorities, single-parent families, people living in civil partnerships and women.
>
> (EP, 2011)

The Venice Commission amicus (Halmai and Scheppele, 2013, pp. 16–22) warns that the Preamble of the Act clearly ranks marriage-based families above other forms of families; the extremely exclusionary definition of family ignores hundreds or thousands of Hungarian families: it does not cover childless de facto partners and registered same-sex partners, and it is not certain whether cohabiting or registered partners raising children who are biologically related to only one of them fall under this category or not; the definition of family creates a direct link between family and marriage, which does not follow from the relevant provision of the Fundamental Law (Article L).

On 23 December 2011, Parliament adopted a new cardinal law on the protection of families (Act CCXI of 2011). In line with the governing parties' well-established practice, the bill was introduced on 2 December 2011 by four individual MPs, all belonging to the Christian Democratic People's Party – which ran a joint party list with Fidesz in the 2010 election but sits formally as a separate parliamentary faction, though it functionally acts as part of the ruling party. As a joint report of the three leading Hungarian human rights NGOs (the Hungarian Helsinki Committee, the Hungarian Civil Liberties Union and the Eötvös Károly Institute) points out, the new law on families is severely biased (HHC, EKI, HCLU, 2012). Article 1 paragraph 2 states that

> The protection of orderly family relations bears special significance in order to secure physical, mental and spiritual health. It continues by stating that The knowledge on the value of human life, healthy lifestyle, preparation for marriage, responsible partnership and family life is part of elementary and secondary education.

This apparently puts fact-based and value-neutral sexuality education at risk.

The Act defines family as follows: "(1) Family is the relationship between natural persons in an economic and emotional community that is based on a marriage between a woman and a man, or lineal descent, or family-based guardianship. (2) Lineal descent is established by way of filiation or adoption" (Article 7). This excludes not only the same sex-couples, but also single parents and their children from the concept of family. The Act also includes obligations for media providers to provide services respecting the institution of marriage and the value of the family and parenting (Article 5); parents are obliged, among others, to arrange for the supervision of their children when they stay in a public area or an entertainment facility at night (Article 9(3)g); school-age children are obliged to meet learning requirements to the best of their abilities, are obliged to abstain from unhealthy lifestyles and are obliged to cooperate with their parents during the course of their caretaking and upbringing (Article 12; HHC, EKI, HCLU, 2012).

Arguably, similarly to the commitment to religion, Hungarian citizens' choices do not reflect how the constitution-makers value commitments. To assess the social embeddedness of the traditional family model preferred by the Fundamental Law, it is important to note that increasingly fewer Hungarians choose the institution of marriage: in 1949, there were 11.7 marriages for 1,000 persons (107,820 weddings were held); in 1980, there were 7.5 (80,331); in 1990, there were 6.4 (66,405); in 2001, there were 4.3 (43.583) and in 2012, when the Fundamental Law entered into effect, there were only 3.6 (36,161) (KSH, n.d., 2014b). The number of divorces (which are of course not independent of the trend observed in marriages) fluctuates somewhat, but on the whole a rising trend is discernible: in 1949, 12,556 marriages were dissolved, leading to a figure of 1.4 per 1000 residents. In 1980, there were 27,997, 2.6 per 1,000 persons. In 1990, this number dropped to 24,888 and a ratio of 2.4; in 2001, it was 24,391 and 2.4, while in 2012, it stood at 21,830 and 2.2 (per 1000 residents, it was 2.5 all throughout 2002, 2003 and between 2005 and 2008 (KSH, n.d., 2014b). The number of births clearly shows a declining tendency: There were 190,398 children born in 1949 (20.6 per 1000 persons); in 1980, there were 148,673 births (13.9); in 2001, there were 97,047 (9.5) and in 2012, the number stood at 90,269 (9.1) (KSH, n.d., 2014b).

An analysis published by TÁRKI in 2014 provides very useful data: It states that the past 25 years brought fundamental changes in Hungarian fertility rates, with birth rates and total fertility rates dropping radically in the decade following the political transition and stagnating since 1999:

> [T]otal fertility rate measures the average number of children a woman is likely to give birth to if she were to experience the exact current age-specific fertility rates (ASFRs) through her lifetime. In 1989, this rate stood at 1.82, but during the 1990s the value dropped to around 1.3 [...] and has been stagnating at this level since.
>
> (Spéder, 2014, p. 64)

Similarly, significant changes took place in regard to personal relationships, with marriage losing ground and common-law marriages emerging as the primary type of relationship:

> The total marriage rate [...], which indicates the probability of someone marrying throughout their lifetime if she were to experience the exact age-specific marriage rate, fell from a level of 0.8 in 1989 to 0.43 in 2012. [...] currently [...], the chances of someone entering into marriage during their lifetime stand at 40 percent.
>
> (Spéder, 2014, p. 65)

Around the political transition, three-fifths of women between 23 and 25 were married. By 2011, the marriage rate dropped below 40 percent even among women at the age of 40. When the new Constitution was adopted, fewer than a quarter of the women between the ages of 23 and 25 lived in long-term relationships, and fewer than a tenth were married. Furthermore, over a quarter of women in their thirties are not in any kind of relationship (Spéder, 2014, pp. 69–70).

The increased diversity of family types is thus an obvious trend. The ratio of people living in relationships that qualify as partnerships is clearly declining, dropping from 75 to 65 percent between 1970 and 2011 (Harcsa and Monostori, 2014, p. 86). The ratio of single-parent households increased from 7 percent in 1970 to 14 percent in 2011. In the past 50 years, the proportion of people living in families with a child under 15 has dropped from 52 to 33 percent. The 1990s alone brought a decline of 7 percent. The ratio of people living alone rose from 5 percent in 1960 to 14 percent in 2011, with a 5 percent increase between 1990 and 2011 (Harcsa and Monostori, 2014, p. 88). In 2011, 11 percent of the population between 25 and 39 years old lived alone (Harcsa and Monostori, 2014, p. 93). In 1990, 66 percent of the population over 20 lived in a relationship; by 2011, this dropped to 56 percent.

Common-law marriages surged: in 1990, 5 percent of people in a relationship lived in common-law marriages; by 2001, this rose to 11 percent and by 2011, it reached 18 percent. The growth was especially rapid among youths: in the age group 25–29, more people lived in common-law marriages than in marriage, while among 30–34-year olds a third and among 35–39 year olds, a quarter of all persons chose to live with their partner without getting married (Harcsa and Monostori, 2014, p. 94). The popularity of common-law marriages is not limited to patchwork families. They are also quite common for relationships where all the children have the same biological parents. While in 1989, only 12.4 percent of children were born to unmarried women, by 2013, it increased to 46.2 percent. Thus, almost half of all births take place in common-law marriages (Spéder, 2014, pp. 69–70).

Patchwork families are also common:

> While back in 1990 78 percent of mothers of newborn children lived with their spouses, by 2001 it was only 65 percent, and in 2011 the ratio had dropped to 53 percent. [...] In the same period, the share of women living in common law marriages surged from 7 percent to 15 percent.
>
> (Harcsa and Monostori, 2014, pp. 100–101)

A growing proportion of children do not live with both biological parents. Among children aged 15 to 18, close to a third did not live with both biological parents in 2001, and in 2011, this share had risen to 40 percent. Many live in single-parent households. In 2001, 30 percent of children aged 15 to 18 lived with only one of their parents; by 2011, it was 37 percent (Harcsa and Monostori, 2014, pp. 102–104). The United Nations Working Group on the issue of discrimination against women in law and in practice (OHCHR UN, 2016) reported that 1 out of 3 pregnancies end in abortion (as compared to 1 out of 5 in the EU).

In sum, the SNC's value biases concerning family values are obvious. In line with the Concluding Observations of the Committee on the Elimination of Discrimination against Women, on the combined seventh and eighth periodic reports of Hungary adopted by the Committee at its 54th session (11 February–1 March 2013), in 2016 the aforementioned United Nations Working Group urged the government to consider that a conservative form of family, whose protection is declared in the constitution as essential to national survival, should nevertheless not be put in an uneven balance with women's political, economic and social rights and empowerment. The Working Group also emphasized that the formulation of family should be interpreted as including the diversity of families, recognized under international human rights law and that it should never be used to undermine women's reproductive rights (OHCHR UN, 2016).

4. Equality of intimate citizenship in the SNC

As mentioned above, the provision on the ban on discrimination of the Fundamental Law of Hungary (Article XV) does not list sexual orientation and gender identity among the grounds of discrimination. While the list is open ended (which means that sexual orientation and gender identity can be protected as one of the "other situations"), it certainly does not involve an unequivocal commitment thereto. The European Parliament considered this to be problematic in its Resolution on the Revised Hungarian Constitution, issued in July 2011 (EP, 2011; Kovács, 2012).

The second opinion of the Venice Commission (2011) on the new Constitution also refers to this feature of the new Fundamental Law: "Article XV lacks any mention of the prohibition of discrimination on the ground of sexual orientation. This however appears to be common to the majority of European Constitutions. [...]the Hungarian Constitution might create the impression that discrimination on this ground is not considered to be reprehensible" (para. 79).

As Kovács (2012, p. 186) argues, the 509-word Preamble does not include equality, and the word only appears three times in the entire text. While Article XV (3) makes provisions concerning the equal rights of women and men, a declaration as a basis for reducing the widely documented gender pay gap, the integration of a constitutional clause involving the common principle of 'equal pay for equal work' never found its way into the text (Kovács, 2012; Majtényi, 2014). As equality scholar Lídia Balogh (2014) points out, the 'equal wages for work of equal value' principle was not only part of the 1989 constitution, but it is also one of the fundamentals of the European Union.[13] Even though the new labor code (Act I of 2012) does endorse this principle, in practice it is mostly applied to regional differences in standards.

A law (Act CLXX of 2010) aiming to improve the situation of women was passed in December 2010, modifying the Act on Social Security Pension Benefits (Act LXXXI of 1997). From 1 January 2011, women with 40 years or more service time may retire even if they have not reached the standard retirement age. Periods of time spent raising children may be counted into the 40 years, but years spent in higher education may not, and the total service time shall include – as a rule of thumb – at least 32 years of paid employment. This reform of the pension system also generated public debate. NGOs and MPs criticized the law, which strengthens the social role of women as housewives, mothers and grandmothers (Ertsey, 2011). The fact that men are excluded from the possibility of acknowledging parental work as service time was also subject to criticism (Juhász, 2012).

The United Nations Working Group on the issue of discrimination against women in law and in practice (OHCHR UN, 2016) reported that among the measures to increase the birth rate, in 2015 the government instituted a program for housing grants plus loans for families with three children or more, which includes single-parent families. Measures for reconciling work with family have been extensively developed. Maternity leave for 24 weeks, paternal leave for five days, and parental leave for up to three years are paid at a high percentage of salary, funded by national insurance. There are also kindergarten programs intended to provide free day care from the age of three months to six years, including free meals. Yet, both the maternity leave percentage payment and the relief from income tax are very effective for middle- or high-income parents but not for low-income parents. The Working Group felt that the 47.4 percent women's labor force participation rate remains low, with a high gender gap of 15.7 percent, and the gap between mothers' and non-mothers' participation in paid work is the second largest in the EU. While Hungary ranks 44 on the UN Human Development Index out of 188 countries, it lags behind on the Gender Gap Index, ranking 99 out of 145 countries. In 86 top companies, the number of women CEOs was only 9 percent and at the two highest levels of management, 17 percent. The number of women on company boards is, in spite of the high level of women with tertiary education, 18 percent, as compared with the

13 Equal pay for equal work is one of the European Union's founding principles, embedded in the Treaties since 1957. Article 157 of the Consolidated version of the Treaty on the Functioning of the European Union (2012) provides that each Member State shall ensure that the principle of equal pay for male and female workers for equal work or work of equal value is applied. EU Gender Equality Recast Directive (2006/54/EC) on gender equality in the area of employment and occupation prohibits direct and indirect discrimination on grounds of sex in relation to pay. Also see, for example, Council Directive 75/117/EEC of 10 February 1975 on the approximation of the laws of the Member States relating to the application of the principle of equal pay for men and women.

EU average of 23 percent. In the agricultural sector, 26 percent of managers in family farms are women though 70 percent of family farm workers are women. According to the UN, the reasons for women's lower gender force participation are multiple: insufficient childcare facilities, the difficulty in finding part-time or flexi-work, the difficulty of reintegration into the labor market after taking long childcare leaves, the early exit of older women from the labor market and the disproportionate allocation of unpaid care duties to women, with women carrying out 80 percent of household and caring tasks and only 2.5 percent of fathers taking child care leave (OHCHR UN, 2016).

Failure to include women in the political elite signals the weakness of the Hungarian society to fully engage in democratic transition. The founding fathers of the new Constitution actually were overwhelmingly males. The Fundamental Law was adopted exclusively by members of the government: out of Fidesz's 225 MPs there were 14 women, while the Christian Democrats had 37 MPs with 2 women on board. The Parliament elected in 2014 has 199 members, among which 18 are female. The 114 member Fidesz group has 8, and the 17 member Christian-Democrat parliamentary group one (!) female member. It is an illuminating signifier of how deeply post-transition Hungarian politics have failed to fulfill the goals of constitutional partnership. Hungary has maintained a political culture that continues to lack commitment to substantive gender equality. Before the 1990s, the ratio of female parliamentarians was at about 30 per cent; after the transition, it has yet to exceed 10 percent (Kövér 2015, p. 114). 2009 opened the era of all-male governments, with now the third in such in power. For example, in 2007, only 18 percent of mayors were women, with this number being the lowest among Budapest districts. Most women were elected in the least strategically important settlements – poorly founded small, disadvantaged villages – where there is no money, only lots of work.[14]

In 2016, the aforementioned United Nations Working Group highlighted that women's 10 percent representation in Parliament has remained the lowest in the EU and one of the lowest globally, ranking 153. In 2016, there were no women in the nine-member Cabinet. In Regional Assemblies, women's representation was 12 percent, with no regional presidents. In local councils, women constituted 20 percent, however this representation is evident mostly in small communities. Out of 15 members of the Constitutional Court, who are appointed by Parliament, there is only one woman. The 19 percent of Hungarian woman MPs in the European Parliament is among the lowest, even though a public opinion survey in 2010 showed a 54 percent majority in favor of quotas for female representation in politics and only 35 percent opposed (OHCHR UN, 2016). The Working Group also pointed out that even though women hold 37 percent of PhDs, they only have 14 percent of university professorships

14 According to the 2014 World economic forum Global Gender Gap Report, Hungary is placed 128 out of 143 in the field of political empowerment, with a 93rd overall gender-gap rank and 25th in the EU (WEF, 2014).

and make up 3.5 percent of the members of the Academy of Sciences and hardly any rectors of universities (OHCHR UN, 2016; Schraad-Tischler and Schiller, 2016, p. 114).

In sum, the Working Group called on the government "not to disguise gender discrimination under an ideology of conservative family values" (OHCHR UN, 2016).

5. Reproductive rights in the SNC

The new constitution's ideological bias is also present in regards of reproductive rights. Article II of the Fundamental Law holds that "Every human being shall have the right to life and human dignity; the life of the foetus shall be protected from the moment of conception." Hence, as Fleck et al. point out (2011, pp. 18–19), it is again the reappearance of Christian values: apart from the Irish constitution of 1937, no other European constitution protects embryonic and fetal life from the moment of conception. This language, by differentiating between in-utero and in-vitro embryos, not only constitutes a restriction on women's right to self-determination, but may also lead to uncertainties regarding artificial reproduction procedures, since in-vitro fertilization methods usually involve the death/destruction of several embryos, either inside or outside of the womb. As Fleck et al. (2011, p. 19) point out, the Fundamental Law does not state explicitly that the embryo and fetus have a right to life, but it supports this interpretation by incorporating the phrase "embryonic and fetal life shall be subject to protection from the moment of conception" into the same sentence as the statement that "every human being shall have the right to life." This not only opens the path for a restrictive legislative or judicial interpretation concerning abortion, but can easily be extended to limiting infertility treatments, especially in vitro fertilization and implantation.

The opinion of the Venice Commission also reflects this concern that the duty to protect fetal life may come into conflict with Article 8 of the European Convention of Human Rights, since "legislation regulating the interruption of pregnancy touches up on the sphere of private life of the woman concerned, since whenever a woman is pregnant her private life becomes closely connected with the developing foetus" (Venice Commission, 2011, para. 62). However, the relevant article of the Fundamental Law "cannot be read as considering the life of the unborn child to be of higher value than the life of the mother and does not necessarily imply an obligation for the Hungarian State to penalise abortion" (Venice Commission, 2011, para. 66). Yet, the "concerns have been expressed that this provision might be used to justify legislative and administrative action restricting or even prohibiting abortion" (Venice Commission, 2011, para. 67).

6. Paternalism and essentialism in the SNC

Herbert Küpper (2012a, p. 9) points to a numerous paternalistic elements in the new Constitution. For example, the:

> end of the preamble[15] attributes an own 'will' to the nation since it suggests that the 'contract' is binding for all Hungarians – regardless of whether they wish to be party to it or not. The 'will' of the nation is superordinated to the freedom of the individuals who constitute the nation.

Küpper (2012a, p. 10) also interprets clause 2 of Article I (1), which states that the protection of human rights "shall be the primary obligation of the State," as a similarly paternalistic element:

> Article 8 (1) of the old Constitution stated that "[t]he respect and protection of these rights is a primary obligation of the State." The notion of 'respect' draws on a liberal approach, for it implies that the state holds back and leaves space for unfolding the citizen's freedom. The protection of rights, however, assumes that the state becomes proactive, it acts, which implies the risk that instead of the individual it will be the state that determines when and in how far individual rights prevail.

He also sees the manifestation of the national as a central value in the Foundation Article P (1). Consider for example the following provisions (Küpper, 2012a, p. 10):

> Natural resources, in particular arable land, forests and the reserves of water, biodiversity, in particular native plant and animal species, as well as cultural assets shall form the common heritage of the nation; it shall be the obligation of the State and everyone to protect and maintain them, and to preserve them for future generations.

It also must be added that the Fundamental Law's Preamble, the so-called National Avowal that was proclaimed in the name of the 'members of the Hungarian nation' (in other words all Hungarians) sets out certain characteristics that Hungarians necessarily possess.[16] Thus, for example,

> [w]e are proud that our king Saint Stephen built the Hungarian State on solid ground and made our country a part of Christian Europe one thousand years ago. We are proud of our forebears who fought for the survival, freedom and independence of our country. We are proud of the

15 "Our Fundamental Law shall be the basis of our legal order, it shall be an alliance among Hungarians of the past, present and future. It is a living framework which expresses the nation's will and the form in which we want to live."

16 The next to last line in the Fundamental Law reads as follows: "We, the Members of the National Assembly elected on 25 April 2010, being aware of our responsibility before God and man and in exercise of our constitutional power, hereby adopt this to be the first unified Fundamental Law of Hungary." Neither does the concluding line of the Preamble, which states that "[w]e, the citizens of Hungary, are ready to found the order of our country upon the common endeavours of the nation."

> outstanding intellectual achievements of the Hungarian people. We are proud that our people has over the centuries defended Europe in a series of struggles and enriched Europe's common values with its talent and diligence. We recognize the role of Christianity in preserving nationhood. We value the various religious traditions of our country. [...] We believe that our national culture is a rich contribution to the diversity of European unity. [...] We deny any statute of limitations for the inhuman crimes committed against the Hungarian nation and its citizens under the national socialist (sic!) and the communist dictatorship. [...] We hold that after the decades of the twentieth century which led to a state of moral decay, we have an abiding need for spiritual and intellectual renewal. We trust in a jointly-shaped future and the commitment of younger generations. We believe that our children and grandchildren will make Hungary great again with their talent, persistence and moral strength. We, the citizens of Hungary, are ready to found the order of our country upon the common endeavors of the nation.

A strict reading of the text would suggest that in terms of their membership in the political community, the status of those Hungarian citizens who disagree with these statements, or at least some portion of them who may agree but happen to be proud of or believe in other things, is thereby questioned. Another example of paternalism is the Foundation's Article G (2) ('Hungary shall protect its citizens') in which the individual is not the subject but the object of the protection offered by the state. Clause 2 of Article I (1) similarly states that

> [t]he inviolable and inalienable fundamental rights of MAN (sic!) be respected. It shall be the primary obligation of the State to protect these rights. Article 8 (1) of the previous Constitution, in contrast, said the following: (1) The Republic of Hungary recognizes inviolable and inalienable fundamental human rights. The respect and protection [sic! in this order!] of these rights is a primary obligation of the State.
>
> (Küpper, 2012a, p. 9)

The respect in question is meant to express the liberal perspective, since it implies that the state withdraws to give citizens the freedom to fully develop their liberties. Protecting rights, by contrast, imply that the state becomes active, that it acts with the concomitant risk that instead of the individual, the state will determine when and to what extent individual rights will apply. Article XV (5) protects "families, children, women, elderly and people with disabilities" in a similar manner.

Küpper (2012a, p. 10) also construes Article XVII (1) of the Fundamental Law as a turn towards paternalism: "Employees and employers shall cooperate with each other with a view to safeguarding jobs and the sustainability of the national economy, as well as other community goals." In his reading,

> employees and employers can only assert their interests in the pursuit of objectives enshrined in the Fundamental Law, and other 'community goals' that are defined by the government as part of its economic policy objectives. In the case of a government that is active in terms of economic policy, there remains little latitude for dialogue, the autonomy of market economy and economic players in the realm of labor relations is done for. [...T]his is strongly reminiscent of the Kádár era's economic regime.
>
> (Küpper, 2012a, p. 11)

Another example of paternalism concerns Article XVI (4), which posits that "[a]dult children shall be obliged to take care of their parents if they are in need." An amendment to the new civil code specifying the details of this obligation even allows third parties, including institutions, to claim expenses from the children. This not only imposes severe restrictions on individuals' decisions on how to conduct personal and family matters, but, in line with the Constitution, allows the state to exit social obligations towards the elderly – and in practice leave women and female offspring in charge.

7. Conclusions

In sum, the new Constitution's ideological commitments (Christian family values, notions such as "family" and the right to life from the moment of conception) create the risk of discrimination against certain groups in society, namely ethnic, religious, sexual minorities, single-parent families, people living in civil partnerships and women. Arguably, by prescribing ideologically based normative value preferences in private relationships, the new constitution violates the autonomy of individuals who do not accept the normative lifestyle models defined on the basis of the Fundamental Law's ideological values, as worded by the Preamble: "the framework in which we want to live" (Fleck et al., 2011, chapter 6, para. 3).

As the second Venice Commission (2011, para. 38) report found,

> while it is not uncommon that the Preamble to a Constitution or the chapter on the general principles includes provisions on the values underlying the Constitution, a Constitution should avoid defining or establishing once and for all values of which there are different justifiable conceptions in society. Such values, as well as their legislative implications, should be left to the ethical debates within society and ordinary democratic procedures, respecting at the same time the country's human rights and other international commitments.

The paternalistic, patriarchal and heteronormative value preferences do not outlaw or prohibit nontraditional lifestyles, but the open endorsement disfavors these citizens, not only symbolically. Furthermore, as this chapter revealed, census data and other research do not support the SNC's firm and selective, normatively formulated ideological biases,[17] such as the Constitution's concept of family, excluding registered (and non-registered) partnerships, single-parent families and non-marriage-based mosaic families. Actually, it refuses to recognize the majority of "families." This chapter also showed that census data and other reliable sources support the claim that the constitutional preferences and biases are actually not supported by Hungarians personal choices or preferences.

Bibliography

Act LXXXI of 1997 on Social Security Pension Benefits.

Act CLXX of 2010 amending the law on Social Security Pension Benefits.

Act CLXXXV of 2010 on media services and mass communication.

Act CXC of 2011 on public education.

Act CCVI of 2011 on the right to freedom of conscience and religion and the legal status of churches, denominations and religious communities of Hungary.

Act CCXI of 2011 on the protection of families.

Act I of 2012 on labour code.

Government order 110/2012 on mandatory national curriculum.

Balogh, L. (2014). Az egyenjogúság értéke vagy a 'gender-ideológia' fenyegetése? A nemek közötti egyenlőség elve és a protestantizmus: viták és narratívák. *Állam- és Jogtudomány*, 55(4), pp. 3–25.

Chronowski, N. (2012). The New Hungarian Fundamental Law in the light of the European Union's normative values. *Revue Est Europa*, (numéro spéciale 1), pp. 111–142.

Chronowski, N., Drinóczi, T. and Kocsis, M. (2012). What questions of interpretation may be raised by the New Hungarian Constitution? *Vienna Journal on International Constitutional Law*, 5(1), pp. 41–64.

Consolidated version of the Treaty on the Functioning of the European Union (2012). *Official Journal of the European Union*, C326, pp. 47–200.

Constitutional Court Decision 6/2013 (III.1).

Constitutional Court Decision 23/2015 (VII.7).

Constitutional Court Decision 28/2012 (XI.14).

Constitutional Court Decision 43/2012 (XII. 20).

Council Directive 75/117/EEC of 10 February 1975 on the approximation of the laws of the Member States relating to the application of the principle of equal pay for men and women (1975). *Official Journal of the European Union*, L045, pp. 19–20.

Directive 2006/54/EC of The European Parliament and of the Council of 5 July 2006 on the implementation of the principle of equal opportunities and equal treatment of men and women in matters of employment and occupation (recast) (2006). *Official Journal of the European Union*, L204, pp. 23–36.

EP (European Parliament) (2011). Resolution on the Revised Hungarian Constitution. 5 July 2011, P7_TA(2011)0315.

Ertsey, K. (2011). A kormány egy éve női szemmel. Ertseykatalin.blog.hu. Available at: http://ertseykatalin.blog.hu/2011/06/05/a_kormany_egy_eve_noi_szemmel [Accessed 31 Dec. 2016].

17 For more see Chronowski (2012); Chronowski, Drinóczi and Kocsis (2012).

Fekete, B. (2011). Történeti elemek az EU-tagállamok alkotmány-preambulumaiban (Historical elements in the preambles of the constitutions of EU Member States). In: V. Lamm, B. Majtényi and A.L. Pap, ed., *Preambulum az alkotmányokban*, (Preambles in constitutions) 1st ed. Budapest: Complex, pp. 33–45.

Fleck, Z. et al. (2011). Opinion on the Fundamental Law of Hungary. Consolidated text as on 1 October 2013. (2013) [online] Available at: http://www.mfa.gov.hu/nr/rdonlyres/8204fb28-bf22-481a-9426-d2761d10ec7c/0/fundamentallawofHUNGARYmostrecentversion01102013.pdf [Accessed 31 Dec. 2016]. First published as Vélemény Magyarország Alaptörvényéről. *Fundamentum*, 15(1), pp. 61–77.

Halmai, G. and Scheppele, K.L. ed. (2012). Opinion on Hungary's New Constitutional Order: Amicus Brief for the Venice Commission on the Transitional Provisions of the Fundamental Law and the Key Cardinal Laws. Princeton, NJ: Princeton University.

Halmai, G. and Scheppele, K.L. ed. (2013). Amicus Brief for the Venice Commission on the Fourth Amendment to the Fundamental Law of Hungary. [online] Available at: http://www.fundamentum.hu/sites/default/files/amicus_brief_on_the_fourth_amendment.pdf [Accessed 31 Dec. 2016].

Harcsa, I. and Monostori, J. (2014). Demográfiai folyamatok és a családformák pluralizációja Magyarországon (Demographic processes and pluralization of family types in Hungary). In: T. Kolosi and I. Tóth, ed., 1st ed. *Társadalmi Riport 2014 (Social Report 2014)*: TÁRKI, pp. 83–109.

HHC (Hungarian Helsinki Committee), EKI (Eötvös Károly Institute) and HCLU (Hungarian Civil Liberties Union) (2012). Fact sheets on some cardinal changes related to the Rule of Law in Hungary. [online] Available at: http://helsinki.hu/wp-content/uploads/Hungary_NGO_Fact_sheets_February2012.pdf [Accessed 31 Dec. 2016].

HHC (Hungarian Helsinki Committee), EKI (Eötvös Károly Institute) and HCLU (Hungarian Civil Liberties Union) (2013). Main concerns regarding the Fourth Amendment to the Fundamental Law of Hungary. [online] Available at: http://tasz.hu/files/tasz/imce/appendix_1_main_concerns_regarding_the_4th_amendment_to_the_fundamental_law_of_hungary.pdf [Accessed 31 Dec. 2016].

Juhász, B. (2012). Orbán's politics – a gender perspective: Working Paper. [online] Available at: http://www.fesbp.hu/common/pdf/Nachrichten_aus_Ungarn_1_2012.pdf [Accessed 31 Dec. 2016].

Keller, T. (2010). Változás és folytonosság a vallásossággal kapcsolatban (Change and continuity in religiosity). *Statisztikai Szemle*, 88(2), pp. 141–153.

Kovács, E. (2012). Equality: The missing link. In: G. Tóth, ed., *Constitution for a disunited nation: On Hungary's 2011 Fundamental Law*, 1st ed. Budapest: Central European University Press.

Kövér, A (2015). Timike and the Sweetie Pies: Fragmented discourses about women in Hungarian public life. In P. Krasztev and J.V. Til, ed. *The Hungarian patient. Social opposition to an illiberal democracy.* Budapest: Central European University Press. pp. 111–132.

KSH (Központi Staisztikai Hivatal) (Hungarian Central Statistical Office) (n.d.). Idősoros éves adatok, 1.1. Népesség, népmozgalom (Annual time-series data, 1.1 Population, vital statistics) [online] Available at: http://www.ksh.hu/docs/hun/xstadat/xstadat_eves/i_wnt001a.html; http://www.ksh.hu/docs/hun/xstadat/xstadat_eves/i_wnt001b.html [Accessed 31 Dec. 2016].

KSH (Központi Staisztikai Hivatal) (Hungarian Central Statistical Office) (2014a). Népszámlálás, 2011: Vallás, felekezet. [online] Available at: http://www.ksh.hu/docs/hun/xftp/idoszaki/nepsz2011/nepsz_10_2011.pdf [Accessed 31 Dec. 2016].

KSH (Központi Staisztikai Hivatal) (Hungarian Central Statistical Office) (2014b). Statisztikai Tükör: Népmozgalom, 2013 [online] Available at: http://www.ksh.hu/docs/hun/xftp/idoszaki/nepmozg/nepmoz13.pdf [Accessed 31 Dec. 2016].

Kuhar, R. (2015). Playing with science: Sexual citizenship and the Roman Catholic Church counter-narratives in Slovenia and Croatia. *Women's Studies International Forum*, 49(March-April), pp. 84–92.

Küpper, H. (2012a). Paternalista kollektivizmus és liberális individualizmus között: az új magyar Alaptörvényben rögzített emberkép normatív alapjai. *Közjogi Szemle* 5(3). pp. 8–11.

Küpper, H. (2012b). Zwischen Staatspaternalismus, Kollektivismus und liberalem Individualismus: Normative Grundlagen des Menschenbilds im neuen ungarischen Grundgesetz In Csehi, Z, Schanda, B. and Sonnevend, *Viva Vox Iuris Civilis. Tanulmányok Sólyom László tiszteletére 70. születésnapja alkalmából* [Viva Vox Iuris Civilis. Essays for the 70th birthday of László Sólyom]. Budapest: Szent István Társulat. pp. 215–239.

Magyar Keresztény Mennonita Egyház v. Hungary [2016] 70945/11, 23611/12, 26998/12, 41150/12, 41155/12, 41463/12, 41553/12, 54977/12 and 56581/12 (the Fourth Section of the European Court of Human Rights).

Majtényi, B. (2014). Alaptörvény a nemzet akaratából. *Állam- és Jogtudomány*, 55(1), pp. 77–96.

Mosse, G. (1985). *Nationalism and sexuality: Respectability and abnormal sexuality in modern Europe*. 1st ed. New York: Howard Fertig.

Nol.hu (2011). Orbán: 2012 az elrugaszkodás éve lesz. *Nol.hu*. [online] Available at: http://nol.hu/belfold/orban__2012_az_elrugaszkodas_eve_lesz-972351 [Accessed 31 Dec. 2016].

OHCHR UN (Office of the High Commissioner for Human Rights, United Nations) (2016). UN Working Group on the issue of discrimination against women in law and in practice finalizes country mission to Hungary. [online] Available at: http://www.ohchr.org/en/newsevents/pages/displaynews.aspx?newsid=20027&langid=e [Accessed 31 Dec. 2016].

Orbán, V. (2014a). A munkaalapú állam korszaka következik. Speech at the Summer Open University of Bálványos. [online] Available at: http://www.kormany.hu/hu/a-miniszterelnok/beszedek-publikaciok-interjuk/a-munkaalapu-allam-korszaka-kovetkezik [Accessed 31 Dec. 2016].

Orbán V. (2014b). Speech at the Europe Forum Conference. [online] Available at: http://2010–2014.kormany.hu/en/prime-minister-s-office/the-prime-ministers-speeches/orban-viktor-s-speech-at-the-europe-forum-conference [Accessed 31 Dec. 2016].

Pap, A.L. (2014). Személyiségkép és alkotmányos identitás a Nemzeti Együttműködés Rendszerében. I. rész. *Közjogi Szemle*, 7(4), pp. 1–11.

Pap, A.L. (2015a). Who are "We, the people"? Biases and preferences in the Hungarian Fundamental Law. In: Z. Fejes, F. Mandák and Z. Szente, ed., *Challenges and pitfalls in the recent Hungarian constitutional development – Discussing the New Fundamental Law of Hungary*, 1st ed. Paris: L'Harmattan, pp. 53–75.

Pap, A.L. (2015b). Személyiségkép és alkotmányos identitás a Nemzeti Együttműködés Rendszerében. II. rész.. *Közjogi Szemle*, 8(1), pp. 1–11.

Pap, A.L. (2015c). Személyiségkép és alkotmányos identitás a Nemzeti Együttműködés Rendszerében. III. rész. *Közjogi Szemle*, 8(2), pp. 1–8.

Plummer, K. (2003). *Intimate citizenship: Private decisions and public dialogues*. 1st ed. Seattle, WA and London: University of Washington Press.

Schraad-Tischler, D. and Schiller, C. (2016). Social justice in the EU – Index Report 2016: Social Inclusion Monitor Europe. [online] Available at: https://www.bertelsmann-stiftung.de/fileadmin/files/BSt/Publikationen/GrauePublikationen/Studie_NW_Social-Justice-Index_2016.pdf [Accessed 31 Dec. 2016].

Simonovits, B. (2014). Nemzeti identitás, kisebbségek és társadalmi konfliktusok – A magyar társadalom attitűdjeinek alakulása 1992 és 2014 között. In: T. Kolosi and I.Gy. Tóth, ed., *Társadalmi Riport 2014 (Social Report 2014)*, 1st ed. Budapest: TÁRKI, pp. 404–431.

Spéder, Zs. (2014). Demográfiai folyamatok: születések, halálozások, korösszetétel. In: T. Kolosi and I. Tóth, ed., 1st ed. *Társadalmi Riport 2014 (Social Report 2014)*: TÁRKI, pp. 63–82.

UN OHCHR, (2012). Hungary's homeless need roofs, not handcuffs – UN experts on poverty and housing. United Nations Office of the High Commissioner, 15 February. Available at: http://newsarchive.ohchr.org/en/NewsEvents/Pages/DisplayNews.aspx?NewsID=11829&LangID=E [Accessed 31 Dec. 2016].

US State Department (2015). Hungary 2015 International Religious Freedom Report. Available at: https://www.state.gov/documents/organization/256409.pdf [Accessed 31 Dec. 2016].

Venice Commission (2011). Opinion on the new constitution of Hungary. 20 June 2011, 621/2011.

Venice Commission (2012). Opinion on Act CCVI of 2011 on the right to freedom of conscience and religion and the legal status of churches, denominations and religious communities of Hungary. 19 March 2012, 664/2012.

Walby, S. (1994). Is citizenship gendered? *Sociology*, 28(2), pp. 379–395.

WEF (World Economic Forum) (2014). Global Gender Gap Report: Hungary. [online] Available at: http://reports.weforum.org/global-gender-gap-report-2014/economies/#economy=HUN [Accessed 31 Dec. 2016].

5 Illiberal multiculturalism

Deceptive premises, misguided policies

As mentioned, these two chapters go beyond the 2010 political transition and, in trying to assess the role of path dependence, focus on two select issues and sociolegal phenomena. This chapter will investigate how the new regime conceptualizes the political community, in particular, its Diaspora and domestic minorities. There is a proverb-like saying within the human rights community that if you want to know what a state or a government is like, take a look at how it treats minorities. Protective measures for racial, ethnic or national minorities can target a number of different things: socioeconomic equality; de facto freedom of religion; protection of potential pogrom victims; prevention of brutal ethnic conflicts; decrease in cultural conflicts between majority and genuine minority or immigrant groups; the combating of racial segregation or apartheid and race-based affirmative measures of compensatory, remedial or transitional justice. In line with this, laws protecting minorities may take several forms, ranging from affirmative action and social protection measures to declarations of religious and political freedom to setting forth cultural or political autonomy or controlling political extremists. The context-dependent meaning of minority protection may also refer to a widely diverse set of policies, such as equal protection (non-discrimination); participatory identity politics (the political participation of identity-based groups in political decision-making); cultural identity politics (the recognition of identity-based groups in cultural decision-making by the state); the protection of historically rooted identity-based sensitivity (the criminalization of hate-speech, holocaust-denial, et cetera); affirmative action; special constitutional constructions form-fitted for the needs of indigenous populations; policies recognizing claims that mirror the state's ethnic kin's Diaspora claims abroad; the right to traditional, pre-colonization life; or simply measures designed to maintain international security.

The importance of the aforementioned 1920 treaty of Trianon, where Hungary lost two-thirds of its territory and the corresponding population, in contemporary Hungarian national identity has already been mentioned. Let us add that the dramatic loss of territory and population also led to a dramatic increase in the ethnic homogeneity of post-WWI Hungary. Nevertheless, aspirations to reunite with ethnic kin have been probably the most important reference point in politics, as well as a foreign policy priority – especially for the political right and conservatives, but not only for conservatives. As Pogonyi (2015) points out, from the 1970s, the Hungarian democratic opposition openly demanded help for Hungarians discriminated against in Romania and Czechoslovakia, and democratization and transborder engagement have become twin projects of the anti-Communist dissidents, nationalists and liberals alike. For example, in 1989, the liberal Free Democrat's Party (SZDSZ) promised to offer nonresident citizenship for transborder Hungarians. After the transition, right-wing parties increasingly used transborder Hungarians to strengthen their national image, while liberals and social democrats accused them of nationalism and even irredentism.

Irredentist ideas dominated the politics of the interwar era. One of the reasons for Hungary's involvement in World War II as an ally of Nazi Germany was the prospect of re-annexation of territories with large Hungarian minorities (Pogonyi, 2015, p. 83). "Responsibility" for ethnic Hungarians living outside the borders, whatever that implies, was codified in the 1989 constitution-making. Throughout the 1990s, when new Central East-European democracies were torn between meeting requirements for European integration and giving in to nationalists revivals, the Hungarian governments made use of all available tools to strengthen ties with the national homeland and ethnic kin in the Diaspora. Bilateral agreements on minority rights were negotiated and signed with neighbouring states (Jeszenszky, 1996). Hungary joined European minority rights treaties and conventions that focused on traditional, national minorities (such as the Framework Convention for the Protection of National Minorities and the European Charter for Regional or Minority Languages), and governments did everything in their powers to pressure neighbouring states to do the same. Of course, their status and position were completely different: Hungary was practically ethnically homogenous in terms of national minorities, with a single ethnic minority: the Roma. In 1990, 271,000 people (2.6 percent of the total population) out of the 10.4 million inhabitants of Hungary claimed to have an ethnic background other than Hungarian, thus 97.8 percent declared themselves to be Hungarian (Tátrai, 2015).

Political (and legal) measures directly fostering Diaspora relations, such as the aforementioned bilateral treaties and a so-called status law,[1] were passed in 2001, instituting a soft version of dual quasi-citizenship: visa-free entry, limited employment opportunities, preference for access to most educational and cultural services in Hungary and a passport-like identity card for ethnic Hungarians in the neighbouring states (Kántor et al., 2004). Granting dual citizenship has been constantly on the political agenda, and an unsuccessful referendum (initiated by an NGO, but supported by Fidesz) was held in 2004. (Voters would have supported the policy, but the voter turnout was too low for it to be binding.) Other, indirect tools have be put into use as well: the law on national and ethnic minorities, adopted under the first right-wing conservative government as early

1 For more, see Pap, 2005a, 2005b.

as 1993, advocated an extremely generous model accommodating multiculturalism for indigenous, meaning traditional, national minorities – specifically for those which have homelands in the neighbouring states with large Hungarian minorities. It was designed in a way to provide a politically marketable model and example for the neighbouring countries – but without a reflective engagement for Hungarian citizens of Europe's largest ethnic minority, the Roma.

This chapter will focus on two developments in post-2010 Hungary's illiberal multiculturalism: first, the adoption of a new citizenship law, which opened the door for all ethnic kin and provided nonresident voting rights, and second, following the path of earlier controversial legislation and rhetoric on multiculturalism, the reconceptualization of the Roma as a national (and not an ethnic) minority community.

***

1. Illiberal transnationalism: The nation and the constitution in internal and external homelands

Let us take a look at Diaspora politics during the second Orbán government. Several important developments took place. First, the new Constitution, the Fundamental Law, reformulated and expanded references to ethnic kin living beyond the borders. The former constitution stated that Hungary "feels responsibility" for the fate of Hungarians living abroad and was dedicated to "promote and foster their relations with Hungary." As mentioned above, the Fundamental Law's lengthy Preamble does not define the subjects of the Constitution as the totality of people living under Hungarian laws, but as the Hungarian ethnic nation: "We, the members of the Hungarian Nation [...] hereby proclaim the following." The new Constitution defines the nation as a community, the binding fabric of which is "intellectual and spiritual": not political, but cultural and built on the concept of a "single Hungarian nation" that transcends borders. The Preamble promises "to preserve the intellectual and spiritual unity of our nation torn apart in the storms of the last century" and stipulates that Hungary "shall bear responsibility for the fate of Hungarians living beyond its borders," which includes helping the "establishment of their community self-governments" and "the assertion of their individual and collective rights" (Körtvélyesi, 2012).

In a report adopted by the Council of Europe's advisory body, the Venice Commission (2011, paras. 39–45) held that

> it is also of particular importance that the constitutional legislator pays proper attention to the principle of friendly neighborly relations and avoids inclusion of extra-territorial elements and formulations that may give rise to resentment among neighboring states. In this respect, the Preamble seems to be premised on a distinction between the Hungarian nation and (other) nationalities living in Hungary. The Hungarian nation, in turn, also includes Hungarians living in other states. According to the Preamble, "we

> promise to preserve the intellectual and spiritual unity of our nation torn apart in the storms of the last century". This statement implies obvious historical references and should be read in conjunction with Art. D, establishing Hungary's "responsibility for the fate of Hungarians living beyond its borders". Such a wide understanding of the Hungarian nation and of Hungary's responsibilities may hamper inter-State relations and create inter-ethnic tension.

The Venice Commission also found that the statement in Article D that "Hungary shall bear responsibility for the fate of Hungarians living beyond its borders",

> [...]touches upon a very delicate problem of the sovereignty of states and, being a rather wide and not too precise formulation, might give reason to concerns. In particular, the Venice Commission finds unfortunate the use, in this context, of the term "responsibility." This term may be interpreted as authorizing the Hungarian authorities to adopt decisions and take action abroad in favour of persons of Hungarian origin being citizens of other states and therefore lead to conflict of competences between Hungarian authorities and authorities of the country concerned. [...] The Venice Commission recalled that, while states may legitimately protect their own citizens during a stay abroad, as indicated in its Report on the Preferential Treatment of National Minorities by their Kin-State "responsibility for minority protection lies primarily with the home-States". [...] Unilateral measures by a State with respect of kin-minorities are only legitimate "if the principles of territorial sovereignty of States, pacta sunt servanda, friendly relations amongst States and the respect of human rights and fundamental freedoms, in particular the prohibition of discrimination, are respected.
>
> (Venice Commission, 2011, paras 40 41)

As mentioned in Chapter 1, besides reformulating a constitutional responsibility clause, the new government amended the 1993 citizenship law, making it available for everybody who was previously a citizen of Hungary or whose ancestors were citizens of Hungary, as well as for everyone of Hungarian descent, and the amendment was accompanied by giving voting rights for nonresident citizens in parliamentary elections.

By 2016 the number of new, nonresident citizens reached 850,000, with a 99.12 percent approval rate and media reports on how the Ukrainian mob and a few select Hungarian law firms organized citizenship applications with falsified documents by 10000s (Index.hu, 2016). The amendment to the citizenship law in the name of "national reunification beyond the borders" was of corollary symbolic importance. The bill was submitted to Parliament only three days after the inaugural session of the new House. Two days later, Fidesz submitted another symbolic proposal on the commemoration of the tragic consequences of the 1920 Trianon Peace Treaties as Hungary's most enduring national catastrophe. The bill, transformed into law as Act XLV of 2010 on National Belonging, held that that Parliament was committed to restoring national unity broken up by the Trianon Treaties and stepping up against the assimilation of Hungarians who were cut from their homelands by shifting borders (Pogonyi, 2015, pp. 84–85).

Transnationalism – ties linking people across borders – is not a new phenomenon, nor are identitarian projects to strengthen symbolic nationness across borders or specific state institution-building projects regarding Diaspora. Based on Gamlen et al. (2013), Pogonyi (2015, pp. 74–75) claims that more than half of the world set up formal institutional arrangements to include expatriates and Diasporas, using them for lobbying in geostrategically important countries or fostering homeland economies, for example, through specifically designed Diaspora investment schemes.

> The most common forms of institutionalized transnationalism include quasi or full non-resident citizenship, facilitated repatriation/return migration policies, official recognition (and even financial support) of diaspora institutions, the introduction of separate government offices (including separate ministries) responsible for overseeing diaspora relations, state sponsored education and cultural events outside the borders, birthright travel frameworks, setting up global television channels and internet forums, and bilateral treaties with states where significant diasporic populations reside.
> (Pogonyi, 2015, p. 80)

As Joppke (2005) and Pogonyi (2015, p. 81) point out, right-wing nationalist parties in traditional emigrant or newly independent (such as several post-Soviet or former Yugoslav) states with large ethnic minorities reach out to co-ethnic populations abroad to counterbalance increasing immigration and to maintain the dominant national group's claims over the state. The peculiarity of the Hungarian case lies in the fact that Diaspora policies are not intended to serve the economic interests of the homeland, and investment is unidirectional: the Hungarian government provides financial support for Hungarian language and culture abroad, expecting no economic geostrategic returns from transborder networks (Pogonyi, 2015, p. 91). Also, nonresident citizenship is not intended to facilitate repatriation to Hungary (Pogonyi, 2015, p. 86). "The new diaspora policies and institutions including birthright travel programs and language courses were intended to folklorize and diasporize Hungarian expatriates and their descendants in the overseas territories rather than mobilize them" (Pogonyi, 2015, p. 73).

Pogonyi argues convincingly that Diaspora engagement policies were mainly designed to strengthen the government's nationalist image within the homeland constituency. Its reasons are purely symbolic, and despite occasional irredentist rhetoric, it does not even include the classic nationalist desire to make the political and national borders congruent.

> It presents national reunification beyond the borders in the rhetoric framework of a borderless Europe in which individuals may cultivate transnational ties and minority rights (including cultural and territorial autonomy)

> are safeguarded by international treaties. One could argue that the Orbán government's romantic transnational nationalism or, more precisely, "trans-state nationalism" promotes a rather innocent deterritorialized conception of symbolic and cultural nationness without irredentist claims.
>
> (Pogonyi, 2015, p. 76)

Hence, Diaspora politics have been tools for electoral gerrymandering (in regard to nonresident voters) and a rhetorical pillar of the new regime.

As Pogonyi concludes, Diaspora politics is path dependent. Hungarian minorities in the neighbouring countries played a central role in political debates since the late 1980s. Before the political transition, the democratic opposition used discrimination against them to contest Communist rule. After 1990, transborder kin politics was an identity banner for right-wing parties, as well as a tool to label left-wing and liberal parties anti-national. After 2010, in something of a perfect storm, the long-held and always denied (even by right-wing governments, including the first Orbán administration between 1998 and 2002) demand by transborder organizations for full nonresident citizenship was fulfilled (Pogonyi, 2015, p. 90).

2. Illiberal multiculturalism: The nation and the minorities

Another characteristic feature of post-2010 Hungary concerns its approach to multiculturalism and accommodating ethno-cultural diversity through minority policies and politics. Similar to the above-mentioned Diaspora issues, the Orbán government's minority politics are path dependent, with a slight twist. Debates and theories applied to multiculturalism in a diversity management context need to be adjusted accordingly when talking about Hungary. Two important demographic and political features need to be stated at the outset.

As for demographics, in the 2011 census, 6.5 percent of the population declared that they belong to one of the minority groups. Immigration figures are very low, and the overwhelming majority of immigrants are ethnic Hungarians from a neighbouring state who do not constitute a cultural minority. With an overall population of about 10 million, the immigration authorities recorded 213,000 foreigners living legally in Hungary in 2012 (Council of Europe, ERICarts, 2016; KSH, 2013). Based on the 2011 census, the number of minorities living in Hungary is as follows: 3571 Armenians; 6272 Bulgarians; 315,583 Roma; 26,774 Croatians; 185,696 Germans; 4642 Greeks; 7001 Poles; 35,641 Rumanians; 3882 Ruthenians; 10,038 Serbs; 35,208 Slovaks; 2820 Slovenians; and 7396 Ukrainians. Roma constitute the largest minority group in the country. In the 2011 population census, about 3 percent of the population identified as Roma (KSH, 2011), but estimations even suggest that the population is closer to 750,000 (EC, 2013). As for the political, again, the almost 100-year-old 1920 Treaty of Trianon left the formerly multinational state practically homogenous but put about a third of the ethnic Hungarians (cca. 3 million people) in the neighbouring states. In 1993, a seminal law on national and ethnic minorities (Act LXXVII of 1993), which has been cited widely in international comparison as a reference point, was in fact designed to provide a politically marketable example for the neighboring countries with substantial Hungarian minorities (Bíró, 2013, p. 26; Pap, 2006). Hungary has thus instituted a cynical legal framework for multiculturalism, which relies on false, or at least deceitful, premises. As we will see in this and the next chapter, at the end of the day it will be the Roma, Hungary's largest minority and only ethnic community[2] (I will return to the difference between ethnic and national minorities shortly), who will pay the price for the inconsistencies encoded in the framework. For the Roma, the legal and policy framework will be highly inadequate, and the paternalistic "culturalism" advocated by, for example, the Orbán government, will foster neither social inclusion nor political empowerment.

Let us first take a closer look at the dishonest Hungarian model of multiculturalism. Thereafter, developments instituted after 2010 will be explained, with a particular focus on how minorities are conceptualized in the new Constitution. Finally, we will look at how the Roma are impacted by recent developments.

2.1. The 1993 framework for multiculturalism and minority protection

The 1993 Minority Act defined national and ethnic minorities as groups that have been present in the territory of Hungary for over 100 years and

> constitute a numerical minority within the population of the country, whose members hold Hungarian citizenship and differ from the rest of the population in terms of their own tongue, cultures and traditions, and who prove to be aware of the cohesion, national or ethnic, which is to aim at preserving all these and at articulating and safeguarding the interests of their respective historically developed communities.

The law also enumerated 13 recognized minorities: Armenian, Bulgarian, Croatian, German, Greek, Polish, Romanian, Ruthenian, Serb, Slovak, Slovenian, Ukrainian and Roma. A complicated procedure was set forth to extend the list, which involves a popular initiative, an advisory opinion of the Hungarian Academy of Sciences and a vote in the Parliament amending the Act, and no such initiatives were successful so far. The Act guarantees cultural and linguistic rights for these groups, contains provisions on the establishment and maintenance of minority education and establishes a unique Hungarian institution, the minority self-governments (hereinafter MSGs). Funded by the local authorities or by the State where national-level bodies are concerned, MSGs operate at the

2 If we were to follow the simplifying definition most commonly used by international law, Ruthenians can also be considered an ethnic minority, as they also lack a nation state.

local, regional and national level and have special competences for protecting cultural heritage and language use; fixing the calendar for festivals and celebrations; fostering the preservation of traditions; participating in public education; managing public theatres, libraries and science and arts institutions; awarding study grants and providing services for to the community (legal aid in particular) (Novak-Lukanovic, 2006). MSGs are elected bodies that function parallel to mainstream institutions and have certain rights regarding decision-making in the areas of local education, language use in public institutions, media, and the protection of minority cultures and traditions. Minority self-government representatives have the right to provide input on public policy matters through access to the local councils' committee meetings.

The function and design of MSGs is quite ambiguous: political representation and empowerment, cultural competences and a vague promise of social integration potential are bundled together. In 2006, the Office for Democratic Institutions and Human Rights of the Organization for Security and Co-operation in Europe (OSCE/ODIHR) published a detailed report and pointed to many problems within the system.[3]

These included unclear competencies, the lack of differentiation between various minority needs, deficiencies in financing, and voter enfranchisement regardless of ethnic affiliation (NDI and OSCE/ODIHR, 2006, p. 5). According to the report, the institution is tinkered with a fundamentally flawed concept that offers the illusion of political power rather than genuine inclusion (NDI and OSCE/ODIHR, 2006, p. 4).

> [...] The MSGs tend to marginalize [...] issues by depositing them in a parallel, fairly powerless, quasi-governmental structure rather than addressing them through established governing bodies. [...] The MSG system is inaccurately named. The local and national MSGs fall far short of the range of competencies that the title "self-government" implies. They lack the authority to take action outside of a very limited scope of issues and function more like NGOs than elected governing bodies. The use of the term "self-government" is not merely inaccurate, but actually damages the credibility and legitimacy of the entire system [...], as it raises unrealistic expectations on the part of constituents regarding what they can accomplish through the MSGs. In truth, the very design of the system prevents it from having a significant impact on issues of greatest concern to most [...] This is due in part to the fact that these were not the government's initial aims in creating the system. Rather, its goal was to give minorities a safeguard for preserving their distinct cultural and linguistic traditions, and [...] to provide the means for encouraging neighboring countries to allow Hungarian minority communities the same privilege.
>
> (NDI and OSCE/ODIHR, 2006, pp. 6–7)

3 For more, see Pap (2001a, 2003, 2006).

The OSCE also pointed to flaws in funding, claiming that financial support, with a budget of approximately 3000 USD per year, with no consideration for the size of the town, is inadequate to carry out either sociocultural projects, per the system's original intent, or additional projects to improve the living standards of community members. Most MSGs cannot even cover a modest salary for a part-time employee (NDI and OSCE/ODIHR, 2006, pp. 6–7). Also, their limited authority makes them a "'half-way house' between a government institution and an NGO, with an undefined, under-funded mandate" (NDI and OSCE/ODIHR, 2006, pp. 22). Due to very limited government funding and rights mostly in education, language and cultural preservation, MSGs have few advantages over NGOs. "In fact, those MSGs that have the greatest impact function much like a local NGO, securing outside resources for small-scale projects" (NDI and OSCE/ODIHR, 2006, pp. 22).

The Hungarian government's Janus-faced policies were apparent to the OSCE:

> the government's stated purpose for creating the Minority Act was to assure the cultural autonomy of minorities [...] However, another important factor in the development of the act was Hungary's desire to protect the rights of the large number of ethnic Hungarians living in neighboring countries. By developing the MSG system and other minority institutions, the government hoped to build that it could use in bi-lateral negotiations with neighboring states on guaranteeing the rights of Hungarians leverage abroad.
>
> (NDI and OSCE/ODIHR, 2006, p. 10)

Several controversial elements characterized this framework. First, the Act, besides defining the two group constituting requirements, contains an enumeration of the 13 minority groups recognized by the Act, which means that the Parliament would need to pass a formal amendment to the provisions if a new group were to qualify. The House (being sovereign), however, is not obliged to vote affirmatively on the question, which is in sharp contradiction with the otherwise clearly defined requirements.[4]

The other, even more controversial element of the Hungarian framework relates to the lack of satisfying legal guarantees regarding individuals' minority affiliations. The Hungarian data protection law prohibits the handling of sensitive data, such as ethnic origin, without the concerned person's explicit permission (Act CXII of 2011). This gives rise to what is commonly known as "ethno-business" or "ethno-corruption" that is, the utilization and misuse of remedial measures for private means that are contrary to the legislators' intentions. In the Hungarian model, the exercise of minority rights is not

4 A number of Parliamentary and Constitutional Court decisions have been passed on petitions of various ethno-national groups, like the Jews, Aegean Macedons, Russians, the Bunyevac, or Huns seeking recognition.

dependent on minimal affiliation requirements. Consequently, several forms of ethno-corruption exist.

Deets documents that school officials pressure parents of "Hungarian" students to declare their children "German." He states, "According to Hungarian government statistics, in 1998, almost 45,000 primary school students were enrolled in German-minority programs, which, by the census, was about 8,000 more than the number of ethnic Germans who are even in Hungary" (Deets, 2002). In its 2011 report, The Minority Rights Ombudsman (2011a, p. 20) drew attention to a school that advertises its German minority class as a "window to Europe," while not requiring either of the parents to speak German, eligibility requirements for the students, or an actual curricula on German ethnography or culture. The Minority Rights Ombudsman also pointed out that in the 2001 census, 62,233 people claimed to be German, while in 2011, there were 46,693 students (aged 6–14 years) enrolled in the German minority education scheme (The Minority Rights Ombudsman, 2011a, p. 39). The Ombudsman also drew attention to the fact that German minority education takes place in several municipalities, where neither the 2001 nor the 1944 census (which predated the mass expulsion of some 380,000 ethnic Germans from Hungary) indicated the presence of a German minority. A similar trend can be seen when looking at minority education initiatives targeting Roma students. In most cases, financial incentives are the obvious reason for this, since schools receive additional public funding for minority education – which is often the only source of extra income for educational institutions in underdeveloped, poor regions or small villages. In order to secure this funding, school administration and teachers will do anything it takes: learning a language, getting training in Roma ethnography and culture and pressuring parents to request minority education (Lakatos, 2010).

As we will see in the next chapter, legal tools developed as instruments for minority protection can, in practice, be abused to provide preference members of the majority community. Minority protection schemes can also be used in a cynically abusive manner, particularly in relation to segregation: either when Roma parents are convinced or forced – without their informed consent – to request specialized minority education for their children.[5] Another scenario concerns cases in which foundations of national minorities are helped to recreate their culture as a way to pressure neighboring states, so that the demand

5 See Balogh (2012a, 2012b). In its report on minority education the Parliamentary Commissioner for (Ombudsman) for Minority Rights (2011a) pointed to several instances where the voluntary, informed choice of parents can be seriously questioned, and evidence points to various forms of pressure in regard to requests for minority education. The ombudsman (2011b) reaffirmed these findings in his report on 2011 preschool report in regard to Roma kindergartens. In one of the minority kindergartens, actually a completely different dialect was taught from what the Roma families spoke (or understood) (The Minority Rights Ombudsman, 2011b, p. 43). Also, Roma language is instructed in several kindergartens, where Romungo Roma live, who have been only speaking Hungarian for generations (The Minority Rights Ombudsman, 2011b, p. 44).

for minority rights is "fuelled by supply" (Carstocea, 2011, p. 19). Deets is correct in concluding that the Hungarian government has an interest in developing programs that offer incentives to local governments to 'create' minority children (Deets, 2002, p. 187).

Minority self-government elections have also been constant sources of fraud, as the decision to vote at these elections was left solely to the political culture and conscience of the majority. After repeated reports on permanent abuse of the electoral scheme, in 2005 a "soft" form of registration was implemented, where minority voters need to sign up in a special register, but no objective criteria or formal requirements for affiliation are set forth. If they are willing to spend some time navigating the bureaucracy, Hungarian citizens, regardless of their ethnic origin, can vote for minority self-government candidates. Although the phenomenon is not widespread, this also enables members of the majority to abuse the system by taking over the minority self-governments. For example, the non-Roma wife of the mayor of Jászladány – a village notorious for segregating Roma primary school children from non-Roma students – held an elected office in the local Roma minority self-government.

According to a poll by the think tank Századvég in December 2012, 49 percent of Hungarians had heard about candidates running in minority elections without actually being a member of the given group (MNO, 2012). Hungarian minority representatives repeatedly claim the fact that some candidates ran as "Gypsies" in one election and then later as Germans the following term (which is permitted by both the law and the concept of multiple identity formation) as proof of the flourishing of local ethno-business (PCNEM, 2006).[6] According to political scientist Andreea Carstocea (2011, p. 20), the minority most affected by the phenomenon was the Romanian minority in Hungary, where approximately 40 percent of the Romanian self-governments were said to be headed by non-Romanians.

In order to demonstrate the fallacies of the legal framework, some Roma politicians publicly decided to run under different labels (in most of the reported 17 cases, they ran as Slovakian). There are also several municipalities in which (according to the national census) nobody identified herself as a member of any minority group, yet numerous minority candidates were registered. Following the 2010 elections, several new members of both the Romanian and Ukrainian minority self-governments were accused by other members of the newly elected self-government of not being actual members of the minority community. A faction of the National Ukrainian Self-government failed to stand up during the Ukrainian national anthem and, claiming to be Hungarian, requested that no Ukrainian be spoken during official sessions, because they did not understand the language (Index.hu, 2011; Nol.hu, 2011). In 2010, a Hungarian

6 In 2005, the law was amended, introducing a self-assessment-based registration requirement for the elections, but, according to analysts and the minority rights ombudsman, no significant changes followed in electoral behaviour and results (PCNEM, 2006).

appellate court actually admitted the existence of ethno-business in minority self-government elections (Beol.hu, 2010). The defendant, the editor-in-chief of a minority newspaper, was brought up on libel charges for calling newly elected members of the Romanian minority self-government "ethno-business doers and no members of the Romanian minority community in Hungary."[7] The court acquitted him (EMASA, 2010).

These loopholes in the legal regime sometimes result in complete absurdity. In order to express their admiration of German football, for example, a small village's entire football team registered as German minority-candidates for the election.[8] In 2010, the mayor of a marginalized village at the edge of bankruptcy and unable to finance its public school requested all 13 students to declare themselves Roma and request minority education (Nagy, 2010). As previously discussed, this qualified the school for extra funds; no Roma officially lived in the village.[9] Ethno-corruption, a symptom of illiberal multiculturalism, is prevalent in many other facets of collective rights. In 2010, the parliamentary commissioner for minority rights (a specialized ombudsman) published a lengthy report showing how members of the majority benefited from a government program designed to employ members of the Roma minority community (The Minority Rights Ombudsman, 2010a; Aurescu, 2012).

2.2. Post-2010 developments

Post-2010 developments in majority-minority relations are manifold. First, for the first time in modern Hungarian history, the prime minister rejected the idea of a multicultural society. The context did not involve ethnic Hungarians or relations with the neighboring states; it concerned the refugee crisis. In an interview with the German daily *Frankfurter Allgemeine Zeitung*, Orbán said, "We do not want a multicultural society" (FAZ, 2015). At the European Parliament in Strasbourg prior to a plenary-session debate regarding the government's stance on immigration and the death penalty, he said, "We regard it to be a value that Hungary is a homogenous country and that it shows a very homogenous face in its culture, way of thinking and customs of civilization" (Politics.hu, 2015). In an interview in the pro-government daily *Napi Gazdaság*, he explained his position:

> Hungary has a multi-nationality root system and cultural background, but this is not multiculturalism. Multiculturalism is the cohabitation of people of various civilizations, the coexistence of Islam, Asian religions and Christianity. We will do everything under our power to spare Hungary from this.

7 For purposes of this discussion, ethno-corruption and ethno-business can be understood as synonymous.

8 See an interview with Antal Heizler, President of the Office for National and Ethnic Minorities, Népszabadság (the leading Hungarian daily), 2002.07.24.

9 Id.

> We gladly see investors, artists and scientists arriving from non-Christian countries, but we do not want to mix with them at the level of large masses of people.
>
> (The Orange Files, 2016)

At the same time, the new regime, adopting a new minority law, basically preserved the earlier institutional and conceptual framework. The path for bogus multiculturalism was not invented by the Orbán government, but the new regime continued down the road, despite Orbán's explicit rejection of multiculturalism in the context of immigration (as refugee integration has been labelled and misrepresented).

Let us first examine how the new constitution conceptualized majority-minority relations. In the constitutional Preamble, the National Avowal, "we Hungarians" proclaim that the "nationalities living with us form part of the Hungarian political community and are constituent parts of the State." According to Article XXIX of the chapter on Freedom and Responsibility:

> (1) Nationalities living in Hungary shall be constituent parts of the State. Every Hungarian citizen belonging to a nationality shall have the right to freely express and preserve his or her identity. Nationalities living in Hungary shall have the right to use their mother tongue, to use names in their own languages individually and collectively, to nurture their own cultures, and to receive education in their mother tongues. (2) Nationalities living in Hungary shall have the right to establish their self-government at both local and national level. (3) The detailed rules relating to the rights of nationalities living in Hungary, the nationalities, the requirements for recognition as a nationality, and the rules for the election of the self-governments of nationalities at local and national level shall be laid down in a cardinal Act. A cardinal Act may provide that recognition as a nationality shall be subject to a certain length of time of presence and to the initiative of a certain number of persons declaring to be members of the nationality concerned.

The Council of Europe's advisory body, the Venice Commission (2011, paras 39–45) opinion, held the following concerning the statement that "*the nationalities living with us form part of the state*":

> While this statement may be seen as an effort towards inclusiveness, it is also to be noted that the Preamble has been written in the name of "we the members of the Hungarian nation", intimating that members of the "nationalities living with us" are not part of the people behind the enactment of the Constitution. The Constitution should be seen as the result of the democratic will-formation of the country's citizens as a whole, and not only of the dominant ethnic group. Therefore, the language used could/should have been more inclusive (such as, for example "We, citizens of Hungary."

The new law brought a peculiar change in terminology – something one may expect to have a reconceptualization in the background. "National and ethnic minorities" subjects and "objects" of the old law were changed to "nationalities" and "nationality self-governments," replacing the old term "minority self-government."

There is no evidence (for example in parliamentary debates or government documents) that this shift in terminology was based on overarching theoretical or conceptual reasoning or that it was accompanied by systematic political commitments. It is not clear what the legislator's problem was with the previous definition of "national and ethnic minority." Presumably, the constitution-maker disputed neither that "nationalities" constitute a numerical minority within society nor that they suffer from certain disadvantages (which the minority law is designed to redress by setting forth minority rights). Furthermore, putting aside the difficulty of differentiating between "national" and "ethnic" minorities, nothing supports the understanding (and even the Hungarian legislator failed to make this claim) that a "nationality" could or would be regarded as a greater set comprising both. Thus, the most accurate description is that it is synonymous with "national minority." It is no coincidence that the terminology used in international documents also employs the aforementioned distinctions and that the original draft of the Fundamental Law talked of "nationalities and ethnic groups." Though no changes were enacted at the level of political communication or in the Preamble of the law, new competencies appeared – somewhat confusingly – codified in a way that makes it difficult to interpret the relevant provisions.

2.2.1. Race, ethnicity, and nationality: Clusters for conceptualizing groups

Let us shortly dwell on terminology and conceptualization (Pap, 2015a). In social sciences and law, the purpose of typologies and classifications is to help us understand the internal logic and substance of concepts and institutions. Despite the fact that lawyers, legislators and drafters of international documents are well versed in creating definitions for concepts that are widely debated in social sciences and philosophy (consider for example the legal definition for poverty or disability) and notwithstanding the fact that the discourse on minority rights and adjacent policy frameworks is essentially law based, most international and domestic documents on minority rights, human rights and social inclusion actually refrain from defining several of their core concepts, and we have to settle for vague descriptions of race, ethnicity and nationality (Pap, 2015a).

Race is a controversial category, and in continental Europe its use is mostly limited to race-based discrimination. In social science literature, it is widely understood to be a social construct rather than a biological trait (in the biological sense, the entirety of humanity constitutes one single race) without a theoretically or politically uniform definition (Tajfel, 1981). Race-based international and domestic legal instruments identify race with the apprehension of physical appearance and put perception and external classifications in the center when prohibiting discrimination or violence on racial grounds. It is rarely distinguished from *ethnicity*, and the two terms are often used interchangeably by lawmakers (and drafters of international documents) and, most of all, judicial bodies. For example, under Article 1 of the 1965 International Convention on the Elimination of All Forms of Racial Discrimination, "the term 'racial discrimination' shall mean any distinction, exclusion, restriction or preference based on race, colour, descent, or national or ethnic origin." Despite academic interest and insistence on differentiating between the two concepts, legal formulations seems to be incognizant and even appear to be unobservant and indifferent concerning a potential difference between the two terms.

One of the most widely cited legal definitions for race and ethnicity comes from the opinion of Lord Fraser of the House of Lords in the Mandla v Dowell Lee ruling (1983), which concerned whether Sikhs were a distinct racial group under the Race Relations Act:

> For a group to constitute an ethnic [sic! – ALP] group [...] it must, [...]. regard itself, and be regarded by others, as a distinct community by virtue of certain characteristics. Some of these characteristics are essential; others are not essential but one or more of them will commonly be found and will help to distinguish the group from the surrounding community. [...] (1) a long shared history, of which the group is conscious as distinguishing it from other groups, and the memory of which it keeps alive; (2) a cultural tradition of its own, including family and social customs and manners, often but not necessarily associated with religious observance. [...] (3) either a common geographical origin, or descent from a small number of common ancestors; (4) a common language, not necessarily peculiar to the group; (5) a common literature peculiar to the group; (6) a common religion different from that of neighbouring groups or from the general community surrounding it; (7) being a minority or being an oppressed or a dominant group within a larger community. [...]

Using these criteria, he held that Sikhs "are a group defined by a reference to ethnic origins for the purpose of the (Race relations!) Act of 1976, although they are not biologically distinguishable from the other peoples living in the Punjab" (Human Rights Commission, Ireland, 2004).

The Permanent Court of International Justice held in the Case of Greco-Bulgarian "Communities" that a minority community is:

> a group of persons living in a given country or locality, having a race, religion, language and traditions of their own, and united by the identity of such race, religion, language and traditions in a sentiment of solidarity, with a view to preserving their traditions, maintaining their form of worship, securing the instruction and upbringing of their children in accordance with the spirit and traditions of their race and mutually assisting one another.
>
> (PCIJ, 1930)

We can argue that if we want to grasp the substance of these definitions, there is one common overarching element: the protection from maltreatment in the form of discrimination, hate crimes, hate speech and physical violence. Reflecting an anti-discrimination logic, the groups need to be defined following the perpetrators' method, which is basing the definition of the group on the perception of either biologically determined characteristics or cultural attributes.

In a sense, however, ethnic minorities are multifaceted groups. While many of their claims are grounded in the anti-discrimination rhetoric employed by racial minorities, some "ethnically defined" groups (such as the Roma) may also have cultural claims (and protections) that national minorities would make. The international legal terminology habitually differentiates between the two groups on the grounds that ethnic minorities are different from national minorities in the sense that they do not have nation states as national homelands (Hannum, 2001). In this way, ethnic minorities constitute a sort of hybrid categorization that blends and often mirrors the claims made by racial and national groups.

The 1995 Council of Europe Framework Convention for the Protection of National Minorities' arguably most important international document on national minorities also fails to provide a definition for its targets. A relevant definition, also endorsed by the European Parliament's resolution (EP, 2005) on the protection of minorities and anti-discrimination policies in an enlarged Europe, is provided by Article 1 of Recommendation 1201 (1993) of the Parliamentary Assembly of the Council of Europe on an additional protocol on the rights of national minorities to the European Convention on Human Rights:

> 'national minority' refers to a group of persons in a state who reside on the territory of that state and are citizens thereof; maintain longstanding, firm and lasting ties with that state; display distinctive ethnic, cultural, religious or linguistic characteristics; are sufficiently representative, although smaller in number than the rest of the population of that state or of a region of that state; are motivated by a concern to preserve together that which constitutes their common identity, including their culture, their traditions, their religion or their language.

When it comes to defining national minorities, I offer to settle for the definition that describes these groups as those based on their claims for collective rights, bypass the anti-discriminatory logic and seek recognition of cultural and political rights, particularly autonomy or the toleration of various cultural practices that differ from the majority's, which often require formal exceptions from generally applicable norms and regulations (Kymlicka, 2001). In this case, we are dealing with claims for preferential treatment. According to Will Kymlicka, cultural minorities can be divided into two types: nations and ethnicities. The former is a historical community, more or less institutionally complete, occupying a given territory or homeland and sharing a distinct language or culture. The latter is a group with common cultural origins whose members do not constitute an institutionally complete society concentrated in one territory (Young, 1997).

Concerning a special form of relationship between these clusters, the (in Hungary not very common, but well documented) case needs to be added, when segregation is achieved by Roma parents being pressured to request specialized minority education, aimed originally at safeguarding Roma culture.[10] The result is that Roma children are provided low-quality Roma folklore classes once a week but are kept in separate, segregated classes with inferior conditions.[11] Based on the claims they make, Will Kymlicka (2001) distinguishes between several ethno-cultural groups in the West: (i) national minorities, complete and functioning societies in historic national homelands that are either substate nations or indigenous peoples; (ii) immigrants, who do not want to engage in competing nation-building strategies but want to negotiate the terms of integration (food, customs, holidays); (iii) voluntarily isolationist ethno-religious groups, unconcerned about marginalization and seek exemption from certain laws and (iv) racial caste groups and Metics.[12] Minority rights claims, he concludes, may vary from immigrant multiculturalism to multination federalism, Metic inclusion or religion-based exemptions from general laws. As the late University of Chicago professor Iris Marion Young argued,

> According to Kymlicka, justice for national minorities requires self-government rights of the national minority to govern their own affairs within their own territory, alongside and distinct from the larger society[...] Polyethnic rights, on the other hand give special recognition to cultural minorities in order to compensate for the disadvantages they would otherwise have in political participation and economic opportunity in the larger society. The objective of polyethnic rights is thus to promote the integration of ethnic minorities into the larger society, whereas self-government rights of national minorities have a separatist tendency. [...] The distinction between national minority and ethnic minority turns out to be a distinction between a cultural group that wishes to and has the right to be a separate and distinct society, on the one hand, and a cultural minority that wishes to or is expected to integrate into a larger nation.
>
> (Young, 1997)

In line with this assessment, instead of a semantic analysis of the types of minorities, a categorical distinction for minorities based on the aim of the particular protection mechanism sought would make more sense. Instead of an empty typology, a more complex set of criteria for distinguishing among minority groups, taking into consideration at least the origin of the group, the basis for group formation and the aspirations, needs and demands of the group towards

10 See Balogh (2012a, 2012b).

11 See The Minority Rights Ombudsman (2011a). The ombudsman reaffirmed these findings in his report on 2011 preschool report in regard to Roma kindergartens (The Minority Rights Ombudsman, 2011b).

12 He admits though that some groups like the Roma in Europe or African Americans are peculiar and atypical.

the majority should be applied. Let us not forget, rights protecting minorities may be dignity-based identity claims, equality-based (synchronic or diachronic) justice claims or even reciprocal diaspora claims.[13]

Also, these questions cannot be separated from discussions concerning which concepts of social justice and equality our decision-makers endorse for particular communities. As McCrudden (2005) points out, there are at least four different meanings of equality, and what is suitable in one context may not be in another. McCrudden's "individual justice model" focuses on merit, efficiency and achievement and aims to reduce discrimination. The "group justice model" concentrates on outcomes and the improvement of the relative positions of particular groups, with redistribution and economic empowerment at its core. Equality as the recognition of diverse identities is yet another dimension, since the failure to accord diversity is a form of oppression and inequality in and of itself. Finally, the fourth conception of equality includes social dialogue and representation, the meaningful articulation of group priorities and perspectives (McCrudden, 2005). Each of these has a different concept at its core that corresponds respectively to direct discrimination; indirect discrimination, group-level marginalization and oppression and cultural and linguistic rights. Participation in political and public policy decision-making is at the center.

A useful set of terminology therefore should center on the substance of legal and policy claims and frameworks. Under this approach, there are three clusters. Minority rights have the recognition and accommodation of cultural claims of both groups and individuals, as well as identity politics in focus. The second array of legal and policy frameworks is individual rights oriented, and has anti-discrimination in focus. The term should be understood in a broad sense, including protection from hate crimes or even hate speech and several other related individual-based human rights claims. The third batch includes those various and diverse social inclusion measures that "ethnicize" social policies or, when endorsing multiculturalism, include recognition of other forms of group-based collective claims. "National minorities" and "nationalities" are adequate terminologies for the first cluster, "racial" and "ethnic" minorities for the second, while the third approach institutionalizes a curious mix of all three.

While acknowledging that in Tajfelian (Tajfel, 1981), the terms "ethnicity" and "nationality" are group-like social constructs (and imagined cultural communities, even if conceptualized and essentialized as biologically determined), and "race" functions as a category created by essentialist external perceptions and criteria, this does not mean that an ethno-national vs. racial binary would not be a useless simplification. Also, while arguably external perceptions and classifications are corollary in defining and differentiating between these approaches, a national vs. ethno-racial binary is similarly reductionist. My point is that the

13 In certain ethno-political situations (in Hungary, for example), the approach to ethnic and national minority rights is defined by reference to ethnic kin Diaspora rights (in the neighbouring states) (Pap, 2006).

recognition of ethno-cultural claims and policies for enhancing certain groups' capabilities for participating in cultural and public life and for preserving their identities needs to be differentiated from measures providing equal treatment or setting forth group-conscious social policies.

Finally, some notes on operationalization. Ethno-national identity can be defined in several ways: through self-identification; by other members or elected, appointed representatives of the group (leaving aside legitimacy or ontological questions regarding the authenticity or genuineness of these actors); classification by outsiders, through the perception of the majority; or by outsiders but using "objective" criteria, such as names, residence, etc. As noted earlier, for anti-discrimination measures, subjective elements for identification with the protected group are irrelevant, and external perceptions serve as the basis for classification. Policies implementing this anti-discrimination principle may rely on a number of markers: skin colour, citizenship, place of birth, country of origin, language (mother tongue, language used), name, colour, customs (like diet or clothing), religion, parents' origin or even eating habits (Simon, 2007). Defining membership criteria comes up in a completely different way when group formation is based on claims for different kinds of preferences and privileges. In this case, subjective identification with the group is an essential requirement, but the legal frameworks may establish a set of objective criteria that need to be met. In the context of drafting affirmative action and ethnicity-based social inclusion policies, external perception, self-declaration and anonymized data collection may be varied and combined. A special form of opting in to groups concerns mixed partnerships or marriages, where protections are extended to victims of discrimination by association. When it comes to choosing legal or policy means to identify community membership, solutions should be tailored to match the policy frameworks. Thus, for hate crimes and discrimination, the perception of the majority and the perpetrators should be taken into consideration. In political representation, the perception of the minority community should matter. In preferential treatment (remedial measures and affirmative action), self-identification along with community identification or endorsement should be key.

Policy makers may even find that attempts to misuse the system will inevitably happen. In fact, "explicit but not exclusive targeting" is currently a dominant approach in the context of the European Union's Roma inclusion policies:

> This approach implies focusing on Roma people as a target group without excluding others who live under similar socio-economic conditions. Policies and projects should be geared towards 'vulnerable groups', 'groups at the margins of the labour market', 'disadvantaged groups', or 'groups living in deprived areas', etc. with a clear mention that these groups include the Roma. This approach is particularly relevant for policies or projects taking place in areas populated by the Roma together with other ethnic minorities or marginalized members of society.
>
> (EC, Directorate-General for Employment, Social Affairs and Inclusion, 2011a)

Returning to the Hungarian case, it is not only unclear whether there would have been an intentional shift in the philosophy of minority rights, but even if there was, it has been shown that terminology itself is not a reliable indicator for policy frameworks. Still, regarding the Roma, the contradictory and ambiguous group terminology may be a useful signal for the underlying issue of inconsistent, confusing and confused policies. This may be the product of decision-makers failing to take sides in broader debates concerning the multicultural or multiethnic nature of the states or avoiding a straightforward commitment to targeted minority rights or privileging individuals over groups (Kaufman, 2014).

For one thing, during the drafting of the new constitution in 2011, the Croatian (Const. Prep Comm., 2010a) and Ruthenien (Const. Prep Comm., 2010c) national minority self-governments welcomed the change in terminology, which was also recommended by the minority rights ombudsman, because for some unexplained reason they considered the term "minority" demeaning. It needs to be added that only four NMSGs took the effort to comment on the draft constitution, as requested by the parliamentary committee in charge. The Roma minority self-government remained silent.

In line with the spirit of the 1993 regulation, the Preamble of the new law only refers to classic minority rights, the preservation of the culture of national minorities, the cultivation and development of their language, the freedom to profess and preserve their identity, active participation in public life, the realization of cultural autonomy, the right to self-administer their real communities (sic!) and their right to self-governance. At the same time, in a stunning solution in terms of legal codification, Article 81 (1) also features equal opportunities, social inclusion and social care as national minority rights.[14] The implications of this will be elaborated in the forthcoming subchapter on Roma.

2.2.2. *Parliamentary representation: Gerrymandering and beyond*

As mentioned above, besides the new terminology, the new regime adopted a new minority law, Act CLXXIX of 2011 on the Rights of Minorities. The law more or less copied the conceptual framework, the enumeration, the (lack of) definition of recognized minorities[15] and, again, the lack of legally defined cri-

14 "Any local government decision affecting the national minority population in its quality as a national minority, in terms of its national minority rights defined in this law, especially the rights of collective language use, education, preserving its traditions and culture, local press, equal opportunities, social inclusion and social care, shall only be taken by the municipal assembly if the local national minority self-government of the national minority population affected by the decision, or, in the absence of a local national minority self-government, the regional national minority self-government, has expressed its consent." For more, also see Chronowski (2012).

15 According to §

> (1) [...] ethnic groups resident in Hungary for at least one century are minorities which are in a numerical minority amongst the population of the State, are distinguished from the rest of the population by their own language, culture and traditions and manifest a sense

teria for membership in the communities, even for the purposes of the various preferential treatment measures the law(s) set forth.[16] The 1993 regulation, which was essentially left unchanged by the new legal framework, was unable to prevent abuses of the privileges accorded to minorities, even though, as we could see, the persistence of such abuses can result in the hollowing out of these privileges. The new regulation did not bring substantial changes in the minority self-government elections. Compared to 2010, there was only a slight rise in the number of those on the voter rolls. There were 228,038 names in 2010, while in 2014 the number rose to 241,030 persons. Only the Roma actually increased its voter registry, from 133,492 to 158,101, by 18 percent. Most national minorities saw their rolls decline: 35 percent in the case of the Bulgarians, 33 percent for Slovenians and 30 percent for Serbs. In terms of participation, there were no substantial changes either. In 2006, turnout had stood at 63.81 percent, in 2010 it was 63.47 percent and in 2014 it reached 65.14 percent (The Minority Rights Ombudsman, 2010b). Nor did the results change appreciably: 2321 local national minority elections were held in 2010, and in 2014 this number increased to 2143.[17]

An important provision of the new law concerns sui generis parliamentary representation for the recognized minorities. Let us not forget the context. First, minority political parties are not relevant actors in Hungarian political life, and their role in parliamentary representation is subsequently insignificant.[18] Second, the size of Parliament was decreased to nearly half (199 MPs from 386), the right to vote was extended to non-resident ethnic Hungarians (whose numbers were multiplied by the new citizenship law), and besides state-sponsored campaigns to mobilize these new (overwhelmingly Fidesz-supporter) voters, electoral districts were redrawn in an explicitly gerrymandered fashion, favouring pro-Fidesz blocks.[19] True, the question of parliamentary representation for minorities has been on the agenda of Hungarian politics and legislation since the 1989 political transition. Laws were passed but never implemented, constitutional court decisions declared the lack of appropriate legislation a form of

---

of collective affiliation that is aimed at the preservation of these and at the expression and protection of the interests of their historically established communities. [...] (3) If a minority other than those listed in Appendix No. 1 wishes to verify that they meet the relevant conditions, minimum one thousand electors forming part of that minority may initiate that the minority be declared an ethnic group native to Hungary. [...] The procedure shall be governed by the provisions of the Act relating to the initiation of national referenda[...] In the course of its procedure, the National Election Committee shall seek the position of the President of the Hungarian Academy of Sciences with respect to the existence of the statutory conditions.

16 For more on the subject of parliamentary representation of minorities, see for example Pap (2001b).

17 See Jogiforum.hu (2010); Valasztas.hu (2010); and Szalayné (2014).

18 See (Dobos, 2013a, 2013b); McGarry (2009); Rövid (2012); and Sobotka (2001).

19 See for example Transparency International (2014); Freedom House (2016); and OSCE/ODIHR (2014).

constitutional omission[20] and dozens of reports by international organizations, the specialized minority rights' ombudsman, minority advocates, and politicians have demanded to remedy the situation.

The legal and political debate was caused by the fact that Article 68 of the 1949 Constitution, in force until 2011, set forth that:

> The national and ethnic minorities living in the Republic of Hungary participate in the sovereign power of the people: they represent a constituent part of the State. (2) The Republic of Hungary shall provide for the protection of national and ethnic minorities and ensure their collective participation in public affairs, the fostering of their cultures, the use of their native languages, education in their native languages and the use of names in their native languages. (3) The laws of the Republic of Hungary shall ensure representation for the national and ethnic minorities living within the country.

In 1992, before the adoption of the comprehensive 1993 minority rights act, the Constitutional Court decision declared a constitutional omission regarding failure to enact such legislation and in 1994, again, referred to its holding (35/1992 and 24/1994). However, the Court's position was not unambiguous – it did not explicitly mention "parliamentary representation" but referred to "general representation." Therefore, the legislation in question could be regarded as completed by 1993. The 1993 Act stipulated parliamentary representation but never actually instituted it, and since there was no direct constitutional language on the issue, the debate was never resolved, but Hungary was repeatedly criticized for not meeting its self-induced obligations. The issue was lingering, and dozens of consultations and meetings were held over the two decades since the political transition.

20 Article 68 of the 1949 Constitution (ACT XX of 1949), in force until 2011, set forth that

> The national and ethnic minorities living in the Republic of Hungary participate in the sovereign power of the people: they represent a constituent part of the State. (2) The Republic of Hungary shall provide for the protection of national and ethnic minorities and ensure their collective participation in public affairs, the fostering of their cultures, the use of their native languages, education in their native languages and the use of names in their native languages. (3) The laws of the Republic of Hungary shall ensure representation for the national and ethnic minorities living within the country.

In 1992, before the adoption of the comprehensive 1993 minority rights act (Act LXXVII of 1993), the Constitutional Court decision declared a constitutional omission in regard to failure to enact such legislation (35/1992), and in 1994, again, referred to its holding (24/1994). However, the Court's position was not unambiguous, it did not explicitly mention "parliamentary representation", but referred to "general representation", thus, the legislation in question could be regarded as completed by 1993. The 1993 Act stipulated parliamentary representation, but never actually instituted it, and since there was no direct constitutional language on the issue, the debate was never resolved, but Hungary was repeatedly criticized for not meeting its self-induced obligations. The issue was lingering and dozens of consultations and meetings were held over the two decades since the political transition.

Recognized minorities are now entitled to win preferential seats in the 199-member Parliament as part of the contingent of 93 seats distributed based on national lists. Should any of the minority lists win a preferential seat, then the seats that must be allocated between party lists will be reduced by the corresponding amount. Minority lists can only be nominated by national (level) self-governments. In other words, the parliamentary representation of minorities is based on representation through minority self-governments, which implies that other players, such as parties, have no influence on the composition of the list and cannot nominate candidates. Each minority can only win a single preferential seat; to win more than one seat, a nationality list can compete for additional seats based on the general election rules, that is, by winning sufficient votes to take the 5 percent threshold. A citizen can choose to vote either for a party list nominated according to the general election rules or, if he or she is registered in the nationality voter roll, for one of the nationality lists. One can only enroll in one minority register, meaning that the expression of multiple identities is not supported in electoral law.

According to the law on Electoral Procedures (Act XXXVI of 2013), the rules for registering in the nationality voter rolls are no different from the rules applicable to the elections of nationality self-governments – essentially a principle of free and unfettered self-identification prevails in this context. The law also provides for a minimum number of votes necessary to win a seat. This effectively implies that some 20,000–25,000 votes are needed for parliamentary representation. This number is considerably less than would be needed based on the generally applicable rules, yet given the demographics of minorities in Hungary, only the Roma and German minorities have a chance to actually succeed in passing this threshold.

According to Article 18 of the Act on the Elections of Members of Parliament, "(1) Any nationality, which drew up a nationality list, but failed to win a mandate by such list shall be represented by its nationality advocate in Parliament. (2) The nationality advocate shall be the candidate who ranked first on the nationality list." Thus, these spokespersons[21] are likely to remain the dominant legal institution in the case of the 11 minorities other than German or Roma. Apart from the limitations on his/her right to vote, and the fact that his/her competencies are limited to nationality affairs, the advocate and his/her status are equal to those of other members of Parliament – she enjoys immunity, receives remuneration, has an expense account, et cetera. Although this has not (yet) been documented as happening, the fact that the House Committee, made up of the Speaker of Parliament, his/her deputies and the leaders of the parliamentary factions, is entitled to decide whether a given item on the agenda pertains to

21 According to Act XXXVI of 2012 on Parliament, the advocate may speak during plenary sessions – if the House Committee (the committee in charge of parliamentary procedures) assesses that a given issue pertains to the rights or interests of nationalities. Indeed, she may even submit proposals for a decision to Parliament, submit questions to the government, members of the cabinet, the Prosecutor General, the president of the National Audit Office or the Commissioner of Fundamental Rights on issues pertaining to the rights and interests of nationalities.

the rights and interests of nationalities, constitutes an inherent limitation of the advocate's powers. It may even decide that such an issue does not exist.[22]

Bearing in mind the above detailed cases for ethno-corruption in the case of minority self-government elections, a cause of major concern is that based on the prevailing rules, politicians belonging to the ethnic majority could be elected to Parliament as representatives of the currently identified 13 minorities, which would constitute an abuse of minority privileges and could significantly influence the election outcome. Though the 2014 election results have not borne out this concern – none of the national minorities won a preferential seat in Parliament (a fact that could also be construed as a key critique of the existing regulations, for it seems that in its current form this institution is incapable of realizing the legislative objective underlying its creation) – in future elections the existence of a 13-member faux minority faction among the 199 MPs could significantly alter election outcomes. This is especially a cause for concern because, as was shown, the persistent practice of ethno-business and the inadequacy of relevant regulations will continue to allow for this possibility in the future. It is worth noting that Commissioner for Minorities Ernő Kállai noted in his opinion on the bill that this was the first legislative proposal by a government pertaining to minority issues that the minority ombudsman was not involved in drafting, wherefore the legislation lacked his professional input. The final bill was sent to Kállai with a deadline to respond in a mere one and a half working days.[23]

Having outlined the general features of Hungarian multicultural legal and policy frameworks, let us turn our attention to the nation's only ethnic minority.

2.2.3. Roma in the hypocritical Hungarian multiculturalist model

2.2.3.1. THE HUNGARIAN ROMA

In Hungary, the Roma are practically the only visible minority and have been present for centuries. Hungarian Roma are citizens. They are documented and linguistically assimilated: they all speak Hungarian, some only Hungarian,

22 As mentioned above, during the constitution-making process, the recognized nationalities mostly remained silent. The Bulgarian, Croatian, German, and Ruthenian National Self-Governments expressed a request for parliamentary representation (Const. Prep Comm. 2010, 2010a, 2010b, 2010c). The Jewish community in Hungary has been divided even on the question seeking recognition as (national or ethnic) minority.

23 The ombudsman concludes:

> One of the fundamental goals of the new national minority law is to prevent abuses of national minority rights. Yet this ambition is undermined by the fact that the bill's creator continues to give primacy to the principle of freely choosing one's identity without providing any safeguards to prevent persons who are not members of a national minority from exercising the rights of national minorities. As a result, therefore, the regulation establishing that the exercise of given national minority rights is contingent merely on a statement by the individual asserting his/her affiliation with the national minority, rather than a recognition by the national minority of his/her membership, continues to prevail.
>
> (The Minority Rights Ombudsman, 2010b)

others are bilingual and they do not differ significantly from the majority in religious affiliation. As mentioned above, they constitute the largest minority group in the country. During the 2001 census less than 2 percent of the general population (190,046 persons) identified as Roma (KSH, 2013), but estimations suggest that this ratio is closer to 7 percent. Before the 2011 census, the president of the National Roma Self-government encouraged the open declaration of ethnicity, and a group of Roma rights activists organized a civil movement "We belong to here" ('Ide tartozunk') campaigning for active declaration. Eventually, slightly more than 3 percent of Hungary's population (308,957 persons) declared themselves to be Roma in 2011 (KSH, 2013).

Also, Roma in Hungary live a sedentary lifestyle. Unlike some Roma communities in Europe, only a very small group of Sinti is semi-sedentary (estimated to be less than 1 percent among the Roma population, some operating travelling carnivals/carousels) (Szuhay, 2003). The Hungarian Roma population is very diverse. There are three main groups (and 27 subgroups) of Roma in Hungary in the cultural and linguistic senses: the Romungros, who are linguistically assimilated and speak Hungarian as a mother tongue; the Boiash (or Beás), who speak a language based on an ancient version of Romanian and the speakers of different dialects of the Romani language (the most widespread version is the Lovari) (Kemény and Janky, 2003). The Hungarian Roma community is extremely heterogenous, unified only by the "othering" of the majority and the political concept of the Roma as constituted by state policies (and to a very limited degree the international Romani movement) (Fosztó, 2003).

As a report by the Hungarian Helsinki Committee shows, members of the Roma community are discriminated against in almost all fields of life, and prejudice runs deep in Hungarian society. A 2009 survey showed that 29 percent of respondents would not accept a Roma person as a coworker, 43 percent would not accept a Roma as a neighbour and 76 percent would not accept a Roma person as a partner (Hungarian Helsinki Committee, 2011). According to a UNDP/EC/WB Survey conducted in 2011, 2 percent of the Roma in Hungary live in absolute poverty, 71 percent in relative poverty and 29 percent of Hungarian Roma do not have secure housing. As major international NGO Minority Rights Group (2012) reports on Hungary, the Roma unemployment rate is estimated at 70 percent, more than 10 times the national average, and most Roma live in extreme poverty. NGOs report racial discrimination in adoption and high rates of removal of children from Roma families by child protective services. According to a 2002 World Bank report, slightly more than 80 percent of Roma children completed primary education, but only one-third continued studies into the intermediate (secondary) level, as compared to 90 percent of non-Roma. In 2013, the European Court of Human Rights ruled in favour of two Roma children who complained that their placement in special schools was based on their ethnic identity. The Court underlined in its ruling that there is a long history of wrongful placement of Roma children in special schools in Hungary (Horváth and Kiss v. Hungary, 2013). Violent attacks against Roma and racist statements by public officials, as well as the activities of extremist paramilitary groups are also widely documented (Harvard, 2014).

2.2.3.2. ROMA IN THE HUNGARIAN MINORITY RIGHTS FRAMEWORK[24]

In order to understand the status and position of Roma in the Hungarian minority rights framework, we need to point out that in terms of identity and advocacy, there are two competing ideologies and movements among Roma intellectuals in Hungary: one centered around a civil rights-oriented emancipatory politics (Vizi, 2013, p. 19; Horváth, 2004) and another with ethno-national cultural identity in focus. The former emphasizes anti-discrimination and desegregation, the latter groupism and cultural rights. András Bíró calls them modernists and culturalists:

> Modernists are mostly drawn from a younger urban elite who see themselves as representatives of an ethnic minority group facing multiple social, economic, educational, but primarily, discrimination problems. Consequently their problems focus on equal opportunities, human rights and integration. Culturalists are located primarily in rural areas and while less visible, are a significant presence in Roma communities. Headed by an older leadership, these prefer retaining tradition to integration.
>
> (Bíró, 2013, pp. 33–34)

The practice of ethno-corruption concerning the minority self-government elections, which are the most important institutions in the legal framework, has already been mentioned. This is not the only or even the most important fallacy of the legislation. The ambiguity of the function and the design of the MSGs is most apparent in regards to the Roma: political representation and empowerment, cultural competences and a vague promise of social integration potential are bundled together. Generally, while acknowledging that it serves as a "training school" for up-and-coming Romani politicians to gain skills that they can use in the mainstream political arena, observers are quite critical of the institutional design. As Melanie Ram notes, the MSG system,

> which at times has been touted as a possible model for other countries, has not brought a substantial improvement in Roma lives. While it has increased participation of Roma to some extent, it has hardly enhanced social inclusion of Roma, largely because its mandate is limited to cultural autonomy (basic education, media, language, and promotion of culture.) [...] The language provisions are simply not so helpful for a community that largely speaks Hungarian at home, and local self-governments do nothing to directly address either discrimination or socioeconomic inequalities.
>
> (Ram, 2014, p. 13)

According to the National Democratic Institute Assessment Report, the minority self-government scheme actually marginalized Roma issues by depositing it

24 This chapter is based on an earlier writing: Pap, A.L. (2015b). Racial, ethnic, or national minority? Legal discourses and policy frameworks on the Roma – In Hungary and beyond. *Social Inclusion*, 3(5), pp. 78–89.

in a powerless, quasi-governmental structure (NDI and OSCE/ODIHR, 2006). Claude Cahn argued that the framework is not only "largely inappropriate for addressing the situation of Roma" but has also "reified the exclusion of non-white minorities in Hungary" (Cahn, 2001; Curejova, 2007). According to the report of the Office for Democratic Institutions and Human Rights of the Organization for Security and Co-operation in Europe and the National Democratic Institute, although Hungary was among the first countries to create a system to promote minority rights and its minority self-government offers a unique approach to fostering Roma participation, many suggest, including Roma activists and analysts, that it is based on "a fundamentally flawed concept that offers the illusion of political power rather than genuine inclusion" (NDI and OSCE/ODIHR, 2006, p. 4). About 10 years ago, the report identified the lack of governance over socioeconomic policy, which was never within the scope of the 1993 minority rights law, a crucial fallacy (NDI and OSCE/ODIHR, 2006, pp. 6–7). In sum, according to the report by the Office for Democratic Institutions and Human Rights of the Organization for Security and Co-operation in Europe and the National Democratic Institute:

> While other minorities are primarily concerned with protection of cultural and linguistic autonomy, the Roma population faces an almost opposite challenge, needing more integration to combat segregated education, discrimination, unemployment, and problems with housing and healthcare.[25]
> (NDI and OSCE/ODIHR, 2006, p. 5)

As Emilia Molnár (currently of the Swedish International Development and Co-operation Agency) and Kai Schaft from Penn State College of Education point out, Hungarian Roma leaders repeatedly call for a redistribution, rather than a recognition-oriented minority policy:

> Roma self-governments see as their main objective the improvement of social conditions in their community rather than the preservation of minority culture and strengthening of minority identity. The ambitions of local Roma leaders are influenced primarily by the marginalization of their community, while the protection of Roma identity remains secondary.
> (Molnár and Schaft, 2013, p. 15)

It also needs to be added that neither of the targeted minority communities ever voiced their demands in a politically compelling way (and Roma representatives certainly would not have advocated such a framework), and, as shown above, the first freely elected Hungarian government acted in a proactive manner, exceeding international minority rights commitments, and created an identity politics-oriented minority rights framework – even if partly or mostly in order to fuel national sentiments and political commitments towards ethnic Hungarians in the Diaspora.

25 For more, see Kováts (1996); Thornberry (2001); and Barany (2002).

In defense of the 1993 law, Balázs Vizi (2013) argues that despite all its flaws, for the first time in Hungarian history, it formally recognized the Roma as a group with legitimate claims for a separate identity. Admittedly, the law facilitated a peculiar nation-building project, conceptualizing a Roma national minority, a distinct political group, incorporating all its diverse subgroups (Fosztó, 2003). Also, to a certain degree, the law successfully endorsed cultural aspirations of certain Roma communities and created a Roma political elite (Bíró, 2013). Its declaration concerning the prohibition of discrimination, a daily fact for Roma in Hungary in all facets of life, received very little attention. For example, the first comprehensive anti-discrimination law was adopted only in 2003, 10 years after the minority rights law, necessitated by EU-accession obligations. And in 2000, only three years before its adoption, the Constitutional Court rejected complaints pertaining to the lack of such a legislation (45/2000). Likewise, the law was unfit to meet social inclusion demands, a dire need for Roma communities. Despite the shocking sweep of market economy that hit the impoverished Roma the hardest, in the first decade or so after the political transition there were no serious attempts to institutionalize social inclusion measures targeting the Roma; Hungarian legislators' priorities concerned enhancing exportable cultural identity for national minorities (Majtényi and Majtényi, 2012).

2.2.3.3. FROM "CIGÁNY" TO "ROMA"

The new minority law in 2011 officially replaced the term "*cigány*" with "*roma.*" Again, no theoretical or political explanation was given. It has been shown that terminology is not a reliable indicator for policy frameworks. It would not be too far-fetched to claim that the inconsistent terminology for the Roma as ethnic, racial and national minority signals the fluidity and the indecisive nature of conceptualizing and targeting.

Roma minority self-governments exemplify a rather curious development in Hungary, as they have formally been involved in social inclusion measures, creating an even more confusingly hybrid, mutant model. As an annex to the 2011 national social inclusion strategy (Ministry of Public Administration and Justice, State Secretariat for Social Inclusion, 2011a), the government signed a framework agreement with the National Roma Self-Government (Ministry of Public Administration and Justice, State Secretariat for Social Inclusion, 2011b), and competences including the supervision of schools, developing new employment schemes and monitoring programs have been assigned to the NRSG. In fact, it has been appointed as one of the core implementing bodies of the Strategy.

The new legislation, backed up by constitutional language, clearly signals that on the one hand the legislator, the right wing populist elite, conceptualizes Roma issues foremost as issues of identity politics. On the other hand, government rhetoric and initiatives (Romagov.kormany.hu, 2014) use cultural identity as a tool for social integration and present it in a simplified, essentialist, manner. Let us see some examples from the National Social Integration Strategy, adopted in order to reflect policy aims set forth by the European Framework for National

Roma Integration Strategies (which, following the "explicit but not exclusive targeting" principle, targets several vulnerable groups) (EC, 2011b; Vizi, 2011):

> The fostering and popularisation of Roma culture [...] should not result in an effect contrary to the desired goal by overly emphasising the cultural "differentness" [...] As the fostering of Roma culture contributes to the positive shaping of the social image of the Roma [...] we must [...] enable the majority society to acquaint themselves with the values of Roma traditions and culture in Hungary and abroad alike (EC, 2011b, pp. 96–98). [...] Learning about the life, values and culture of the other community is an effective means of the fight against stereotypes. We must therefore lay particular emphasis on providing information in public education on the culture and history of the Roma as a part of the multifaceted Hungarian culture as well as on presenting the effects of the Roma culture on the national and Eastern European culture.
>
> (EC, 2011b, pp. 100–102)

This approach is further articulated in the updated version of the integration plan (Ministry of Human Resources, 2014), which emphasizes the role of maintaining cultural traditions, can function as a source of pride and confidence and "which is a prerequisite for the self-esteem, the consciousness-raising, and the re-creation of the integrity of Roma community." While the document sets forth the goal to "reshelve projects fostering Roma culture from social issues to cultural identity," (Ministry of Human Resources, State Secreteriat for Social Issues and Social Inclusion, 2014, pp. 87–88) it also calls for the integration of a social inclusion approach to Roma educational and cultural programs (Ministry of Human Resources, State Secreteriat for Social Issues and Social Inclusion, 2014, p. 91).

Flaws in the Strategy and its policy environment have been thoroughly criticized in the monitoring report commissioned by the Decade of Roma Inclusion Initiative and compiled by an NGO coalition involving most of the relevant organizations (Balogh et al., 2013). For example, it points out that effective anti-discrimination and equal opportunity policies are missing, which is even more acute due to the abolishment of the independent institution of the Parliamentary Commissioner for the Rights of National and Ethnic Minorities and the move of this function to the portfolio of the deputy of the Commissioner for Fundamental Rights. Also, authorities were found to be lenient in sanctioning hate speech, and, as we will see, criminal provisions designed to protect groups facing bias are more often applied by the authorities to sanction Roma rather than non-Roma (Balogh et al., 2013, pp. 9–10). Correspondingly, connecting public security measures with Roma inclusion gives the impression that ethnic origin is intrinsically linked with criminality (Balogh et al., 2013, p. 37).

3. Conclusion

This chapter showed that the hypocritical model for multiculturalism, which was originally designed to foster minority-friendly legislation for ethnic

Hungarians in the neighboring states, was not overridden in the Orbán era. The path-dependent Janus-faced framework was modified in a way to allow for a dual-powered electoral gerrymandering: providing non-resident citizenship, voting rights for Hungarians in the Diaspora and introducing a set of preferential mandates for traditional minorities in a legal framework that allows for abusing minority rights and large-scale ethno-corruption. At the end of the day, it will be the marginalized, abandoned sole ethnic minority, the Roma, who will lose in this scheme. Not only were they most severely affected by the economic consequences of the political transition, but also the newly emerging political structures and legal regimes were inadequate for the historic challenges they have faced.

As for the broader relevance of the Hungarian case, it shows that confusing terminology (in our case of ethnic and national minorities and nationalities) reflects and reveals confused conceptualization and the lack of clearly defined political and policy objectives. Here, the collectivist, essentialist and patronizing approach and the relabelling of the Roma as a nationality are accompanied by a neglect of the individual justice-based, anti-discrimination-oriented approach. This clears the path for far-right rhetoric, centered on ethnicizing criminality and the collective responsibility of the Roma, for an unwillingness to adopt Hungarian middle-class norms and lifestyle.In sum, the terminology and institutional framework originally designed to lobby for minority rights for ethnic Hungarians in the neighbouring states, as well as the new constitution, laws and policy frameworks, each fail to comprehend the complexity of Roma-related issues and even the essential difference the various policy models (minority rights, anti-discrimination and social inclusion) carry and require.

Bibliography

ACT XX of 1949. The Constitution of the Republic of Hungary.

Act XXXVI of 2012 on Parliament.

Act XXXVI of 2013 on Electoral Procedures.

Act LXXVII of 1993 on the Rights of National and Ethnic Minorities.

Act CXII of 2011 on Informational Self-Determination and Freedom of Information.

Act CLXXIX of 2011 on the Rights of Minorities.

Aurescu, B. (2012). The June 2012 opinion of the Venice Commission of the Council of Europe on the act on the rights of nationalities of Hungary. *Lex et Scientia*, 19(2), pp. 166–179.

Balogh, L. (2012a). Minority cultural rights or an excuse for segregation? Roma minority education in Hungary. In: D. Pop, ed., *Education Policy and Equal Education Opportunities*, 1st ed. New York: Open Society Foundations, pp. 207–222.

Balogh, L. (2012b). Jog a kultúra őrzésére – vagy ürügy a szegregációra? A roma nemzetiségi oktatás mint kétélű kard Magyarországon (The right to protect culture or a reason for segregation?). *Pro Minoritate*, 16(1), pp. 207–223.

Balogh et al. (2013). *Civil society monitoring report on the implementation of the National Roma Integration Strategy and Decade Action Plan in 2012 in Hungary.* 1st ed. Budapest: Decade of Roma Inclusion Secretariat Foundation. [online] Available at: http://www.romadecade.org/cms/upload/file/9270_file8_hu_civil-society-monitoring-report_en.pdf [Accessed 31 Dec. 2016].

Barany, Z. (2002). *The East European gypsies. Regime change, marginality and ethnopolitics.* 1st ed. Cambridge: Cambridge University Press.

Beol.hu, (2010). Nem rágalmazás, az etnobiznisz létezik. *Beol.hu* [online] Available at: http://www.beol.hu/bekes/kozelet/nem-ragalmazas-az-etnobiznisz-letezik-335133/ [Accessed 31 Dec. 2016].

Bíró, A. (2013). The price of Roma integration. In: W. Guy, ed., *From victimhood to citizenship: The path of Roma integration. A debate*, 1st ed. Budapest: Kossuth Kiadó, pp. 11–40.

Cahn, C. (2001). Smoke and mirrors: Roma and minority policy in Hungary. European Roma Rights Centre [online] Available at: http://www.errc.org/cikk.php?cikk=1255 [Accessed 31 Dec. 2016].

Carstocea, A. (2011). Ethno-business – the manipulation of minority rights in Romania and Hungary. In: T. Bhambry, C. Griffin, T. Hjelm, C. Nicholson and O. Voronina, ed., *Perpetual motion? Transformation and transition in Central and Eastern Europe & Russia*, 1st ed. London: UCL, School of Slavonic and East European Studies.

Curejova, L. (2007). Hungary: Self-abusive governance. *Transitions online.* [online] Available at: http://www.tol.org/client/article/18943-self-abusive-governance.html [Accessed 31 Dec. 2016].

Chronowski, N. (2012). The New Hungarian Fundamental Law in the light of the European Union's normative values. *Revue Est Europa, (numéro spéciale 1)*, pp. 111–142.

Const. Prep Comm. (2010). Opinion submitted to the parliamentary sub-committee on preparing the new constitution by the Bulgarian National Minority Self-Government, Budapest, http://www.parlament.hu/biz39/aeb/info/bolgar_onk.pdf [Accessed 31 Dec. 2016].

Const. Prep Comm. (2010a). Opinion submitted to the parliamentary sub-committee on preparing the new constitution by the Croatian National Minority Self-Government, Budapest, http://www.parlament.hu/biz39/aeb/info/horvat_onk.pdf [Accessed 31 Dec. 2016].

Const. Prep Comm. (2010b). Opinion submitted to the parliamentary sub-committee on preparing the new constitution by the German National Minority Self-Government, Budapest, http://www.parlament.hu/biz39/aeb/info/mnoo.pdf [Accessed 31 Dec. 2016].

Const. Prep Comm. (2010c). Opinion submitted to the parliamentary sub-committee on preparing the new constitution by the Ruthenian National Minority Self-Government, Budapest, http://www.parlament.hu/biz39/aeb/info/ruszin_onk.pdf, [Accessed 31 Dec. 2016].

Constitutional Court Decision 24/1994 (V.6).

Constitutional Court Decision 35/1992 (VI.10).

Constitutional Court Decision 45/2000 (XII.8).

Council of Europe (1993). Additional protocol on the rights of minorities to the European Convention on Human Rights. Recommendation 1201 (1993).

Council of Europe, ERICarts (2016). Compendium of cultural policies and trends in Europe, 15th edition. [online] Available at: http://www.culturalpolicies.net/web/hungary.php?aid=424 [Accessed 31 Dec. 2016].

Deets, S. (2002). Reconsidering East European minority policy: Liberal theory and European norms. *East European Politics and Society*, 16(1), pp. 30–53.

Dobos, B. (2013a). The role of elections in minority contexts: The Hungarian case. In: E. Nimni, O. Alexander and D. Smith, ed., *The challenge of non-territorial autonomy: Theory and practice*, 1st ed. Oxford: Peter Lang Academic Publishers, pp. 163–180.

Dobos, B. (2013b). Roma political parties in Hungary after 1989. In: E. Dácz, ed., *Minderheitenfragen in Ungarn und in den Nachbarländern im 20. und 21. Jahrhundert*, 1st ed. Baden-Baden: Jahrhundert.Nomos, pp. 279–291.

EC (European Commission), Directorate-General for Employment, Social Affairs and Inclusion. (2011a). The 10 common basic principles on Roma inclusion. Vademecum. [online] Available at: http://www.coe.int/t/dg4/youth/Source/Resources/Documents/2011_10_Common_Basic_Principles_Roma_Inclusion.pdf [Accessed 31 Dec. 2016].

EC (European Commission) (2011b). Communication from the Commission to the European Parliament, the Council, the European Economic and Social Committee and the Committee of the Regions. An EU framework for national Roma integration strategies up to 2020. COM(2011) 173.

EC (European Commission) (2013) The European Union and Roma – Country Factsheet, Hungary. http://ec.europa.eu/justice/discrimination/files/roma_country_factsheets_2013/hungary_en.pdf [Accessed 31 Dec. 2016].

EMASA (2010) Pert nyert az újságíró a román önkormányzattal szemben, May 23. [Accessed 31 Dec. 2016].

EP (European Parliament) (2005). Protection of minorities and anti-discrimination policies in an enlarged Europe. 2005/2008(INI).

FAZ (Frankfurter Allgemeine Zeitung) (2015). "Wir wollen keine multikulturelle Gesellschaft". *Frankfurter Allgemeine Zeitung* [online] Available at: http://www.faz.net/aktuell/politik/europaeische-union/viktor-orban-im-interview-ueber-russland-und-umgang-mit-fluechtlingen-13411128.html [Accessed 31 Dec. 2016].

Fosztó, L. (2003). Diaspora and nationalism: An anthropological approach to the international Romani movement. *Regio – Minorities, Politics, Society*, 3(1), pp. 102–120.

Freedom House (2016). Freedom in the world: Hungary. [online] Available at: https://freedomhouse.org/report/freedom-world/2016/hungary [Accessed 31 Dec. 2016].

Gamlen, A., Cummings, M., Vaaler, P. and Rossouw, L. (2013). Explaining the rise of diaspora institutions. IMI Working Paper 78, International Migration Institute, University of Oxford.

Hannum, H. (2001). International law. In: *Encyclopedia of nationalism*, 1st ed. Academic Press, pp. 405–419.

Harvard (2014). Accelerating patterns of anti-Roma violence in Hungary. A report from the François-Xavier Bagnoud Center for Health and Human Rights, Harvard School of Public Health and Harvard University, Boston.

Horváth, A. (2004). Magyar nemzet, roma nemzet. *Népszabadság*, 12 July.

Horváth and Kiss v. Hungary [2013] 11146/11 (the Second Section of the European Court of Human Rights).

Hungarian Helsinki Committee, (2011). General climate of intolerance in Hungary. [online] Available at: http://helsinki.hu/wp-content/uploads/General_climate_of_intolerance_in_Hungary_20110107.pdf [Accessed 31 Dec. 2016].

Human Rights Commission, Ireland (2004). Travellers as an ethnic minority under the Convention on the Elimination of Racial Discrimination. A Discussion Paper.

Index.hu (2011). Megalakult a szerb és ukrán kisebbségi önkormányzat. *Index.hu* [online] Available at: http://index.hu/belfold/2011/02/05/megalakult_a_szerb_es_ukran_kisebbsegi_onkormanyzat/ [Accessed 31 Dec. 2016].

Index.hu (2016). Továbbra is boldog-boldogtalannak adunk kettős állampolgárságot. *Index.hu* [online] Available at: http://index.hu/gazdasag/2016/07/08/

tovabbra_is_boldog-boldogtalannak_adunk_kettos_allampolgarsagot/ [Accessed 31 Dec. 2016].

Jeszenszky, G. (1996). Hungary's bilateral treaties with the neighbours and the issue of minorities. *Ethnos-Nation. Eine europäische Zeitschrift*, 4(1–2.), pp. 123–128. [online] Available at: http://www.hungarianhistory.com/lib/jeszenszky/jesz5.pdf [Accessed 31 Dec. 2016].

Jogiforum.hu (2010). Választás 2010 – Kisebbségi önkormányzatok – 1.592 településen 2.315 eredményes választás zajlott le vasárnap. *Jogiforum.hu* [online] Available at: http://www.jogiforum.hu/hirek/23865 [Accessed 31 Dec. 2016].

Joppke, C. (2005). *Selecting by origin: Ethnic migration in the liberal state*. 1st ed. Cambridge: Harvard University Press.

Kántor, Z., Majtényi, B., Ieda, O., Vizi, B. and Halász, I. ed., (2004). *The Hungarian status law: Nation building and/or minority protection*. 1st ed. Sapporo: Hokkaido University.

Kaufman, E. (2014). Immigration and integration in Britain: The great nationalism debate. *Nationalities Papers*, 42(6), pp. 1072–1077.

Kemény, I. and Janky, B. (2003). A 2003. évi cigány felmérésről (About the gypsy survey in 2003). In: E. Kállai, ed., *A magyarországi cigány népesség helyzete a 21. század elején (The situation of the gypsy population in Hungary at the beginning of the 21st century)*, 1st ed. Budapest: MTA Etnikai-Nemzeti Kisebbségkutató Intézet, pp. 24–25.

Körtvélyesi, Zs. (2012). From "We the people" to "We the nation". In: *G. Tóth, ed., Constitution for a disunited nation: On Hungary's 2011 Fundamental Law*, 1st ed. Budapest: Central European University Press, pp. 85–110.

Kováts, M. (1996). The Roma and minority self-governments in Hungary. *Immigrants & Minorities: Historical Studies in Ethnicity, Migration and Diaspora*, 15(1), pp. 42–58.

KSH (Központi Staisztikai Hivatal) (Hungarian Central Statistical Office) (2011). Personal Questionnaire [online] Available at: www.ksh.hu/nepszamlalas/docs/kerdoivek/szemely_angol.pdf [Accessed 31 Dec. 2016].

KSH (Központi Staisztikai Hivatal) (Hungarian Central Statistical Office) (2013). A népesség anyanyelv, nemzetiség és nemek szerint (Population according to native language, nationality and gender) [online] Available at: www.ksh.hu/nepszamlalas/docs/tablak/teruleti/00/1_1_6_1.xls [Accessed 31 Dec. 2016].

Kymlicka, W. (2001). Western political theory and ethnic relations in Eastern Europe. In: W. Kymlicka and M. Opalski, ed., *Can liberal pluralism be exported?*, 1st ed. Oxford: Oxford University Press, pp. 13–107.

Lakatos, S. (2010). A romani nyelv közösségi használatának és közoktatási helyzetének vizsgálata Magyarországon. PhD. Pécsi Tudományegyetem, "Oktatás és Társadalom" Neveléstudományi Doktori Iskola.

Majtényi, B. and Majtényi, G. (2012). *Cigánykérdés Magyarországon, 1945–2010*. 1st ed. Budapest: Libri.

Mandla v Dowell Lee [1983] 1 All ER 1062 (House of Lords).

McCrudden, C. (2005). Thinking about the Discrimination Directives. *European Anti-Discrimination Law Review*, (1), pp. 17–23.

McGarry, A. (2009). Ambiguous nationalism? Explaining the parliamentary underrepresentation of Roma in Hungary and Romania. *Romani Studies*, 19(2), pp. 103–124.

Ministry of Human Resources (2014). Magyar Nemzeti Társadalmi Felzárkózási Stratégia II. Tartósan rászorulók – szegény családban élő gyermekek –romák (2011–2020) Frissített változat, Emberi Erőforrások Minisztériuma, Szociális és Társadalmi Felzárkózásért Felelős Államtitkárság. Available at: http://www.kormany.hu/

download/1/9c/20000/Magyar%20NTFS%20II%20_2%20mell%20_NTFS%20II.pdf [Accessed 31 Dec. 2016].

Ministry of Public Administration and Justice, State Secretariat for Social Inclusion (2011a). National social inclusion strategy – Extreme poverty, child poverty, the Roma – 2011–2020. Budapest. [online] Available at: http://romagov.kormany.hu/download/5/58/20000/Strategy%20-%20HU%20-%20EN.PDF [Accessed 31 Dec. 2016].

Ministry of Public Administration and Justice, State Secretariat for Social Inclusion (2011b). Annex 2 to the National social inclusion strategy – Extreme poverty, child poverty, the Roma – 2011–2020. Framework agreement between the government of Hungary and the national Roma self-government, Budapest. [online] Available at: http://romagov.kormany.hu/download/8/58/20000/Annex%202.PDF [Accessed 31 Dec. 2016].

Minority Rights Group (2012). World directory of minorities and indigenous peoples: Roma. [online] Available at: http://minorityrights.org/minorities/roma-8/ [Accessed 31 Dec. 2016].

MNO (2012) Etnobiznisz: magas az új szabályozás lakossági támogatottsága, *Magyar Nemzet Online*, December 21. http://mno.hu/belfold/etnobiznisz-magas-az-uj-szabalyozas-lakossagi-tamogatottsaga-1126477 [Accessed 31 Dec. 2016].

Molnár, E. and Schaft, K.A. (2003). Preserving cultural autonomy or confronting social crisis? The activities and aims of Roma local minority self-governments. *Review of Sociology of the Hungarian Sociological Association*, 9(1), pp. 27–42.

Nagy, J. (2010) Angyalok kertje. *Népszabadság*, July 7.

NDI (National Democratic Institute) and OSCE/ODIHR (Organization for Security and Co-operation in Europe, Office for Democratic Institutions and Human Rights), (2006). The Hungarian minority self-government system as a means of increasing Romani political participation. [online] Available at: http://www.osce.org/odihr/25974?download=true [Accessed 31 Dec. 2016].

Nol.hu, (2011). Kakukktojások? Balhé a román kisebbségnél. *Nol.hu* [online] Available at: http://nol.hu/belfold/kakukktojasok__balhe_a_roman_kisebbsegnel-974661 [Accessed 31 Dec. 2016].

Novak-Lukanovič, S. (2006). Euromosaic III: Presence of regional and minority language groups in the new member states, Office for official publications of the European communities, pp. 111–164.

OSCE/ODIHR (Organization for Security and Co-operation in Europe, Office for Democratic Institutions and Human Rights) (2014). Parliamentary elections 6 April 2014 OSCE/ODIHR limited election observation mission final report [online] Available at: http://www.osce.org/odihr/elections/hungary/121098?download=true [Accessed 31 Dec. 2016].

Pap, A.L. (2001a). Ethnicity and politics – definitions and scopes. *East Central Europe/L'Europe Du Centre-Est. Eine wissenschaftliche Zeitschrift*, 28(2), pp. 41–68.

Pap, A.L. (2001b). Ethnic minorities in parliaments. *Columbia Journal of Eastern European Law*, 7(2), pp. 261–339.

Pap, A.L. (2003). Ethnicization and European identity policies: Window-shopping with risks. *Dialectical Anthropology*, 27(3–4), pp. 227–248.

Pap, A.L. (2005a). The Hungarian status law: Nation building and/or minority protection. *Acta Juridica: Hungarian Journal of Legal Studies*, 46(3–4.), pp. 287–299.

Pap, A.L. (2005b). The status law syndrome: The Hungarian status law: Nation building and/or minority protection (review). *Central European Political Science Review*, 5(16), pp. 99–106.

Pap, A.L. (2006). Minority rights and diaspora-claims: Collision, interdependence and loss of orientation. In: O. Ieda, ed., *Beyond sovereignty: From status law to transnational citizenship?*, 1st ed. Sapporo: Hokkaido University, Slavic Reserach Center, pp. 243–252.

Pap, A.L. (2015a). Is there a legal right to free choice of ethno-racial identity? Legal and political difficulties in defining minority communities and membership boundaries. *Columbia Human Rights Law Review*, 46(2), pp. 153–232.

Pap, A.L. (2015b). Racial, ethnic, or national minority? Legal discourses and policy frameworks on the Roma—In Hungary and beyond. *Social Inclusion*, 3(5), pp. 78–89.

PCIJ (Permanent Court of International Justice) (1930). Greco-Bulgarian Communities, Advisory Opinion, ser. B., No. 17 (July 31).

PCNEM (2006) Annual report of the Parliamentary Commissioner for National and Ethnic Minority Rights 2005, Budapest.

Pogonyi, S. (2015). Transborder kin-minority as symbolic resource in Hungary. *Journal on Ethnopolitics and Minority Issues in Europe*, 14(3), pp. 73–98.

Politics.hu (2015). Quotable: Viktor Orbán on Hungary and multiculturalism. *Politics.hu* [online] Available at: http://www.politics.hu/20150522/quotable-viktor-orban-on-hungary-and-multiculturalism/ [Accessed 31 Dec. 2016].

Ram, M.H. (2014). Europeanization and the Roma: Spreading the norms of inclusion and exclusion. In: 10th Biennial Conference of the European Community Studies Association-Canada. [online] Available at: http://www.ecsa-c.ca/wp-content/uploads/2014/11/4A_Ram.pdf [Accessed 31 Dec. 2016].

Romagov.kormany.hu, (2014). Balog Zoltán: A kultúrára kell építeni a felzárkóztatást. [online] Available at: http://romagov.kormany.hu/balog-zoltan-a-kulturara-kell-epiteni-a-felzarkoztatast [Accessed 31 Dec. 2016].

Rövid, M. (2012). Options of Roma political participation and representation. *Roma Rights*, pp. 9–17. [online] Available at: http://www.errc.org/cms/upload/file/roma-rights-1-2012-challenges-of-representation.pdf [Accessed 31 Dec. 2016].

Simon, P. (2007). "Ethnic" statistics and data protection in the Council of Europe Countries. Study Report. 1st ed. Strasbourg: Council of Europe.

Sobotka, E. (2001). The limits of the state: Political participation and representation of Roma in the Czech Republic, Hungary, Poland and Slovakia. *Journal on Ethnopolitics and Minority Issues in Europe*, 2(1), pp. 1–23.

Szalayné Sándor, E. (2014). A 2014. évi választások a magyarországi nemzetiségekért felelős biztoshelyettes szemszögéből. *Kisebbségkutatás*, 23(1), pp. 7–14.

Szuhay, P. (2003). "Ez egy eredeti cigányélet". *Beszélő*, [online] 8(4). Available at: http://beszelo.c3.hu/cikkek/%E2%80%9Eez-egy-eredeti-ciganyelet%E2%80%9D [Accessed 31 Dec. 2016].

Tajfel, H. (1981). *Human groups and social categories: Studies in social psychology*. 1st ed. Cambridge: Cambridge University Press.

Tátrai, P. (2015). Transformations of the ethnic structure in Hungary after the turn of the millennium. *Human Geographies – Journal of Studies and Research in Human Geography*, 9(1), pp. 76–96.

The Minority Rights Ombudsman (2010a). Rövid összegzés a nemzeti és etnikai jogok országgyűlési biztosának a Romák foglalkoztatása a közigazgatásban és az igazságszolgáltatásban" című program vizsgálatáról. [online] Available at: http://kisebbsegiombudsman.hu/hir-526-rovid-osszegzes-nemzeti-es-etnikai.html [Accessed 31 Dec. 2016].

The Minority Rights Ombudsman (2010b). Beszámoló a Nemzeti és Etnikai Kisebbségi Jogok Országgyűlési Biztosának tevékenységéről, J/2427 [online] Available at: http://www.kisebbsegiombudsman.hu/data/files/205796771.pdf [Accessed 31 Dec. 2016].

The Minority Rights Ombudsman (2011a). Jelentés a nemzeti és etnikai kisebbségi általános iskolai nevelés-oktatás helyzetéről, NEK-411/2011. [online] Available at: http://www.kisebbsegiombudsman.hu/data/files/217986220.pdf [Accessed 31 Dec. 2016].

The Minority Rights Ombudsman (2011b). Jelentés a nemzeti és etnikai kisebbségi általános iskolai nevelés-oktatás helyzetéről, NEK-368/2010. [online] Available at: http://http://www.kisebbsegiombudsman.hu/data/files/205104474.pdf [Accessed 31 Dec. 2016].

The Orange Files (2016). Notable quotes: Prime Minister Viktor Orbán. [online] Available at: https://theorangefiles.hu/notable-quotes-prime-minister-viktor-orban-by-subject/ [Accessed 31 Dec. 2016].

Thornberry, P. (2001). An unfinished story of minority rights. In: A. Bíró and P. Kovács, ed., *Diversity in action: Local public management of multi-ethnic communities in Central and Eastern Europe*, 1st ed. Budapest: Local Government and Public Service Reform Initiative – Open Society Institute, pp. 46–73.

Transparency International (2014). Hungary's elections: Free but not fair. [online] Available at: http://www.transparency.org/news/feature/hungarys_elections_free_but_not_fair [Accessed 31 Dec. 2014].

Treaty of Peace between The Allied and Associated Powers and Hungary and Protocol and Declaration (1920). Signed at Trianon June 4, 1920. [online] Available at: https://wwi.lib.byu.edu/index.php/Treaty_of_Trianon [Accessed 31 Dec. 2016].

Valasztas.hu. (2010). 2010: Önkormányzati Választások. *Valasztas.hu* [online] Available at: http://www.valasztas.hu//hu/onkval2010/576/576_0_index.html [Accessed 31 Dec. 2016].

Venice Commission (2011). Opinion on the new constitution of Hungary. 20 June 2011, 621/2011.

Vizi, B. (2011). The Hungarian presidency of the Council of the European Union: Focus on the neighbourhood and on a European Roma strategy. *Journal on Ethnopolitics and Minority Issues in Europe*, 10(1), pp. 123–134.

Vizi, B. (2013). *Európai kaleidoszkóp. Az Európai Unió és a kisebbségek*. 1st ed. Budapest: L'Harmattan.

Young, I. (1997). A multicultural continuum: A critique of Will Kymlicka's ethnic-nation dichotomy. *Constellations*, 4(1), pp. 48–53.

6 Communitarians, dignity and privacy

Personhood and transparency in the System of National Cooperation

Following the lengthy assessment of how the Hungarian model of illiberalism conceptualizes and operationalizes the nation, national and ethnic minorities and the multiethnic and multinational character of the state, this analysis focuses on the relationship between the individual and the state, in particular, the ethno-cultural majority. The chapter investigates how the Fundamental Law and subsequent recent legislation conceptualizes and operationalizes personhood and constitutionally recognized groups. This not only uncovers constitutional preferences in the Fundamental Law but also shows how the Hungarian model of "illiberal democracy" denies the primacy of individual freedom over collective values and interests. The main argument of this chapter is that the illiberal nature of the Hungarian illiberal democracy concerns not only illiberalism vis-à-vis democracy, that is, the dismantling of checks and balances, democratic control mechanisms, the rule of law or gerrymandering, but also how personhood is conceptualized in the constitutional regime. As the chapter on intimate citizenship showed, the new constitution operates with outright value preferences. In Orbán's regime, the disregard for individual liberties and freedom primarily has not yet surfaced in the blatant denial of fundamental rights (such as habeas corpus, free speech, et cetera); it is visible in the theoretical foundations of the constitutional conceptualization of the new political community, which is not built on individual freedom and liberties. As this chapter will show, the recognition of individual dignity is conditional on membership in the (most often majority) community, which is defined by the constitutionally cemented value preferences. Also, the new Constitution protects the dignity of communities – including but not limited to the ethnic majority community – not individual freedoms, liberties and autonomy, on which the post-WWII, human rights-based political consensus is built and most classic liberal democracies identify as the foundations of their "social contracts." The dignity of communities is a concept that is difficult to operationalize in liberal democracies (Sajó, 2011). People within the human rights community are routinely involved in theoretical and practical debates on whether legal (and political) protection and activism should center on civil liberties and limits on government control or on equality and human dignity, which require a more severe restriction of free speech and other civil liberties in order to efficiently protect victimized and vulnerable groups from threats and harm caused by other nonstate actors. These internal conflicts come up all the time among human rights activists and scholars, all of whom endorse the same principles: human rights, social justice and combating violence. The question of hate speech (and say, the criminalization of genocide-denial) or the legalization or a client-based abolition of prostitution are the most notable cases. The Hungarian legislator and the constitution makers were not too concerned with these dilemmas. Constitutional, civil and criminal protections are provided for the dignity of certain communities: often the majority, even against various minorities (be they ethnic, ideological or lifestyle). The legislature swiftly ended a two-decade long debate on hate speech, which involved a series of constitutional court decisions.

Besides dignity, the other core concept in this chapter will be privacy. As will be shown, in Hungarian illiberalism privacy will be used as a tool to obstruct transparency and political accountability. Furthermore, as the case study of the last subchapter will show, a peculiar and cynical approach to data protection can even be used to discriminate and further marginalize certain communities. As in the case of the ill-conceived model of multiculturalism, the Roma will again fall victim to these conceptual and legal frameworks. I will demonstrate how legal protection for privacy is used to reject the recognition and registration of ethnicity by authorities. This, in turn, leads both to under- and over-policing, insufficient prosecutions of racially motivated hate crimes and inadequate monitoring of ethnic profiling.

As a last preliminary note, some of the legislation and legal practices predate the Orbán regime, especially when privacy interests and arguments have overruled transparency and public access interests and arguments. This can be explained in part by the close legacy of communism. In the 1990s, providing powerful guarantees for protection against the gaze of Big Brother defined and dominated the agenda of the Constitutional Court and the first Parliamentary Commissioner (Ombudsman) for Data Protection; access to public data did not seem to be a priority. It is quite telling that even though the title of the relevant law (Act LXIII of 1992) included both data protection and access to public data, in the media, professional and academic language and press releases, the law and the specialized ombudsman (supervising the enforcement of the entire law) were referred to only as the data protection law and the data protection ombudsman. Still, similarly to the developments discussed in the previous chapter, it would be a mistake to identify post-2010 developments as entirely path-dependent. Even though illiberal traditions and practices have been continuous in several areas and not newly introduced by Orbán's regime, in several cases law enforcement and judicial reflexes simply became constitutionally and legally cemented. The path was certainly there, but Orbán had the political power to go against it. Instead, illiberal traditions were used as important pillars for building the new regime.

***

1. Communities as primary agents of dignity

This subchapter shows how the ethno-cultural majority and certain select minorities are the primary agents of constitutionally recognized dignity. In its declaration (which incidentally follows the Universal Declaration of Human Rights) stating that "individual freedom can only be complete in cooperation with others," the Preamble of the Fundamental Law embraces a markedly collectivist and communal approach to fundamental rights and civil liberties, rather than one based on individual autonomy. This is reinforced by Article G (2) of the chapter entitled Foundations, which states, "Hungary shall protect its citizens." Herbert Küpper (Küpper, 2012, p. 9). argues that here "the individual ceases to be a subject and is only an object of the state's protection."

The contours of the SNC's position emerge even more markedly in the context of freedom of speech and the community-based protection of dignity. Article IX (5) of the Fundamental Law's chapter on Freedom and Responsibility states that

> [t]he right to freedom of speech may not be exercised with the aim of violating the dignity of the Hungarian nation or of any national, ethnic, racial or religious community. Persons belonging to such communities shall be entitled to enforce their claims in court against the expression of an opinion which violates the community, invoking the violation of their human dignity, as provided for by an Act.

Protection against offensive speech is a highly debated issue, with vastly different standards of jurisprudence on the two sides of the Atlantic; even where curtailing hate speech and the protection of dignity on the basis of identity is allowed, it usually only arises in the context of some sort of documented vulnerability in regards to the protected group or as a threat of potential or actual exclusion or marginalization. When it involves restricting the right for free expression, the arguments that carry the greatest weight are not those that seek to justify restrictions on hate speech with regard to general notions of dignity, but rather those that would legitimate such measures on the basis of protecting minorities. That is, they would offer additional protections for groups with a reduced ability to assert their interests or groups that, as a consequence of, for example, some historical trauma, are prevented from participating in the democratic discourse on a level that is commensurate with the majority's involvement. The prohibition of hate speech therefore usually serves as a means to right a historical wrong (Uitz, 2000) or as an instrument for protecting groups that cannot ignore the hate they encounter or lack the wherewithal to take effective action against it. It is unclear how being part of the ethnic/national majority or the Hungarian nation in today's Hungary could have implications that threaten individuals within this majority with a stigma and vulnerability requiring special legal protections. A feudal-type unconditional, blank-check protection for communities is not an accepted practice.

In sum, this is an utterly disturbing provision, as under classic constitutional doctrine in Europe, the concept of human dignity is generally intended to protect the individual rather than the community. Additionally, there are recent policies concerning the protection of certain groups, such as women in relation to speech (Recommendation of the European Parliament and of the Council, 2006). Be that as it may, with concern to new avenues for the protection of the dignity of communities, it is safe to say that it is difficult to justify the protection of the "majority" (ethnic or political), in particular, against minorities. Balázs Majtényi argues that this provision can be used to curtail government criticism if it is interpreted (by agents of the very criticized entity) as a violation of dignity. This is not an impossible scenario. As an analogy, consider, for example, the arguments defensive courts may use for criticism: if a politician comments on a judicial decision, it is often rebutted as a violation of the separation of powers and the autonomy of the court. Seeing criticism as a violation of constitutional competences and authority, especially if it concerns the government or Parliament, who, based on a direct electoral authorization, speak on behalf of the nation, is not far-fetched from seeing it as a violation of dignity. Again, here the binding interpretation of what amounts to the violation of dignity lies in the hands of the agent that has been the target of criticism.

1.1. Minorities vs the majority

Relying on a peculiar legislative logic, the Fundamental Law's mentioned Article IX states on the one hand that the "right to freedom of speech may not be exercised with the aim of violating the dignity of the Hungarian nation or of any national, ethnic, racial or religious community," while, at the same time, in the next clause, it is the dignity of individuals, as members of communities, that serves as the grounds for restricting the right to free expression.

The constitutional language had been transformed into civil legislation. A newly adopted Civil Code (Act V of 2013) that entered into effect on 15 March 2014 – the day of press freedom – was adopted after several decades of preliminary codification work. The author of the personal rights section in the new Code was former Fidesz government commissioner László Székely, who serves as the current Commissioner for Fundamental Rights. Article 2:54 (5) gives the individual the right to initiate litigation against the offender in cases involving hate speech[1] – even if according to the general rules of continental civil law, a

1 "Any member of a community shall be entitled to enforce his personality rights in the event of any false and malicious statement made in public at large for being part of the Hungarian nation or of a national, ethnic, racial or religious group, which is recognized as an essential part of his personality, manifested in a conduct constituting a needlessly serious violation in an attempt to damage that community's reputation, by bringing action within a thirty-day preclusive period. All members of the community shall be entitled to invoke all sanctions for violations of personality rights [...]" It also needs to be mentioned that the term "needlessly offensive" cannot be interpreted in any meaningful way, for with regard to limiting free expression, it appears irrelevant

community is not a legal subject and hence lacks a personality and is not entitled to the protection of civil law. A civil law relation is (conceptually) always a relationship between two individuals, and thus the legislator's approach does not mesh with the logic of civil law, neither substantive nor procedural law. Nor does it harmonize with classical constitutional law doctrines, for the right to human dignity[2] can only be construed in the context of individual persons. A further marked example for illiberalism is that the state, via the prosecutor, is authorized to initiate proceedings (in lieu of an individual, in his/her representation, but in the name of the offended community), even if no member of the involved communities feels a need to do so!

The protection of the majority is not without precedent in pre-SNC history of constitutional law. A 2008 Constitutional Court decision (96/2008) written by Justice, later Chief Justice, Péter Paczolay (who, in this capacity assisted in Orbán's constitutional capture and the castration of the Court's competences) struck down a 2007 amendment of the Civil Code that was to sanction hate speech only in regards to members of minority communities. The Court argued that it would amount to discrimination if such protections were not awarded to members of the majority (Mahlmann, 2012, pp. 370–396).

1.2. Identity or vulnerability protection?

The Hungarian Civil Liberties Union (Hegyi and Simon, 2013) argued that the law is discriminative to begin with, as it only protects members of the Hungarian nation and national, ethnic, racial or religious communities; however, gender, gender identity, sexual orientation, disability and age are not included. Also, the requirement that the infringing speech must be made before a wide public audience is unconstitutionally vague and may even include speech that does not reach a single member of the protected communities.

Hate speech is also regulated by Article 332 of Act C of 2012 on the Criminal Law. This provision establishes that incitement against a community is committed by someone who incites to hatred against "the Hungarian nation; any national, ethnic, racial or religious group; or certain societal groups, in particular on the grounds of disability, gender identity or sexual orientation." Here, the Hungarian nation is specified as a protected legal object, unlike in Article 216 codifying hate crime as "violence against members of the community,"[3] which

---

whether a statement or a conduct was – in an everyday sense of the term – justifiably or needlessly offensive. The formulation used in the law suggests that there are the following distinct and relevant degrees of a(n objective) rights infringement: an expression is (subjectively speaking) inoffensive, it is (subjectively) offensive, it is (objectively) justifiably offensive or (objectively) gratuitously offensive.

2 See for example Mahlmann (2012, pp. 370–396); McCrudden (2008); Dupré (2012) and Jones (2012).

3 "Any person who displays an apparently anti-social behavior against others for being part, whether in fact or under presumption, of a national, ethnic, racial or religious group, or of a certain societal group, in particular on the grounds of disability, gender identity or sexual

does not specify the Hungarian nation as a protected group but provides for an open-ended list by including "*certain societal groups.*"

As will be shown, the question of specifically codified hate crime sanctions for members of a minority (again, in Hungary it will mostly concern a single minority, the Roma) in relation to crimes committed against a member of a majority (especially if this involves members of racist hate groups) will be of paramount importance. The issue concerns the core question of defining hate crimes. Can and should any group be protected as a hate crime victim, or should protection only apply to members of discrete and insular, underprivileged, vulnerable communities that lack sufficient numbers or power to seek redress through the political process or may face discrimination because of their inherent (unchangeable, fundamental, immutable) characteristics? The debate concerning hate crimes is generally an intriguing one: should the political message, the more severe criminalization of bias motivation and the heightened protection be extended to all kinds of identities, or is it intrinsically a minority protection mechanism? The entire concept of imposing a more severe punishment for bias or hatred has been criticized for introducing 'thought policing' (Washington, 2007).

Legislation in the past years by international and national organizations brought a proliferation of protected grounds and has been extended to basically any socially recognized identity; often open-ended lists are used, making reference to "any other status." While hate crime legislation has been endorsed, and sometimes implicitly or explicitly required by international organizations such as the OSCE, the UN, the EU and the Council of Europe,[4] this element has never been clarified. It appears that the language and concept set forth by the Hungarian legislator, where membership in the majority nation qualifies equally as well as membership in a minority community when seeking protection, seems to be in line with international standards. The Hungarian lawmaker explicitly stated in a commentary on the new Penal Code[5] that hate crimes are identity-protecting and not minority-protecting provisions, and this position is supported by several international examples.

The case of Hungarian illiberalism nevertheless shows that even contrary to commitments made by international organizations such as the OSCE and the EU's Fundamental Rights Agency, the concept of hate crimes should be limited to hate incidents committed against members of minority communities. Instances of members of minority communities being systematically charged

---

orientation, of aiming to cause panic or to frighten others, is guilty of a felony punishable by imprisonment not exceeding three years. (2) Any person who assaults another person for being part, whether in fact or under presumption, of a national, ethnic, racial or religious group, or of a certain societal group, in particular on the grounds of disability, gender identity or sexual orientation, or compels him by force or by threat of force to do, not to do, or to endure something, is punishable by imprisonment between one to five years" (Act C of 2012).

4 See for example OSCE (2009) and Framework Decision on Combating Certain Forms and Expressions of Racism and Xenophobia by Means of Criminal Law (2008).

5 Bill T/6218, amending various laws in order to protect public order and the justice system.

with racially motivated hate crimes committed against the majority point to a substantive difference from anti-discrimination legislation, where 'the more the better' principle is in place. Here, less is more!

Judicial practice is uneven, and some high court decisions adopted the position that hate crime provisions are indeed minority-protection mechanisms. In 2015, the high court[6] nevertheless reiterated that members of the majority community can be victims of hate crimes. In the SNC, dignity as constitutional principle and the source of fundamental rights does not seem to be perceived as an inherent characteristic of the individual, but it rather as something that human beings have because of their membership in various communities. The community-based protection of dignity becomes particularly problematic when it serves the protection of the majority community. The SNC, however, overcame this dilemma by constitutionally enshrining this possibility, or, in an alternative interpretation, this obligation. The Hungarian Constitutional Court held as early as 1992 that the dignity of communities can be a legitimate reason to curtail the freedom of expression. Interestingly, this principle was actually not applied uncritically in a 2011 decision, when the court struck down certain provision of the media law (165/2011). This demonstrates that here too, the path was paved but not cemented; the SNC chose to follow traditions that were in line with its goals.

2. Liberal instruments for illiberal objectives: Privacy as a tool to obstruct public accountability and to protect the dignity of government institutions and officials

It is a peculiar feature of the SNC that despite its communal and collectivist commitments and biases, privacy has been used as a tool to obstruct the transparency and accountability of public officials. Here, an individual-oriented liberal instrument serves an illiberal goal of limiting public oversight of public power. It needs to be noted that here too, this legislative and judicial attitude precedes the SNC. The path had been paved, but if were not compatible with the SNC, the supermajority and the newly established legal and judicial elite could have abandoned it. Hence, path-dependency is a difficult argument to make and should not be confused with the continuity of pre-2010 illiberal practices, models and reflexes.

As mentioned in the introduction to this chapter, the primacy of privacy over public accountability was due to several factors: the proximity of the totalitarian regime before 1990 and the successful activism of human privacy rights advocates, NGOs and academics. A mere two years after the political transition, a progressive and very powerful privacy law (Act LXIII of 1992) was adopted with a specialized ombudsman who was very active and also acted decisively against data collectors in the private sector. To mention just one example: Hungary for a while was among the few European countries where Google Street View was only allowed to go public contingent on compliance with strict requirements,

6 Supreme Court uniformity decision 2015 B.3 (3/2015 "büntető elvi döntés").

thanks to an intervention by the data protection commissioner (Kulcsár, 2011). Nevertheless, from the very start the issue of access to public data and freedom of information received less emphasis. This is not to imply, of course, that this is a zero sum game. A society can very well be transparent when it comes to the public sphere even if there is a strong privacy/data protection regime in place. Before his office was abolished, the last specialized ombudsman specifically advocated for a new perspective and a modified, more harmonious balance in the activism concerning these two protected legal interests.[7]

Let us consider a few illuminating examples of how privacy is actually used to prevent public scrutiny. An emblematic case concerns recording the images of police officers that exercise public power and represent the state's monopoly on violence. Despite a 2000 Constitutional Court decision (54/2000), which held that

> in the interest of effectively protecting the rights of citizens it is necessary to identify the persons who exercise public power in the name of the state, and [...] members of the uniformed service, [...], do not perform their duties as part of a 'faceless mass' but as officials authorized to exercise public power. Hence they need to be individually identifiable in the interest of personal accountability

there are even law firms that specialize in this issue, and from time to time, more often than not succeed in convincing courts to award damages against media outlets that disseminate identifiable images of police officers (Index.hu, 2012; Hvg.hu, 2014a). This existing judicial practice, which was affirmed by one of the data protection commissioners, became the subject of an intensive legal debate involving several actors, but had not changed much after all. A 2012 decision of a seven-member panel on harmonizing jurisprudence of Hungary's high court, the Curia,[8] led by the court's president, the chief justice, held that

> the performance of official duties in public spaces does not qualify as an act by a public figure, which is why visual or audio recordings of police officers, firefighters, prison officers, postal carriers, paramedics, street cleaners, etc. taken or made during the public performance of their duties may only be published with consent of the person in question [...] a police officer who performs his/her work and takes official measures cannot be regarded as a public figure just because he/she is the employee of an official body that discharges public power functions. [...] it is not necessary to publish the

7 To quote a press release: "In many cases data protection prevails at the expense of freedom of information. Achieving transparency [...] is often hindered by obstacles stemming from the (often presumed) needs of data protection. [...] data protection [...] ought not turn into an objective pursued for its own sake, and it especially ought not impede the legitimate interest in freedom of information." (Office of the Data Protection Commissioner, 2010).

8 Supreme Court uniformity decision 1/2012 BKMPJE.

> image of police officers who perform official actions in order to hold officials accountable for acts performed in the exercise of public power, nor is it necessary for the sake of transparency.

A 2014 decision by the Constitutional Court (28/2014) resulted in a peculiar situation, for it left the Curia's judgement unchanged but struck down as unconstitutional a decision by the Budapest Appellate Court, arguing that

> if the police officer is faceless then the accountability of public power is lost and personal accountability is undermined. [...] Recorded images of police action may be published without the consent of the officer or officers in question as long as their public dissemination is not gratuitous, in other words as long as it is part of a visual coverage of current public affairs involving information that the public has a legitimate interest in knowing, based on the circumstances of the given case and with regard to the exercise of public power in the applicable context.

Nevertheless judicial, and most of all, media practice followed the arguments of dissenting justices, all Fidesz appointees. István Balsai, Orbán's former justice minister, and Egon Dienes-Oehm held that the decision "gives unfounded preference to the rights of free expression, free press and free speech over the protection of personal data."

Uncovering police officers is not the only noteworthy case. According to the Hungarian Supreme Court's jurisprudence (Kfv. III.39.302/2010/8), for example, mayors who utter racist statements during municipal assembly sessions or before the press are not subject to anti-discrimination law, which bans discrimination and harassment by public officials and agencies, because they cannot be assumed to be speaking in an official capacity and thus may not qualify as public figures (Pap, 2012). The Hungarian Civil Liberties Union (HCLU) once even had to sue the Constitutional Court for not disclosing the name of a petitioner, a Member of Parliament seeking the constitutional review of a provision of the Criminal Code on an official letterhead. The court, in line with the Constitutional Court (the ultimate guarantor of fundamental rights!) was of the opinion that cases initiated by Members of Parliament may amount to private data and can be exempt from disclosure. The case reached the Supreme Court, with the HCLU's requests denied at all instances (HCLU, 2005). Finally, the European Court of Human Rights ruled for the NGO (HCLU v. Hungary).

An appellate court held that official communication between a former prime minister and other heads of governments and states need not be of public concern (Index.hu, 2010), and another court ruled that the budgetary appropriations of a nuclear plant need not be disclosed.[9] Pursuant to a suggestion by Fidesz's Vice Chairman Gergely Gulyás in September 2014, the Parliament's ad

9 The appellate court overruled the judgment. See Hvg.hu (2011).

hoc committee on nominating the members of the Constitutional Court voted in a closed session about the nominees "in the interest of safeguarding [their] personal data" (Index.hu, 2014a).

Frequently those who are implicated in cases involving public officials or the use of public funds simply declare that they do not consider themselves public figures and hence refuse to divulge information. The media and the investigating authorities tend to accept this position uncritically. This attitude was also characteristic of the debates involving the attendance of the 2014 soccer World Cup in Brazil by the prime minister's son, Gáspár Orbán, for example, and the question of who bore the costs of his VIP booth ticket (444.hu, 2014) or the conviction of the prime minister's infamous guru and advisor, Árpád Habony, in a criminal case in court (Hidvégi, 2013; Hvg.hu, 2013). An embezzlement case involving the socialist politician Gábor Simon, who was found to have hundreds of millions in a secret account, was similarly symbolic. Simon resigned from his seat in Parliament and from his party positions; when journalists subsequently sought him out for a reaction he refused on the grounds that he was now a private person and threatened the journalists with legal reprisals (Hirado.hu, 2014).

A 2014 decision the Constitutional Court (7/2014) ruled that a provision of the newly adopted Civil Code that only allowed the broader criticism of public figures in the context of public affairs contingent on the presence of a "legitimate public interest," ran afoul of the freedom of speech and expression laid down in Article IX of the Fundamental Law. Here too most of the new judges who had been elected by the governing majority that had also adopted the Fundamental Law wrote dissenting opinions, which reflects the legislators' preferences in terms of reasoning and attitudes. Justice, later Chief Justice, Barnabás Lenkovics held that

> [T]here is an increasing social desire [...] for the public power to defend the rights of free speech and free expression against the influence and domination of the press and media powers [...] [T]here is a growing expectation vis-à-vis the law that it protect free speech and free expression from becoming deformed and morphing into libertinism, turning on itself. [...] the exercise of all fundamental rights and liberties implies responsibilities, and may only occur responsibly.
>
> (p. 247, para. 103)

So far, we have seen how privacy enjoys primacy over monitoring public power and freedom of information, as this applies even when the person involved is a public figure or an official exercising public power. One notable exception is expressed in the constitution: under Article U (4) of the Fundamental Law, "[t]he holders of power under the communist dictatorship shall be obliged to tolerate statements of facts about their roles and acts related to the operation of the dictatorship, with the exception of deliberate statements that are untrue in essence; their personal data related to such roles and acts may be disclosed to the public." The Fundamental Law thus declares that those who previously exercised public power in the communist regime (and of the two totalitarian regimes in the 20th century, this provision only applies to the communist; fascism is not included) are quasi-public figures who, in the name of historical justice, are subject to less severe privacy protections. Yet, the new constitution fails to apply similar provisions to other public figures.

Authorities and other public institutions are traditionally adverse to making their activities transparent. Journalists and civil organizations had to turn to the courts with freedom of information requests in cases where such requests would have been automatically granted in most liberal democracies, even without a judicial verdict to that effect. The Office of the President of the Republic, for example, sought to keep secret the names of the persons whom President Pál Schmitt had pardoned (HCLU, 2012a). The foreign ministry needed a court order to answer a question raised by an MP as to whether the spin doctor Árpád Habony owned a diplomatic passport (Index.hu, 2015). (It is a recurring political and freedom of information litigation issue that NGOs and opposition politicians ask the prime minister and other government politicians about the contractual or employment status of Mr. Habony, who has been identified by the media as one of the most influential government advisors and regularly appears in public with top government officials. The response is always a flat denial of any kind of relationship.) The National Consumer Protection Authority routinely fails to specifically name the products that it finds poisonous (Index.hu, 2011a). As we will see, the media is happy to report the news without these key details.

In 2016, a highly publicized scandal erupted; it concerned the 1962 gang rape conviction and jailing of the head coach of the national swimming team. The National Authority for Data Protection and Freedom of Information, headed by a former data protection ombudsman, first blocked access to the case files and later fined the Budapest archives for 3 million forints (approximately 11,000 USD, 9,800 EUR) for violating the coach's privacy by allowing access.[10]

The HCLU, the anti-corruption portal K-Monitor, Transparency International Hungary and the International Press Institute (IPI) argued that Act CXII of 2011 on Informational Self-Determination and Freedom of Information (the so-called "Privacy Act") imposes an undue restriction on access to public interest data and on the transparency of the government's operations and thereby increases the risk of corruption (FreedomInfo, 2013). The government pushed through several subsequent legislative actions curtailing access to public data (444.hu, 2016), introducing the concept of "abusive data requests" in 2013, abolishing anonymous data requests, allowing government offices to charge (even very high amounts) for processing access to data in 2015 and making certain public areas, such as the postal services or certain national budget-calculations, exempt from disclosure requirements.

The denial to refuse access to information has deep moral and constitutional reasoning: the dignity of the government. The prosecutor general, former Fidesz

10 See Origo.hu (2016); The Daily News Hungary (2016); The Guardian (2016); and U.S. News (2016).

parliamentary candidate Péter Polt, has initiated dozens of lawsuits concerning political and journalistic criticisms of his office and his person, mostly in response to opinion statements. According to a decision by the Metropolitan Court of Budapest, the daily *Népszava* committed libel against the Prosecutor General's Office and Prosecutor General in person and ordered that the respondent pay each of the plaintiffs 1 million forints (approximately 3600 USD, 3300 EUR) in damages, as well as a public interest fine of 500,000 because they published that the "Prosecutor General's Office is led by a governing party politician, Péter Polt, who is free to decide himself which controversial case makes it into the judicial phase and which court it will be heard by" (Népszava, 2013a).

The Prosecutor General filed similar suits against the weekly *Élet és Irodalom*, as well as against an iconic dissident and former liberal MP philosophy professor János Kis, in response to an article published in April 2011, which stated the following: "[T]he prosecutor general was elected last year and will hold this office until 2019. During his previous term in office he amply demonstrated that he does not exercise his duties as an independent public servant but in service of the people who had selected him for this office." In this case, neither the Metropolitan Court of Budapest nor the Budapest Court of Appeal took Polt's position; they held that the author stated a political opinion and had not exceeded the limits of free expression, as his text had contained neither disparaging nor defamatory statements.[11]

In another case, the court held that the daily *Népszabadság* libeled the Prosecutor General's reputation and was sentenced to pay 800,000 forints (approximately 3000 USD, 2600 EUR) in non-pecuniary damages for writing about a case involving two figures who had been tied to fictional corporations allegedly set up by operatives close to Fidesz, claiming that "Péter Polt successfully extricates his comrades from even the most suspicious cases." In a book titled *The Real Orbán*, the author Péter Kende claimed – in the context of investigations initiated during the (center-left) Medgyessy government (between 2002 and 2004), which were then terminated per the instructions of the Prosecutor's Office – that the "prosecutor's office [was] blocking" investigations. In an extensive chapter, the author analyzed what considerations had underlain the decisions not to bring these cases to a conclusion. Mr. Polt and the Prosecutor General's Office had compiled their objections in almost 50 counts, 13 of which were ultimately affirmed by the court, which held that the author made false statements of facts regarding the operations of the Prosecutor's Office, which libeled the institution and had given rise to false impressions. He was fined to pay non-pecuniary damages amounting to 1 million forints (approximately 3600 USD, 3300 EUR) to each of the plaintiffs.

In another case, socialist politician (and former foreign minister and EU Commissioner) László Kovács said that "The Prosecutor's Office is not engaged in law enforcement; in fact, the positions it takes in several cases create the appearance that it serves as an accessory to criminal activities." The first instance court held that that though the politician used strong and polarizing language, he ultimately

11 Budapest Court of Appeal Case No. 8.Pf.20.008/2013/6. Also see Kovács (2011).

voiced an opinion. The Budapest Court of Appeal reversed, ordering an apology (Lencsés, 2011).[12] Taking legal action each time someone criticizes the office or its leader reflects the concept of seeing the civil code as another tool to protect the honor of public institutions or the dignity of public officials. In political debates, not only actual people but also government institutions and even companies may enjoy privacy protection and preference over the public's right to information.

2.1. The judiciary

The Hungarian judicial system generally endorses the obstruction of access to information. The past years have seen a significant improvement in terms of the availability of judicial decisions in electronic databases. Without knowledge of the case-number (!), however, it is still very difficult to find specific judgements. This is mostly because almost everything has been rendered anonymous in the registries, citing the need to protect personal data. The cases are sometimes absurd: when I looked up the above-mentioned case concerning the weekly *Élet és Irodalom* vs. the Prosecutor General, regarding the above-mentioned lawsuits involving media, the courts used the following language:

> [A] report series entitled '? III.' about the constitution-making process was published in the public affairs and literary weekly É.I. [...] The author [...] concludes that as long as the 'F.[...] party alliance is in government it practically removes the governing majority from the checks of the other independent branches of government.' [The author] uses untrue and offensive expressions concerning the co-plaintiff and through his/her person the entire staff of the Prosecutor's Office.[13]

Another judgment rendered by the Metropolitan Court of Budapest obviously did not make the intelligibility of the text or even the understanding of the full underlying story a priority:

> The court determines that the co-respondent violated the co-plaintiff's right to reputation by stating falsely in a caption ('caption') under an image depicting the co-plaintiff (name of co-plaintiff, the Deputy Prosecutor General) and the person in charge of the plaintiff's institution (Prosecutor General's Office) at the time – the image was used as an illustration accompanying an article entitled 'title of article' published on June 14, 2010 on the www.first website operated by the co-respondent – that the co-plaintiff (name of co-plaintiff) is the corrupt prosecutor alluded to in the article.[14]

12 Efforts to track down the case numbers and the corresponding judgments proved unsuccessful in the public available judicial databases.

13 Budapest Court of Appeal, Decision No. 8.Pf.20.008/2013/6.

14 Judgment by Judge Renáta Bérces, in a December 8, 2011 decision by the Metropolitan Court of Budapest registered in the database as No. P. .../2010/13 (official indexing).

The Budapest Court of Appeal's website featured a judgement in September 2014, which talked of a "Mayor G.P." (Index.hu, 2014b). Another very illustrative case is a judgment by Judge János Pap of the Csongrád County Court, anonomized in the following fashion:

> The judgment was preceded by the plaintiff's criminal charges filed against the mayor on account of the fact that following a corresponding proposal by the municipal assembly, the mayor had ordered the free distribution to high school students of copies of the novel entitled Fateless by a Hungarian Nobel laureate.[15]

Anonymizing is completely absurd because not only can the author be identified by the book title, but there has only been one Hungarian Nobel-laureate, Imre Kertész, who was not even directly involved in the case. There are countless cases in which information that is blacked out is de facto public and easily identified with a simple Google search. It is also quite telling that Act 125 of 2003 on Equal Treatment, the law transposing the EU's racial and other equality directives, identifies the publication of the names of those found guilty in discrimination as a separate sanction that the Equal Treatment Authority, the equality body established by the law, may (!) apply. The practice of the relatively newly formed organization reflects the above attitude: concerning its activities for example in 2013, the Authority proudly reported that of the 1496 complaints they received, of which a mere 11 were actually made public (Equal Treatment Authority, 2012).[16]

2.2. *The far right*

The most absurd cases concern lawsuits by extremist and far right politicians for being labeled as such. They argue that their privacy has been violated. The most memorable case concerned history professor László Karsai, who called the Jobbik party a neo-Nazi organization on a television channel's morning show. The party sued for slander. The historian asked the court to reject the plaintiff's action, arguing that the issue for the court to decide was not whether Jobbik is a neo-Nazi party but rather to protect academic free speech. The Metropolitan Court of Budapest[17] held that the party's right to a good reputation (!) had been violated, and the historian was ordered – in addition to paying court costs and fees amounting to 66,000 forints (approximately 240 USD, 210 EUR) in total – to express his regret for his impugned statement as a form of "redress" for the injured party. It is worth adding that Jobbik MP György Gyula Zagyva, who is an honorary president of the far-right Sixty-Four Counties Youth Movement

15 Csongrád County Court 2.P.21.514/2008/4.

16 In 2015 every third decision was published (ETA, 2016).

17 Metropolitan Court of Budapest 19.P.22.708/2012/10.

(Hungarian: Hatvannégy Vármegye Ifjúsági Mozgalom, HVIM), subsequently made the following statement: "And they always say that we need to be stopped in the name of this democracy and that democracy. Interestingly, however, when this grand democracy thing would protect us, then suddenly it no longer applies! So fascists need to be trampled underfoot, right?" (Harkai, 2011) (It is worth mentioning that shortly after delivering the judgment, the judge resigned, started a diplomatic career and was appointed consul in Romania.) Though the Budapest Court of Appeal changed the first instance decision and rejected Jobbik's action in its decision of January 2014,[18] on the whole this episode is a good illustration of the prevailing attitude and corporate culture in the administration of justice. In another case, brought against the same (opposition) television channel, Jobbik won once again, this time because the party was referred to as far right. The Media Authority held that there was a violation of the media law's prohibition on combining the reading of political news with an opinion, for Jobbik is a "value-based, conservative and national Christian party, which employs radical methods, but is not a far-right party."[19] The high court affirmed the Media Authority's decision.[20] Tamás Szigeti of the HCLU points out that this was not the first time that a far-right group contested being labeled as fascist or neo-Nazi. In a highly publicized case, a radio host lost a suit against a far-right motorcycle gang for calling them fascists. The peculiarity of the current case lies in the fact that a court ruled that a parliamentary party, which cannot actually have "dignity" (the constitutional foundation of good reputation in the case of persons) enjoys the same level of legal protection of its reputation as a private person. It is also unusual in democracies that a court would engage in the legal investigation of whether political opinions concerning a political party are objectively justified.

> A politician with hurt feelings will often find the courts sympathetic to his/her plight. As things stand today, is not to say that the freedom of speech has been extended to Nazis, but that it is becoming limited to them. [...] One may not offend the sensibilities of the anti-Semitic party or motorcycle club, [...] but right-wing extremists calling for the liquidation of Roma citizens is acceptable.
>
> (Szigeti, 2013)

> Another case that received considerable media attention was one in which Jobbik chairman Gábor Vona filed a lawsuit against the columnist György Balavány, because the latter had accused Jobbik's leader of sympathizing with the Názis and the Hungarian fascist Arrow Cross movement.
>
> (Bánlaki D., 2013)

18 Judgment No. 2.Pf.20.695/2013/7.

19 Decision No. 799/2013. (V.8.) by the National Media and Infocommunications Authority's Media Council, http://mediatanacs.hu/dokumentum/158523/m079920130508.pdf.

20 No. Kfv.III.37.033/2014/3. Also see for example: Index.hu (2014c).

2.3. *The media*

Media responsibility needs to be mentioned. Media reporting follows the state authorities' approach and fails to choose an alternative. The media does not choose to risk penalties that may result from civil disobedience and does not take up strategic litigation. Thus, the media would report in leading daily newspapers or news portals that officials found illegal, toxin-laced meat products in a supermarket chain, but would not disclose the name of the company. News reports, televised or printed, habitually refrain from publishing the full names of people featured in reports and use initials or first names at best – even if those mentioned are politicians or other public figures. For example, following the official press release of the police and MTI, the official Hungarian News Agency, media organs used the label 'György H.' to refer to György Hunvald, the mayor of District 7 of Budapest, who was arrested for charges of corruption – despite that fact that the identity of the mayor is known to almost everybody in the country. Similarly, for the corruption cases concerning General O. of the Ministry of Defense (Index.hu, 2011b), even if a simple Google search would show the involved public officials' names.

Though there were several news items on news portals and in press outlets concerning the revocation of the immunity of a judge (who, incidentally, was the judge in charge of hearing the Roma murders, which was one of the most extensively covered court cases) who had been caught shoplifting toothbrushes, perfumes, and nail polish (Hvg.hu, 2014b), it did not occur to any of the countless journalists and reporters covering the issue that the name of the judge may be of relevance to the public. Just as no journalist thought that he/she should be able to or should write down the full name of Pál Sipos, but only refer to him as 'Pál. S.' A nationally known recipient of several professional awards with a long career as a teacher and television editor had become the subject of a serious public debate and official investigation in 2014 due to charges of pedophilia. S.'s name was kept confidential even though the press had presumably uncovered the case precisely with the intention of bringing the affair, which had been hushed over repeatedly, out in the open (Magyari, 2014). Likewise, even self-proclaimed progressive news portals and print dailies initialized the name of the director-general of a major Budapest public hospital who severely battered and sprayed women with acid (Népszava, 2013b) or police officers that brutalized citizens (Hvg.hu,2014c).

The media uncritically accepts that police officers' faces need to be obscured (on occasion replaced by funny cartoon characters as an ironic protest move, Index.hu, 2014d), even though they happily pose on the police.hu, the force's news portal after a successful investigation. This is despite the fact that the Forum of Editors-in-Chief, which comprises the leaders of the major Hungarian media outlets, drew up a list of norms entitled Self-Regulation Ethics Guidelines, which advises against this practice (Editor-in-Chiefs' Forum Hungary, 2012).

This chapter has shown that in the SNC, the protection of dignity by the state is a concept that does not primarily come up in the context of the individual, but rather constitutionally recognized communities, most of all the ethnic (ethno-cultural) majority, and state agencies and government offices (and their representatives). These agents are also given privacy protections (extended to even extremist political organizations), and in general, privacy has been used as a tool to obstruct transparency and accountability of public officials. Here, the initially individual-focused liberal instrument serves an illiberal goal limiting public oversight of public power. The only exception from privacy concerns former communists. The previous chapter illustrated how the conceptual and codified inconsistencies of approaching multiculturalism sanctioned the nation's only ethnic minority, the Roma. In part, this was instituted through a legal framework that allowed for a widespread practice of ethno-corruption explained and excused by privacy considerations. The final part of this chapter will provide a case study of how the abuse of privacy can be used as a tool for ethnic discrimination and the further marginalization of the Roma. The previous chapter has shown how the failure to properly define the beneficiaries of the affirmative action and collective rights framework of the minority rights law can allow non-Roma to make use of the preferential treatment that was supposed to benefit (only) the given group; this last subchapter will show how the failure to recognize and register ethnicity (or race) by authorities leads to both under- and over-policing, a reduction in prosecutions of racially motivated hate crimes and inadequate monitoring of ethnic profiling.

3. Privacy as a tool for ethnic discrimination and marginalization

Few arguments and examples in this subchapter will contain post-2010 developments, and even those are not on as grand a scale as the ramifications of a new Criminal or Civil Code, nor are these phenomena directly related to the illiberal U-turn. Their discussion is nevertheless relevant, both for showing a complex picture of the illiberal use of privacy and to demonstrate that even privacy will intersect in a consistent and persistent pattern with majority-minority dynamics, where, given the specificities of the Hungarian case, there is only one (notable) minority, the Roma, who will be systematically disadvantaged.

In Hungary, as in many places across Europe, there are tragic, historical precedents when censuses and other administrative lists have been used to identify people as enemies of the state and to discriminate against them. There is, therefore, an understandable shyness towards practices that include collecting ethnic data without explicit permission from the concerned persons or policies that would curtail the free choice of (ethnic) identity. However, such a restrictive approach to ethno-national data classification causes severe constitutional problems.

In line with European legislation,[21] Hungarian law allows for the handling of data on racial and ethnic origin only with the consent of the person concerned.[22]

21 See Article 8 of the Directive 95/46/EC of The European Parliament and of the Council (1995).

22 The law, of course, does not prohibit the anonymous collection of census data and law can, in principle, prescribe other circumstances when ethnic data can be collected.

According to the Hungarian Privacy Act (Act CXII of 2011, Article 5, (2)), such data are "special" (or "especially sensitive"). Under the Act, special data may be processed under the following circumstances: (a) when the data subject has given his consent in writing; or (b) when processing is necessary for the implementation of an international agreement promulgated by an act concerning the data, if prescribed by law in connection with the enforcement of fundamental rights afforded by the Fundamental Law, for reasons of national security or national defense, or law enforcement purposes for the prevention or prosecution of criminal activities; or (c) when processing is necessary for the performance of a task carried out in the public interest. In the approach widely accepted in Hungarian professional literature, the term "data" must be interpreted extensively to mean any fact, information or knowledge that can be linked to a person.

According to a comprehensive and influential analysis, co-authored by László Majtényi, the most authoritative privacy expert and former Hungarian Data Protection Commissioner:

> Hungary's information rights regulations do not distinguish between data and information; legal professionals use the two terms interchangeably. Beyond data identifying natural persons, personal data includes everything that can be correlated with a specific person with the help of the identifying data. The information does not necessarily have to be factually true. [...] In this way, data implying Roma origin is regarded as personal data even if the subject in question does not happen to be Roma as well as in cases where he does declare himself to be Roma. Finally, the notion of 'data' also comprises inferences drawn from one or[...] several pieces of information. For instance, information must be considered personal (even sensitive) data if it is an inference, whether well-founded or unjustified, from other data (such as a surname more often borne by Roma individuals than by others) that does not in itself necessarily imply minority status.[23]
>
> (Majtényi, Székely and Szabó, 2006, p. 10)

Under this approach, even the following statements may constitute a violation of data protection laws: "Nelson Mandela was a black human rights activist," or "Benjamin Netanjahu is Jewish" (Majtényi and Pap, 2009). Furthermore, not only inferred data (on which journalism is built), but also false data – for example the statement that "Barack Obama is white" – would be illegal under data protection laws.

This subchapter will show how privacy arguments are used as obstacles to monitor and combat ethnic profiling by the police and as potential reasons against prosecuting racially motivated hate crimes. I will argue that in this legal and socio-political climate, institutional discrimination takes a special form

23 Although the analysis refers to the 1992 law, which was replaced in 2011, but it remained intact in all parts relevant for our discussion.

where ethno-politics are trapped by populist rhetoric and the Murphy law of ethnic data collection (Pap, 2008). By this I refer to the phenomenon that when it comes to discrimination or hate crimes, perpetrators will never have difficulties identifying their victims, yet when it concerns legal remedies, ill-interpreted legal provisions (some formally adopted on behalf of the minorities) or obstructing practices, mostly centered around privacy (data protection) provisions prohibiting ethno-racial classifications (the processing of ethno-national data) will prevent action. This institutionalized cynicism has far-reaching consequences. For example, combating ethnic profiling by the police, a thoroughly proven phenomenon (Pap, 2011; Kádár and Pap, 2009) is made difficult by various factors. First, the monitoring of stop and search procedures (desegregated by ethnic data) is deemed contrary to data protection measures. But also, the argument commonly voiced in the Western world – that racial profiling yields a high number of false positive and false negative stops, thus making it an inefficient use of police resources – simply does not work in a society that is deeply prejudiced.

For example, Zsolt Bayer, a prominent far-right commentator and founding member of the governing Fidesz Party and close friend of the prime minister, responded in a column in the daily *Magyar Hírlap* to the stabbing of two Hungarian youths allegedly by Roma perpetrators, saying,

> A significant part of the Roma are unfit for coexistence. They are not fit to live among people. These Roma are animals, and they behave like animals. When they meet with resistance, they commit murder. They are incapable of human communication. Inarticulate sounds pour out of their bestial skulls [...] These animals should not be allowed to exist.
>
> (FRA, 2013, p. 28)

As a report by the EU's Fundamental Rights Agency finds,

> Hungarian practice of attributing news value to ethnicity only in case when the perpetrator is Roma, but not when he or she belongs to some other minority living in Hungary (or to the majority, for that matter), has naturally contributed to the strenuous assumption of a direct connection between Roma identity and criminality. Although [...] criminality is not any higher among Roma than in groups of a similar social standing, these results have not influenced public opinion about Roma.
>
> (FRA, 2013, p. 30)

In Hungary, human rights-centered language is politically unprofitable. In a country where the concept of "Roma criminality" (the essentialist view that criminal behaviour is connected to ethnicity) is the mantra of not only the extreme right but also part of the mainstream political discourse and media representations, taxpayers will actually perceive discriminatory police actions as effective and efficient, since in the securitized and prejudiced discourse, Roma are perceived as posing a real risk of criminality.

Consider these pre-2010 incidents: In February 2009, Orbán himself spoke about a dramatic increase in severe criminal offences committed by Roma people, while statistical evidence reveals that the number of severe violent criminal offences was decreasing in the past years, and the ethnic affiliation of perpetrators is not recorded in any statistics. On April 2009, Máté Szabó, Parliamentary Commissioner (Ombudsman) for Civil Rights (!) stated in an interview with an online news portal, amongst other things, that criminality categorized on an ethnic basis – "Gypsy crime" – does exist, identifying it as a type of crime performed to earn a living. He also referred to Roma as being "a collectivist, almost tribal level social group," comparing them to the individualist Hungarian society. On 30 January 2009, head of the Miskolc Police Headquarters Albert Pásztor held a press conference concerning robberies committed in the city of Miskolc (the third biggest city of Hungary, with approximately 190,000 inhabitants), where he mentioned that all the robberies in the preceding two months had been committed by Roma perpetrators. He said, "We can conclude that the robberies perpetrated in public premises are committed by Gypsy persons. Hungarians seem to rob banks or patrol stations, but all the other robberies are committed by Gypsies," and that it is the duty of the police to raise the awareness of the inhabitants concerning the Roma issue, and the ethnic confrontation may not be solved by remaining silent about the problem. He also stated that Hungarians shall refrain from attending bars in certain parts of the city, since they may become victims of Roma perpetrators. He said, "cute Gypsy children often become rude and cruel perpetrators" and that the ethnic affiliation of the defendants may be taken into consideration in the course of criminal proceedings. Upon the instruction of the Minister of Justice and Law Enforcement, the National Police Headquarters initiated an inquiry into the case, and Pásztor was suspended. Following a massive demonstration in his favour, Pásztor was reinstated as police chief (HHC, 2011).

3.1. Data protection as a tool for over-policing by obstructing the monitoring and combating of police ethnic profiling

There are long-standing allegations of police harassment of Roma and other visible minorities in Europe in the course of crime prevention. Profiling by law enforcement agencies has become one of the most widely researched and debated questions in legal discussions relating to ethnic and racial discrimination in the criminal justice system. Data on its presence and effects on the Roma is scarce in Central-Eastern Europe, most of all due to the lack of statistics that would include the ethnicity of the people stopped – again, due to privacy considerations.

As argued above, in Hungary anti-Romany prejudices are particularly strong. According to a survey in 2006, almost two-thirds (62 percent) of the Hungarian adult population agreed fully or to some degree with the claim that "the tendency to commit crime is in the nature of the Roma" (TÁRKI, 2006). A 2011 survey of attitudes towards Roma in Hungary found that 60 percent of a representative general population sample shared the view that "the inclination to criminality is in the blood of Gypsies" (FRA, 2013, p. 29). Another 42 percent agreed that "it is only right that there are still pubs, clubs and discos where Gypsies are not let in" (FRA, 2013, p. 28).

In the light of empirical sociological research,[24] police officers are highly biased against the Roma, which may seriously influence the way they treat victims of Roma origin and conduct investigations in racially motivated crimes. A qualitative research study in 2005 showed that there is an assumption among police officers that correlation between ethnic identity and potential criminal behaviour exists. It is also worth mentioning that in May 2009 one of the police trade unions (Tettrekész Magyar Rendőrség Szakszervezet, "Action-ready Hungarian Police Union") – having around 5000 members in a police force of 45,000 – signed an agreement of cooperation with the racist radical right-wing party "Jobbik" (Jobbik Magyarországért Mozgalom Párt – Movement for a Better Hungary Party), which put "Gypsy criminality" in the focus of its campaigns (HHC, 2011).

These attitudes are persistent. A 1997 survey by the Ministry of Interior showed that 54 percent of police perceived criminality as a central element of Roma identity (Csepeli, Örkény and Székelyi, 1997), and in 2002–2003, the Hungarian Helsinki Committee carried out a research on discrimination against Roma in the criminal justice system, finding deep-running traces of racial profiling by the police within Roma communities. By scrutinizing court files, the research focused on how perpetrators were initially detected by the authorities.

The findings of the survey appeared to be fully in line with similar Anglo-American studies that analyze discrimination in the criminal justice procedure against visible minorities. The researchers found that Roma offenders and suspects were significantly more likely to have been identified via police stops and searches, whereas in the case of non-minority suspects, other investigatory methods – particularly being caught in the act – were the dominant causes that lead to the suspects' capture (Farkas et al., 2004).

Since the mid-1990s, ill treatment of Roma in Hungary has been widely documented by human rights NGOs such as the Legal Defense Bureau for National and Ethnic Minorities (NEKI), the Hungarian Helsinki Committee (HHC), the Romani Civil Rights Foundation (RPA) and the Parliamentary Commissioner for National and Ethnic Minorities. Even the European Commission against Racism and Intolerance (ECRI) expressed concern that "at evidence that severe problems in the administration of justice exist as regards discrimination against members of the Roma/Gypsy community [...]" (ECRI, 2000, p. 7, para. 14).

Circumstantial evidence from other stages of the criminal procedure also indicates the likeliness of racial profiling. According to the 2001 EUMAP report (EUMAP, 2002, p. 241.) "research indicates that Roma are more likely than non-Roma to be remanded in pre-trial detention or ill-treated by the police, and tend not to have legal representation during investigation." ECRI has expressed

24 See for example Balogi et al. (2008); Pap (2007, 2011).

concern "at evidence that severe problems in the administration of justice exist as regards discrimination against members of the Roma/Gypsy community [...]. There are authoritative reports that Roma/Gypsies are kept in pre-trial detention for longer periods and more frequently than non-Roma, although the prohibition of the recording of the ethnic origin of suspects makes it difficult to evaluate the extent of such discrimination" (ECRI, 2000, p. 7, para. 14). According to the 2001 EUMAP report (EUMAP, 2002, p. 245), "NGOs estimate that only five percent of Roma complaints of police abuse lead to convictions" (NEKI, 1999). The conclusion that a disproportionate number of cases brought by Roma are either "terminated" after investigation or do not lead to convictions is supported in data from the town of Hajdúhadház, where 15 cases brought by Roma against police officers in recent years remain either unresolved or ended in acquittal.[25]

The high proportion of Roma in prisons can also be seen to indicate racial profiling, even though it obviously cannot explain it alone.[26] Research was published in the mid '90s revealing estimates on the ratio of Roma inmates (Huszár, 1997). This showed that based on self-definition of inmates, about 40 percent of the prison population is Roma, with prison directors giving much higher estimates, on average 60 percent (Póczik, 1997). The presence of ethnic profiling of Roma in Hungary has also been confirmed by a comparative study conducted under the sponsorship of the Open Society Justice Initiative as part of a comparative research program exploring ethnic differences in experiences of police stops and ID checks in Bulgaria, Hungary and Spain (Pap, 2007).

In 2008, the Helsinki Committee (HHC) (Kádár et al., 2008) carried out a pilot research project, which, upon the approval of the data protection and the minority rights ombudsmen, alongside the participation of Roma observers, included the registration of the presumed ethnicity of the people stopped. The research showed that only 1 percent of ID checks led to an arrest, 2 percent led to a short-term arrest and 18 percent to petty offense procedures. If ID checks related to traffic offenses are removed, the remaining checks resulted in 2 percent arrest, 3 percent short-term arrest, 19 percent petty offense procedure and 76 percent no further action taken. For comparison, in the UK nationally 10–13 percent of stop and searches lead to arrest (Jones and Singer, 2008).

The data also showed that Roma were disproportionately targeted for ID checks. Within the framework of the project, 22 percent of all persons checked by the police were of Roma origin (according to the assessment of the officer performing the check), as opposed to 75 percent being identified as "white." The remaining 3 percent were identified as "black," "Asian," "Arab" or other. According to reliable sociological research, the estimated proportion of Roma people within the total Hungarian population (of 10,045,000) was approximately 6.2 percent (i.e., their actual number is around 620,000) (Hablicsek, 2007, p. 63).

25 Half of the town's police force was under investigation for abusive conduct at the time (HRW, 2000, p. 272).

26 Along with other determinants such as precarious social status or inadequate legal defense (Huszár, 1999).

Thus, Roma were more than three times more likely to be stopped than their percentage of the general population would indicate. The proportion of Roma youth between age 14 and 16 who were stopped and checked during the project period was significantly higher than the already high general representation of Roma within the sample (32 percent as opposed to 22 percent). The data in the research also showed that ID checks of Roma were no more likely to yield results than measures enforced in relation to non-Roma. It is often argued that a disproportionate targeting of ethnic minority groups is justified by differential rates of criminal involvement. The hit rate of police checks, however, showed no significant differences by ethnic group. On a national level, 78 percent of ID checks involving Roma were "unsuccessful" in the sense that no further measure was required after the check. For non-Roma this ratio was 79 percent. The percentage of checks followed by a petty offense proceeding for Roma and non-Roma was 19 percent and 18 percent, respectively. Rates of arrests and short-term arrests were practically the same within the Roma and the non-Roma sample. In the country's capital of Budapest, 80 percent of the checks of Roma did not require any further police action, whereas the same proportion for non-Roma was 59 percent. If we compare this with the fact that 33 percent of all the persons checked are of Roma origin, it becomes evident that there is a serious over-representation relative to their proportion of 5–10 percent in Budapest (Kádár, Pap and Tóth, 2009).

Monitoring stop and search practices, including the registration of the ethnicity of the people stopped, is the only way to combat this phenomenon. However, due to data protection constraints, despite a singular event in which both the data protection and the minority rights ombudsman endorsed a pilot project,[27] this is something Hungarian authorities would firmly reject.

In a 2011 case launched before Hungary's equality body (Egyenlő Bánásmód Hatóság, Equal Treatment Authority), the Hungarian Helsinki Committee (HHC, 2012; Iván and Pap, 2012) successfully argued that in the village of Rimóc (in Northern Hungary), 97 percent of the bikers stopped and penalized for the lack of bicycle accessories were Roma. The case ended in a settlement between the Nógrád County Police Headquarters and the HHC. The police acknowledged that the cumulative effect of the lawful police measures might have led to ethnic disproportionality but argued that it could not have been substantiated or recognized by the police for the lack of data on the offenders' ethnic affiliation – a trait that in the majority of cases, as the Open Society points out, is highly visible (Bobis, 2012).

3.2. Data protection as a potential reason for not prosecuting hate crimes

Although the causal relationship is difficult to establish since there is no data or research on how police officers and prosecutors decide on classifying and

27 See the above mentioned 2008 Hungarian Helsinki Committee project.

qualifying incidents, arguably, the above described "culture of reluctance to recognize ethnicity" may be a contributing factor to the number of prosecuted hate crimes being strikingly low in Hungary, especially when Roma or other minorities are the victims. According to the available official data,[28] the number of prosecuted "violence against member of a community" offences and the number of final court decisions establishing that a hate crime was committed, which was the following in the last years in Hungary:[29] According to a research by criminal lawyer Henriett Dinók (2013, 2014, 2015), the number of sentences delivered for "violence against member of a community" by courts in 2010 include 5 cases and 11 convictions; in 2011, 8 cases and 15 convictions; and in 2012, 12 cases and 23 convictions. In 2013, there were 14 cases and 34 convictions. According to the Internal Ministry, in 2014 there were 31 and in 2015 16 indictments. The cynicism of the Hungarian legal practice can be observed in full bloom by the phenomena where authorities are very much able to identify members of minority communities, as perpetrators of hate crimes committed against members of the majority, even against hate groups, and of course, in the "traditional" form of over-policing minorities, in police stop and search practices, where their higher criminality is a widely held belief.

As pointed out by Hungarian human rights NGOs, one of the reasons for the low number of criminal offences officially qualifying as hate crimes is that authorities fail to take into consideration the bias motivation of crimes in the course of criminal proceedings, which results in qualifying the given crime as a less serious criminal offence than a hate crime. This may happen intentionally, when police officers or prosecutors decide to avoid collecting evidence for the perpetrators' bias motivation and opt instead for the simple and safe qualification and classification of "bodily harm" instead of "violence against a member of a community." As noted by the EUMC over a decade ago, and its relevance and accuracy has not faded,

> [i]n Hungary, the low levels of registration under the various specific racially motivated crimes were attributed to law enforcement agents, as well as prosecutors and courts, being very reluctant to recognize racial motivation in violent and non-violent crimes committed against Roma.
>
> (Oakley, 2005, p. 17)

28 Source of data: website of the Prosecution Service (www.mklu.hu) and data requests from the Prosecution Service.

29 Criminal data – including data on crimes motivated by hatred or prejudice – is available via two databases, both maintained by the General Prosecutor's Office (*Legfőbb Ügyészség*): Unified Criminal Statistics of the Investigation Authorities and the Public Prosecution *(Egységes Nyomozóhatósági és Ügyészségi Bűnügyi Statisztika – ENYÜBS)* on cases registered by the police and prosecution, and Prosecution Information System *(Vádképviseleti Informatikai Rendszer – VIR)* on criminal court cases. The data in both databases refer to the articles of the 1978 Criminal Code (Act IV of 1978), or from July 2013, to the articles of the 2012 Criminal Code (Act C of 2012). However, there is no comprehensive mechanism for monitoring and data collection on hate crimes and racial/ethnic incidents in Hungary.

The phenomenon may also be explained by the lack of necessary professional knowledge, as well as the lack of relevant instructions and guidelines. Hungary is, thus, one of the (many) countries where legal restrictions on the collection of non-anonymous data concerning ethnic, national or religious identity are interpreted by the police and prosecutors in a way that often leads to the refusal to acknowledge that ethnicity is of significance in criminal activity. As mentioned above, the data protection law prohibits the handling of sensitive data, such as ethnic origin, without the concerned person's explicit permission. Unable or unwilling to distinguish between perceived ethnicity and the expressions of personal declarations regarding ethno-national affiliation, officials habitually claim that the recording of racial violence victims would run against statutory provisions, even though the Criminal Code acknowledges certain racially motivated crimes (Balogh, 2011), such as "violence against members of a community" (formerly national, ethnic or racial minorities and religious groups) or "incitement against a community," all of which presuppose membership in the given (e.g., racially or ethno-nationally defined) community.[30] The determination of the nature of the crime upon which the indictment will be brought to court is in the sole competence of the prosecutor, who will, *inter alia* referring to data protection constraints, hardly ever acknowledge the quintessential ethnic component (the racial motivation) of a hate crime.

In Hungary, in line with the legally articulated declaration to refrain from any kind of involuntary official classification of ethnicity, no specific legally binding instructions exist for the determination of racially motivated criminal activity. Law enforcement officers, who are the primary decision-makers of the legal classification of a given offense, become very reluctant to classify incidents and conflicts as racially motivated.

Although it will always be the law-school-graduate prosecutor who will decide on what grounds to indict the defendant, she will usually follow the police's determination of the nature of the criminal offense in question. As for the police, in order to avoid making an uncomfortable and (given the widespread anti-Roma or xenophobic sentiments in Hungarian society) unpopular decision, and lacking

30 The current Criminal Code (Act C of 2012) which entered into force on July 1, 2013, contains the following provisions: (i) '*Violence against a member of a community*' (Article 216); the protected grounds are membership (or perceived membership) in a national, ethnic or racial group, or in "other social groups", particularly based on disability, gender identity or sexual orientation; the available sanction ranges from 2 up to 8 years imprisonment, preparation for the crime: up to 2 years imprisonment; (ii) '*Incitement against a community*' (Article 332); the protected communities are: the Hungarian nation, national, ethnic or racial groups, or in "other social groups", particularly based on disability, gender identity or sexual orientation; the available sanction is up to 3 years imprisonment; (iii) '*Public denial of the crimes committed by the Nazi or Communist regimes*' (Article 333); the provision covers the questioning, minimalisation and the legitimisation of the crimes of the above mentioned totalitarian regimes, including the Holocaust, the available sanction is imprisonment up to 3 years, (iv) '*Using a totalitarian symbol*' (Article 335); the provision list the following symbols: swastika, SS-badge, arrow-cross, hammer-and-sickle, red star –, the offence is considered to be a delinquency.

any legally binding guidance, we see a very strong reluctance to recognize racial motivation in violent criminal behaviour.

Also, there is no governmental strategy or policy framework in place on countering racism, xenophobia and related intolerance. On 18 September 2013, the government adopted the new National Crime Prevention Strategy for the next 10 years, as well as an Action Plan for 2013–2015, but the document does not include any specific measure aimed at combating crimes motivated by bias or hatred. Furthermore, no protocols for dealing with hate crimes are established for the police or the prosecution in terms of investigation or indictment. Not much has changed since 2005, when the European Monitoring Centre on Racism and Xenophobia (Oakley, 2005) pointed out that in Hungary there are no instructions on how to determine whether a crime is racially motivated; specialist training programs on dealing with racist crime and violence are not provided; and no measures to publicize police initiatives and guidelines for working with victims of racist crime and violence exist.[31] In 2008, in its fourth periodic report on the country, the European Commission Against Racism and Intolerance (ECRI, 2009) voiced criticism about the implementation of existing provisions of criminal law on racially motivated criminal offenses, including not only the lack of sufficiently vigorous implementation of the existing laws, but also the lack of reliable statistics in this field. It recommended for Hungary to introduce a systematic and comprehensive monitoring of all incidents that may constitute racist offences, covering all stages of proceedings. In its report "Field Assessment of Violent Incidents against Roma in Hungary: Key Developments, Findings and Recommendations," OSCE ODIHR (2010) pointed out that

> current interpretations of Hungarian law render the collection of [relevant] data, or even the identification of ethnic bias as a motivation for a crime, extremely difficult. [...] Only the citizenship, gender and the age of victims are recorded on the statistical sheet [...], and there are no data on their ethnicity. As a result, there is no statistical information on crimes committed against Roma. Recorded cases of hate crimes are also not disaggregated further by bias motivation, so there are no available data of how many of the cases were based on bias against Roma. There are no records kept on cases where the hate motivation was considered as a base motivation and evaluated as an aggravating circumstance. As such, there is no statistical information on the extent and pattern of hate crimes.

31 "A number of possible explanations were advanced [...] as to why bias motivations are often overlooked by the police. Among these, the latent climate of intolerance and prejudice that also exists within the police force was mentioned. [...]Another contributing factor could be that proving hate crime is more complex, resource intensive and time consuming than proving other types of crime. Police officers are often focused on closing cases quickly rather than on investing considerable resources in identifying bias motivations" (FRA, 2013, p. 39).

In this context, ODIHR recommended *inter alia* that the Hungarian authorities should reconcile the aim of effectively investigating crimes with a possible hate motivation and the Hungarian regulations on ethnic data collection and processing. Although the incident and report predate the SNC, the diagnosis is still valid.[32]

Another issue needs to be mentioned, where under-policing curiously intersects with over-policing. Having shown the fallacy of Hungarian authorities to properly respond to hate crimes, when the victims are Roma and other minorities, it is particularly striking to see that in more and more cases involving violence between members of the majority, often members of racist hate groups and members of the Roma community, Roma are charged with racially motivated hate crimes (HHC, 2011).

3.2.1. Under-policing intersecting with over-policing: Protecting racist hate groups from the minority

As already touched upon in this chapter, there is a peculiar case where the question of protecting the majority needs to be revisited: in cases of violence between members of racist hate groups and members of the Roma community, often Roma are charged with racially motivated hate crimes.

Let us take a look at some of the most highly publicized incidents. A case that came to judgment recently happened in Miskolc, a city with a high Roma population. In March 2009, to set the scene, a series of targeted murders against Roma was ongoing, an incident in Tatárszentgyörgy had recently resulted in the death of two Roma, and members of the extreme right-wing paramilitary group the Hungarian Guard – an association later dissolved by the Supreme Court for carrying out racist activities – were marching around in different Hungarian villages. Text messages circulated among the members of the Roma community in Miskolc, alleging that skinheads were planning to attack the local Roma. At around 1 a.m. two unfamiliar cars drove around the homes of the Roma several times. At some point, a car was attacked by 25 to 40 Roma who assumed that the people in the cars were skinheads or members of the Hungarian Guard. The perpetrators had no firearms and they used wooden sticks and stones. The damage caused to the car was 104,000 HUF (approx. 350 EUR). Eleven perpetrators

32 In November 2011, the Government adopted the National Social Inclusion Strategy (aka the Roma Inclusion Strategy, Ministry of Public Administration and Justice, State Secretariat for Social Inclusion (2011)). As a reaction, a group of Roma and pro-Roma NGO's submitted a joint statement on the document, pointing out – among others – that there are "no concrete anti-prejudice or anti-discrimination measures or tools" identified in the Strategy, and "there are is concrete action, measure, tool, accountable person/body in charge, or dedicated funding to enforce the fight against racially or ethnically motivated crimes" (Amnesty International Hungary et al., 2012). In September, 2012, the participating NGOs of the Hate Crime Working Group expressed concerns over the structural rearrangement of the National Police, resulting in an unclear situation regarding the units responsible for the investigation of hate crimes (e.g., the investigation of some crimes fall within regional level – county the capital city–law enforcement authorities while others do not) (Hate Crime Working Group, 2013).

were identified by the police (the others fled and were never identified) and taken into pre-trial detention by the court. One piece of evidences against the Roma defendants included a wooden stick found in the crime scene with the sentence "Death to the Hungarians" written on it, however, it has not been clarified by whom the stick was prepared or used. It was proven that one of the victims had right-wing ties, and the passengers carried several litres of gasoline with them. Furthermore, the only witness (a defendant himself), initially stating that he heard that others made "anti-Hungarian" statements during the attack, claims that he was subject to forced interrogation by the police and made a false statement under duress, in the absence of a lawyer, and that the other defendants made no "anti-Hungarian" statements (Index.hu, 2013a).

In the case, which Petra Bárd (2014, p. 36) calls "fear crime" as opposed to a hate crime, in October 2010 in the first instance decision the court found that all the perpetrators were guilty in violence against member of a community, committed in a group and armed. The highest sentence imposed was 6 years imprisonment (Magyarnarancs.hu, 2010). On October 8, 2013, the appellate court (3.Bf.2023/2012/51) changed the legal qualification of the case and convicted the men for antisocial behaviour with a significantly lower penalty. The court noted that the indictment and the first instance decision referred to members of the Hungarian Guard, skinheads and Hungarians as the protected group interchangeably. The court found that members of the Hungarian Guard and skinheads are not protected by the provision on violence against a member of a community. Hungarians as a group are protected, but there was not enough evidence to prove the motivation, as there was no evidence that the stick was used in the attack – its engraving was known by the attackers, and the witness testimony is questionable.

Another similar case (which was closed only recently) happened in Sajóbábony, a small town close to Miskolc. On 14 November 2009, the extreme right-wing Jobbik party organized a public forum. Roma were not allowed to enter, and after the forum some were threatened. The next evening, three out of the approximately 100 members of the New Hungarian Guard (the "successor" of the dissolved Hungarian Guard) were attacked by Roma locals, one of their cars was seriously damaged by wooden sticks and axes, and passengers suffered light injuries. The victims claimed that their Hungarian ethnicity was the cause of the attack, while defendants argued that they wanted to protect their families from the neo-Nazi (New) Hungarian Guard. Nine Roma suspects were placed in pre-trial detention and were accused of violence against member of a community. In May 2013, the first instance court ruled that they indeed committed a hate crime "against members of the Hungarian nation," and the perpetrators were sentenced to imprisonments between 2.5 and 4 years. The decision was appealed, and the second instance court decided to raise the sentences imposed on all defendants in its decision issued on 30 September 2013 (Index.hu, 2013b).

The decisions came under severe criticism from human rights NGOs (HHC, 2011; Hate Crime Working Group, n.d). According to the Hungarian Civil Liberties Union, the perpetrators were clearly not motivated by prejudice but by a fear of racism and were driven to chase the extremists away, and this is not hate crime. The court also erred in holding that the acts were aimed "against members of the Hungarian nation," as the defendants attacked the car of people they believed to be members of the Guard, which cannot be identified as the Hungarian nation even if the perpetrators used the term "Hungarian" (habitually used by Roma to refer to non-Roma).

> The judgment […] fuels our worries about the increase in the number of cases where Roma are accused of racism whereas Roma are the main target of racist violence in Hungary. However, hate crimes against Roma are systematically under-classified if procedures are at all started, and very often these cases get thrown out during inspection. The decision by the […] Court failed to take into account a long history of exclusion, severe discrimination, and inequality that affects the Roma […] The court applied the hate crime law […] against a population that had been traumatized by a series of murders by racist extremists. HCLU believes that these decisions are examples of wide-spread […] discrimination in the criminal justice system.
>
> (HCLU, 2012b, 2013)

Judicial practice is uneven. In a 2011 case involving a physical assault against persons who belonged to the far-right paramilitary Hungarian Guard, the Supreme Court took the position that

> criminal law can logically not extend special protections to persons who are members of an organization that was established against certain national, ethnic, racial, religious or other social groups, obviously in violation of the law – especially if this group has already been dissolved by a legally binding court decision. […] Members of an organized group based on joint ideology (which might be an association, a movement, etc.) only enjoy special criminal law protections if the organization respects the principles laid down in the constitution and carries out its activities in compliance with the law. Members of groups established in opposition to national, ethnic, racial, religious or other social groups, and in obvious conflict with legal provisions, clearly cannot enjoy special criminal law protections, since in that case the principle of the unity of the legal order would be seriously impaired.[33]

Overall, in its recent decisions, the high court seems to be committed to the position that hate crime provisions cannot be applied to members of hate groups as victims.[34]

How can we sum up the above-demonstrated fallacies of the continuous practice that predates the SNC? It is a unique, special form of institutional

33 Bfv.III.87/2011/5.

34 Bfv. II. 590/2012/18., Bfv.III.87/2011/5, also see LB-H-BJ-2011–106.

malfunctioning of legal regimes triggered by the socio-legal specificities of the region. It is no less than institutional discrimination taken to the next level. It is the distinguishing feature of institutional discrimination that individually more or less legal and justified decisions (for example stopping and frisking pedestrians or drivers, for which officers have a broad margin of discretion) add up to an institutionalized practice that will disproportionately affect (harass and torment) certain groups. What we have seen here is that the somewhat inconsistent approach of international organizations and the intrinsically ambiguous legal nature for conceptualizing identity, sensitive data collection and ethnic bias is systematically interpreted in a way that will be unfavourable for members of the minority. This practice fits neatly into the corporate culture of police officers, prosecutors and judges (and as we have seen, journalists as well), who are either endorsing or at least have no inclination to go against the widespread and politically and culturally substantially unchallenged anti-Roma and anti-democratic public sentiments. One of the puzzle pieces in this picture is what Lynne Haney calls penal nationalism (Haney, 2011), a special form of penal populism, where the social construction of Roma criminality evolves and gains power from its mythical nature, stemming partly form restrictions on collecting empirical data on the race/ethnicity of criminal defendants and offenders.

4. Concluding thoughts

This chapter has shown that in the National System of Cooperation, individual dignity (or at least its recognition) is conditional on belonging to a community (foremost one of those explicitly preferred by the constitution). The dignity of communities – including the ethnic majority community – is protected (in ways unknown in liberal democracies) based on civil and criminal law alike, even against various minorities (ethnic, ideological or lifestyle minorities). In the chapter devoted to the effectuation of a personal liberty, namely, the protection of personal data, I argued that a special feature of the SNC is that, in a divergence from the otherwise pronounced collectivist commitment in the Fundamental Law, this right often enjoys greater protection than community objectives. Yet the liberal construct serves an illiberal goal: limiting the possibility of monitoring public power. Privacy could emerge as an impediment to public debate and to the transparency of public affairs. Based on the Civil Code, which, after decades of preparation, was adopted to reflect the SNC's own image, public figures and those exercising public power are insulated not only against criticism, but from publicity in general (to an unprecedented degree in a liberal democracy). One of the characteristic features of the SNC is also that public institutions and intolerant and radical political parties that engage in the politics of exclusion are also entitled to personal rights protections based on the concept of dignity. The media, the independence of which is not curtailed in this regard, also fails to provide a democratic counterbalance in these cases. By all this, as in other areas, the country's only ethnic minority, the Roma, will end up in further marginalization and discrimination.

Bibliography

444.hu (2014). Orbán Gáspár levelet írt a *444-nek*: Ne közöljenek velem foglalkozó cikket. *444.hu* [online] Available at: http://444.hu/2014/07/15/orban-gaspar-levelet-irt-a-444-nek-ne-kozoljenek-velem-foglalkozo-cikket/ [Accessed 31 Dec. 2016].

444.hu (2016). Benyújtották a törvényt, aminek nyomán soha többet semmi sem fog kiderülni. *444.hu* [online] Available at: http://444.hu/2016/02/10/benyujtottak-a-torvenyt-aminek-nyoman-soha-tobbet-semmi-sem-fog-kiderulni [Accessed 31 Dec. 2016].

Act IV of 1978 on Crimincal Code.

Act V of 2013 on the Civil Code.

Act LXIII of 1992 on the Protection of Personal Data and the Disclosure of Information.

Act C of 2012 on the Criminal Law.

Act CXII of 2011 on the Right of Informational Self-Determination and on Freedom of Information.

Amnesty International Hungary et al. (2012). Recommendations to the Hungarian national social inclusion strategy. Prepared by a group of Hungarian non-governmental organizations. [online] Available at: http://www.habitat.hu/files/CivilekRomaStrat_angol_vegleges_marc6.pdf [Accessed 31 Dec. 2016].

Balogi, A. et al. (2008). Racism and police stops – Adapting US and British debates to continental Europe. *European Journal of Criminology*, 5(2), pp. 161–191.

Balogh, L. (2011). Racist and related hate crimes in Hungary – recent empirical findings. *Acta Iuridica Hungarica*, 52(4), pp. 296–315.

Bánlaki D. (2013). Mi a közös bennük? *Index.hu*. [online] Available at: http://index.hu/belfold/2013/08/08/kozszereplo_vagyok_mindent_szabad/ [Accessed 31 Dec. 2016].

Bárd, P. (2014). A gyűlölet-bűncselekmények hatékony üldözésének társadalmi feltételrendszere. In: A. Borbíró et al. ed., *A büntető hatalom korlátainak megtartása: A büntetés mint végső eszköz. Tanulmányok Gönczöl Katalin tiszteletére.*, 1st ed. Budapest: ELTE Eötvös Kiadó, pp. 29–40.

Bill T/6218, amending various laws in order to protect public order and the justice system.

Bobis, Z. (2012). Fined for being Roma while cycling. *Opensocietyfoundations.org. [online]* Available at: https://www.opensocietyfoundations.org/voices/fined-being-roma-while-cycling [Accessed 31 Dec. 2016].

Budapest Court of Appeal decision, Case No. 8. Pf.20.008/2013/6.

Constitutional Court Decision 7/2014 (III.7).

Constitutional Court Decision 28/2014 (IX.29).

Constitutional Court Decision 54/2000 (XII.18).

Constitutional Court Decision 96/2008 (VII.3).

Constitutional Court Decision 165/2011 (XII.20).

Council of the European Union (2008).

Csepeli, G., Örkény, A. and Székelyi, M. (1997). Szertelen. In: K. Csányi, ed., *Szöveggyűjtemény a kisebbségi ügyek rendőrségi kezelésének tanulmányozásához*, 1st ed. Budapest: OSI-COLPI, pp. 130–173.

Dinók, H. (2013). A gyűlölet-bűncselekmények, különösen a közösség tagja elleni erőszak kapcsán felmerülő jogalkalmazási nehézségek. *Fundamentum*, 17(4), pp. 93–103.

Dinók, H. (2014). A gyűlölet-bűncselekmények szabályozásának általános kérdései – a kiemelt büntetőjogi figyelem mellett és ellen szóló érvek. *Állam- és Jogtudomány*, 55(4), pp. 26–50.

Dinók, H. (2015). A Gyűlölet-bűncselekmények, különös tekintettel a Büntető törvénykönyv speciális tényállására, a "közösség tagja elleni erőszakra". PhD. Szegedi Tudományegyetem, Állam- és Jogtudományi Kar.

Directive 95/46/EC of The European Parliament and of the Council of 24 October 1995 on the protection of individuals with regard to the processing of personal data and on the free movement of such data (1995). *Official Journal of the European Union*, L281, pp. 31–50.

Dupré, C. (2012). Dignity, democracy, civilisation. *Liverpool Law Review*, 33(3), pp. 263–280.

ECRI (European Commission against Racism and Intolerance) (2000). Second Report on Hungary. CRI (2000)5 [online] Available at: http://hudoc.fcnm.coe.int/XMLEcri/ENGLISH/Cycle_02/02_CbC_eng/02-cbc-hungary-eng.pdf [Accessed 31 Dec. 2016].

ECRI (European Commission against Racism and Intolerance) (2009). Report on Hungary (fourth monitoring cycle), adopted on 20 June 2008, CRI(2009)3 [online] Available at: http://www.coe.int/t/dghl/monitoring/ecri/Country-by-country/Hungary/HUN-CbC-IV-2009–003-ENG.pdf [Accessed 31 Dec. 2016].

Editor-in-Chiefs' Forum Hungary (2012). Self-regulatory ethical guidelines. [online] Available at: https://foszerkesztokforuma.files.wordpress.com/2012/01/english_ethical-guidelines_-final.pdf [Accessed 31 Dec. 2016].

Equal Treatment Authority (2012). Az Egyenlő Bánásmód Hatóság 2012. évi tevékenysége a számok tükrében. [online] Available at: http://www.egyenlobanasmod.hu/app/webroot/files/img/articles/321a316770b8f66c2c5dddaecdd3399b/2012.%20%C3%A9vi%20tev%C3%A9kenys%C3%A9ge%20a%20sz%C3%A1mok%20t%C3%BCkr%C3%A9ben.pdf [Accessed 31 Dec. 2016].

Equal Treatment Authority (2016). Az Egyenlő Bánásmód Hatóság 2015. évi tevékenysége a számok tükrében, [online] Available at: http://www.egyenlobanasmod.hu/article/view/az-egyenl%C5%91-b%C3%A1n%C3%A1sm%C3%B3d-hat%C3%B3s%C3%A1g-2015-%C3%A9vi-tev%C3%A9kenys%C3%A9ge-a-sz%C3%A1mok-t%C3%BCkr%C3%A9ben/mid:7 [Accessed 31 Dec. 2016].

EUMAP (2002) *Monitoring the EU accession process: Minority protection*. Budapest: OSI EU Accession Monitoring Program.

Farkas, L., Kézdi, G., Loss, S. and Zádori, Z. (2004). A rendőrség etnikai profilalkotásának mai gyakorlata (The current police practice of ethnic profiling). *Belügyi Szemle (Interior Affairs Review)*, 52(2–3), pp. 30–50.

FRA (European Union Agency for Fundamental Rights) (2013). *Racism, discrimination, intolerance and extremism: Learning from experiences in Greece and Hungary, thematic situation report*. Luxembourg: Publications Office of the European Union.

Framework Decision on Combating Certain Forms and Expressions of Racism and Xenophobia by Means of Criminal Law. 2008/913/JHA (2008). Official Journal of the European Union, L328, pp. 55–58.

Freedominfo.org (2013). Hungarian NGOs Call FOI Changes as Unconstitutional. [online] Available at: http://www.freedominfo.org/2013/07/hungarian-ngos-call-foi-changes-as-unconstitutional/ [Accessed 31 Dec. 2016].

Hablicsek, L. (2007). Kísérleti számítások a roma lakosság területi jellemzőinek alakulására és 2021-ig történő előrebecslésére. *Demográfia*, 50(1), pp. 7–54.

Haney, L. (2011). The politics of punishment in postsocialist Eastern Europe. Straus Institute Working Paper 06/11. [online] Available at: http://www.law.nyu.edu/sites/default/files/siwp/WP6Haney.pdf [Accessed 31 Dec. 2016].

Harkai, P. (2011). Oi korban élünk, August 11, 2011, http://www.commmunity.eu/2011/08/15/oi-korban-elunk/ [Accessed 31 Dec. 2015].

Hate Crime Working Group (n.d.). Szakmai anyagok. [online] Available at: http://gyuloletellen.hu/node/3 [Accessed 31 Dec. 2016].

Hate Crime Working Group (2013). A Gyűlölet-bűncselekmények Elleni Munkacsoport véleménye a Rendőrség nyomozó hatóságainak hatásköréről és illetékességéről szóló rendelet tervezetéről. [online] Available at: http://gyuloletellen.hu/sites/default/files/hataskorirendelet_2013–06–05.pdf [Accessed 31 Dec. 2016].

HCLU (Hungarian Civil Liberties Union) v. Hungary [2009] 37374/05 (the Second Section of the European Court of Human Rights).

HCLU (Hungarian Civil Liberties Union) (2005) Valaki nem mond igazat, 2005. július 5., http://tasz.hu/informacioszabadsag/valaki-nem-mond-igazat [Accessed 31 Dec. 2016].

HCLU (Hungarian Civil Liberties Union) (2012a). Schmitt Pál kegyelmi határozatai titkosak. [online] Available at: http://tasz.hu/informacioszabadsag/schmitt-pal-kegyelmi-hatarozatai-titkosak [Accessed 31 Dec. 2016].

HCLU (Hungarian Civil Liberties Union) (2012b). Romas sentenced for hate crime against Hungarians. [online] Available at: http://tasz.hu/node/2785 [Accessed 31 Dec. 2016].

HCLU (Hungarian Civil Liberties Union) (2013). Those racist Roma again. [online] Available at: http://tasz.hu/node/3543 [Accessed 31 Dec. 2016].

Hegyi, S. and Simon, É. (2013). Szólásszabadság elleni fegyver lett belőle *Ataszjelenti.blog.hu*. Available at: http://ataszjelenti.blog.hu/2013/02/15/baj_van_az_uj_ptk-val_4_resz_szolasszabadsag_elleni_fegyver_lett_belole [Accessed 31 Dec. 2016].

Holström, L. ed. (2000). Hungary. Third Periodic Report. Conclusions and recommendations issued by the Committee against Torture at its 360th meeting (twenty-first session) held on 19 November 1998. In: *Conclusions and Recommendations of the UN Committee against Torture*, 1st ed. The Hague: Kluwer Law International, pp. 97–99.

HHC (Hungarian Helsinki Committee) (2011). General climate of intolerance in Hungary. [online] Available at: http://helsinki.hu/wp-content/uploads/General_climate_of_intolerance_in_Hungary_20110107.pdf [Accessed 31 Dec. 2016].

HHC (Hungarian Helsinki Committee) (2012). Practice of racial profiling against the Roma community is acknowledged by the police. [online] Available at: http://www.helsinki.hu/en/practice-of-racial-profiling-against-the-roma-community-is-acknowledged-by-the-police/ [Accessed 31 Dec. 2016].

Hidvégi, F. (2013). Habonyodalom. *Ataszjelenti.blog.hu*. Available at: http://ataszjelenti.blog.hu/2013/03/18/habonyodalom [Accessed 31 Dec. 2016].

Hirado.hu (2014). Korózs: Senkiháziaknak nincs helye közöttünk. *Hirado.hu* [online] Available at: http://www.hirado.hu/2014/02/14/korozs-senkihaziaknak-nincs-helye-kozottunk/ [Accessed 31 Dec. 2016].

HRW (Human Rights Watch) (2000). *World Report, 2000*. New York: Human Rights Watch.

Huszár, L. (1997). Romák, börtönök, statisztikák. *Amaro Drom*, 7(8), pp. 9–11.

Huszár, L. (1999). Roma fogvatartottak a büntetés-végrehajtásban. *Belügyi Szemle*, 47(7–8), pp. 124–133.

Hvg.hu, (2011). Nem lát el közfeladatot a Paksi Atomerőmű – a TASZ szerint abszurd az ítélet. *Hvg.hu* [online] Available at: http://hvg.hu/itthon/20110208_paksi_atomeromu [Accessed 31 Dec. 2016].

Hvg.hu, (2013). Közszereplés: elkaptuk Habony Árpádot a parlamentben egy kamerával. *Hvg.hu* [online] Available at: http://hvg.hu/itthon/20130705_Video_Habony_Arpad_kozszereplo [Accessed 31 Dec. 2016].

Hvg.hu (2014a). rendőröknek mától nincs arcuk. *Hvg.hu* [online] Available at: http://hvg.hu/itthon/20140315_A_rendoroknek_matol_nincs_arcuk [Accessed 31 Dec. 2016].

Hvg.hu (2014b). Bolti lopáson érték a romagyilkosságokat tárgyaló bírónőt. *Hvg.hu* [online] Available at: http://hvg.hu/itthon/20140711_Bolti_lopason_ertek_a_romagyilkossagokat [Accessed 31 Dec. 2016].

Hvg.hu (2014c). Elengedték főnökük fiát a rendőrök, mégis rosszul jártak. *Hvg.hu* [online] Available at: http://hvg.hu/itthon/20140730_rendorseg_eljaras_bantalmazas_felmentes [Accessed 31 Dec. 2016].

Index.hu (2010). Kende megint vesztett Németh Miklós ellen. *Index.hu* [online] Available at: http://index.hu/belfold/2010/09/28/kende_megint_vesztett_nemeth_miklos_ellen [Accessed 31 Dec. 2016].

Index.hu (2011a). Ólomszennyezett arcpakolást talált a fogyasztóvédelők. *Index.hu* [online] Available at: http://index.hu/gazdasag/magyar/2011/07/21/olomszennyezett_arcpakolast_talalt_a_fogyasztovedelok/ [Accessed 31 Dec. 2016].

Index.hu (2011b). Az ügyészségen már olvasták Budai beadványát Juhász Ferencről (At the prosecutor's office, they've already read Budai's statement on Ferenc Juhász). *Index.hu* [online] Available at: http://index.hu/belfold/2011/02/21/az_ugyeszsegen_olvassak_budai_bedvanyat_juhasz_ferencrol/ [Accessed 31 Dec. 2016].

Index.hu (2012). Ki kell takarni a rendőrök arcát. Index.hu [online] Available at: http://index.hu/belfold/2012/11/26/ki_kell_takarni_a_rendorok_arcat/ [Accessed 31 Dec. 2016].

Index.hu (2013a). Halál a magyarokra! – fordulat a verekedő romák tárgyalásán. *Index.hu* [online] Available at: http://index.hu/belfold/2013/06/04/halal_a_magyarokra_fordulat_a_verekedo_romak_targyalasan/ [Accessed 31 Dec. 2016].

Index.hu (2013b). Másfélszeres büntetés a sajóbábonyi romáknak. *Index.hu* [online] Available at: http://index.hu/belfold/2013/09/30/sajobabony_masodfok/ [Accessed 31 Dec. 2016].

Index.hu (2014a). Ők lehetnek az új AB-tagok. Index.hu [online] Available at: http://index.hu/belfold/2014/09/15/zart_ulesen_targyalnak_a_leendo_ab-tagokrol/ [Accessed 31 Dec. 2016].

Index.hu (2014b). Kispesti önkormányzat: mégsem sértettek törvény Gajda-féle füzetcsomagok. *Index.hu* [online] Available at: http://index.hu/belfold/2014/09/25/kispesti_onkormanyzat_megsem_sertettek_torveny_gajda-fele_fuzetcsomagok/ [Accessed 31 Dec. 2016].

Index.hu (2014c). Nem szélsőjobbozható a tévében a Jobbik. *Index.hu* [online] Available at: http://index.hu/kultur/2014/06/03/nem_szelsojobbozhato_a_teveben_a_jobbik/ [Accessed 31 Dec. 2016].

Index.hu (2014d). A bíróság szerint is vicces, ha egy rendőrnek dinoszaurusz feje van (The court agrees: putting a dinosaur's head on a police officer's image is funny). *Index.hu* [online] Available at: http://index.hu/kultur/media/2014/07/04/elso_fokon_nyertunk_lehet_trollarca_a_rendoroknek [Accessed 31 Dec. 2016].

Index.hu (2015). Végre kiderül, van-e Habonynak szolgálati útlevele, vagy sem. *Index.hu* [online] Available at: http://index.hu/belfold/2015/03/24/vegre_kiderul_van-e_habonynak_szolgalati_utlevele_vagy_sem/ [Accessed 31 Dec. 2016].

Ivány, B. and Pap, A. (2012). Rendőri etnikai profilalkotás az Egyenlő Bánásmód Hatóság előtt. *Fundamentum*, 16(3), pp. 103–111.

Jones, A. and Singer, L. (2008). *Statistics on race and the criminal justice system – 2006/7.* London: Ministry of Justice.

Jones, J. (2012). Human dignity in the EU Charter of Fundamental Rights and its interpretation before the European Court of Justice. *Liverpool Law Review*, 33(3), pp. 281–300.

Kádár, A., Körner, J., Moldova, Z. and Tóth, B. (2008). *Control(led) Group. Final report on the strategies for effective police Stop and Search (STEPSS) Project.* 1st ed. Budapest: HHC (Hungarian Helsinki Committee).

Kádár, A. and Pap, A. (2009). Police ethnic profiling in Hungary – an empirical research. *Acta Iuridica Hungarica*, 50(3), pp. 253–267.

Kádár, A., Pap, A. and Tóth, B. (2009). Police ethnic profiling in Hungary. *European Police Science and Research Bulletin*, 1(1), pp. 4–6.

Kovács, K. (2011). A befejezett mondat. *Szuverén.* [online] Available at: http://www.szuveren.hu/archiv/jog/a-befejezett-mondat [Accessed 31 Dec. 2016].

Kulcsár, Z. (2011). Jóri zöld utat adott a Google Street View-nak. *Dr. Kulcsár Zoltán adatvédelmi szakértő blogja.* Available at: http://www.adatvedelmiszakerto.hu/2011/07/jori-zold-utat-adott-a-google-street-view-nak/ [Accessed 31 Dec. 2016].

Küpper, H. (2012). Paternalista kollektivizmus és liberális individualizmus között: az új magyar Alaptörvényben rögzített emberkép normatív alapjai. *Közjogi Szemle* 5(3). pp. 8–11.

Lencsés, K. (2011). A megsértett Polt Péter. *Nol.hu.* [online] Available at: http://nol.hu/belfold/20130626-a_megsertett_polt_peter-1396217 [Accessed 31 Dec. 2016].

Lenkovics, B (2014), Constitutional court decision (7/2014) dissent, Az Alkotmány-Bíróság Határozatai, 2014. 7.

Magyari, P. (2014). Utána minden állat szomorú. *444.hu.* [online] Available at: http://444.hu/2014/07/09/koitusz-utan-minden-allat-szomoru/ [Accessed 31 Dec. 2016].

Magyarnarancs.hu (2010). Rasszizmusért elítélt miskolci romák – Az önmaga ellen fordult törvény. *Magyarnarancs.hu* [online] Available at: http://magyarnarancs.hu/belpol/rasszizmusert_elitelt_miskolci_romak_-_az_onmaga_ellen_fordult_torveny-75090 [Accessed 31 Dec. 2016].

Mahlmann, M. (2012). Human dignity and autonomy in modern constitutional orders. In: M. Rosenfeld and A. Sajó, ed., *The Oxford Handbook of Comparative Constitutional Law*, 1st ed. Oxford: Oxford University Press.

Majtényi, B. and Pap, A.L. (2009). Should ethnic data be standardized? Different situations of processing ethnic data. In: M. Szabó, ed., *Privacy protection and minority rights*, 1st ed. Budapest: Eötvös Károly Policy Institute, pp. 63–88.

Majtényi, L., Székely, I. and Szabó, M. (2006). Roma támogatások és jogosultságok egyéni követésének lehetőségei. [online] Ekint.org. Available at: http://www.ekint.org/az-allam-atlathatosaga-informacioszabadsag/2007–01–17/roma-tamogatasok-es-jogosultsagok-egyeni-kovetesenek-lehetosegei [Accessed 31 Dec. 2016].

McCrudden, C. (2008). Human dignity and judicial interpretation of human rights. *The European Journal of International Law*, 19(4), pp. 655–724.

Ministry of Public Administration and Justice, State Secretariat for Social Inclusion (2011). National Social Inclusion Strategy – Extreme Poverty, Child Poverty, the Roma – 2011–2020. Budapest. [online] Available at: http://romagov.kormany.hu/download/5/58/20000/Strategy%20-%20HU%20-%20EN.PDF [Accessed 31 Dec. 2016].

Miskolc Regional Court Decision 3.Bf.2023/2012/51.

NEKI (Legal Defence Bureau for National and Ethnic Minorities) (1999). *White booklet: The annual report of the Legal defence Bureau for National and Ethnic Minorities (NEKI)*. 1st ed. Budapest: Másság Alapítvány.

Népszava (2013a). Jó hírét félti a legfőbb ügyész. *Népszava* [online] Available at: http://nepszava.hu/cikk/657767-jo-hiret-felti-a-legfobb-ugyesz [Accessed 31 Dec. 2016].

Népszava (2013b). RTL Klub: egy budai kórház vezetője lehet az óbudai savas támadó (RTL Klub). *Népszava* [online] Available at: http://nepszava.hu/articles/article.php?id=631427 [Accessed 31 Dec. 2016].

Oakley, R. (2005). Policing racist crime and violence: a comparative analysis. European monitoring Centre on Racism and Xenophobia. [online] Available at: http://fra.europa.eu/sites/default/files/fra_uploads/542-PRCV_en.pdf [Accessed 31 Dec. 2016].

Office of the Data Protection Commissioner (2010). Információszabadság napja 2010 "Adatvédelem kontra adatnyilvánosság – új egyensúly?" (Freedom of Information Day 2010, Data protection v. freedom of information – a new balance?). [online] Available at: http://abi.atlatszo.hu/index.php?menu=0/sajtokozlemenyek&dok=20100907_abi_1 [Accessed 31 Dec. 2016].

Origo.hu (2016). Zárolta az adatvédelmi hatóság a Kiss-ítéletet. *Origo.hu* [online] Available at: http://www.origo.hu/itthon/20160411-kiss-laszlo-itelet-peterfalvi-attila-naih.html [Accessed 31 Dec. 2016].

OSCE/ODIHR (Organization for Security and Co-operation in Europe) (2009). Decision No. 9/09 on combating hate crimes. MC(17) Journal No. 2, Agenda item 8. [online] Available at: http://www.osce.org/cio/40695?download=true [Accessed 31 Dec. 2016].

OSCE/ODIHR (Organization for Security and Co-operation in Europe, Office for Democratic Institutions and Human Rights) (2010). Addressing Violence, Promoting Integration – Field Assessment of Violent Incidents against Roma in Hungary: Key Developments, Findings and Recommendations. [online] Available at: http://www.osce.org/odihr/68545 [Accessed 31 Dec. 2016].

Pap, A.L. (2007). Police ethnic profiling in Hungary – Lessons from an international research. *Regio - A Review of Studies on Minorities, Politics, Society*, 7(1), pp. 117–140.

Pap, A.L. (2008). Human Rights and Ethnic Data Collection in Hungary. *Human Rights Review*, 9(1), pp. 109–122.

Pap, A.L. (2011). Ethnic profiling and discrimination: The international context and Hungarian empirical research findings. *Acta Iuridica Hungarica*, 52(4), pp. 273–295.

Pap, A.L. (2012). A Legfelsőbb Bíróság ítélete az Egyenlő Bánásmód Hatóság határozatának hatályon kívül helyezéséről. Zaklatásnak minősülhet-e egy polgármester rasszista megnyilatkozása? Legf. Bír. kfv. II. 37 551/2010/5. *Jogesetek Magyarázata*, 3(1), pp. 91–100.

Póczik, Sz. (1997) Cigányság, bűnözés, bűnüldözés: nyitott kérdések, adatok és tapasztalatok. *Belügyi Szemle*, 6, pp. 5–11.

Recommendation of the European Parliament and of the Council of 20 December 2006 on the protection of minors and human dignity and on the right of reply in relation to the competitiveness of the European audiovisual and on-line information services industry (2006/952/EC) (2006). *Official Journal of the European Union*, L378 pp. 72–77.

Sajó, A. (2011). *Constitutional Sentiments*. 1st ed. New Haven: Yale University Press.

Supreme Court (Kúria) decision (2011). Kfv. III.39.302/2010/8 of 18 October 2011.

Supreme Court (Kúria) uniformity decision 2015 B.3 (3/2015 "büntető elvi döntés").

Supreme Court (Kúria) uniformity decision 1/2012 BKMPJE.
Supreme Court decision (Kúria) (2011) Bfv.III.87/2011/5.
Supreme Court decision (Kúria) (2011) Bfv.III.87/2011/5
Supreme Court (Kúria) decision (2011) LB-H-BJ-2011–106.
Supreme Court decision (Kúria) (2012) Bfv. II. 590/2012/18.
Szigeti, T. (2013). A feje tetejére állított szólásszabadság. *Szuverén*. [online] Available at: http://www.szuveren.hu/jog/a-feje-tetejere-allitott-szolasszabadsag [Accessed 31 Dec. 2016].
TÁRKI (2006). Továbbra is erős roma-ellenes előítéletek. [online] Available at: http://www.tarki.hu/kozvelemeny/kitekint/20060201.html [Accessed 31 Dec. 2016].
The Daily News Hungary (2016). Parliament restricts public access to Hungarian Post Data. *The Daily News Hungary* [online] Available at: http://dailynewshungary.com/parliament-restricts-public-access-to-hungarian-post-data/ [Accessed 31 Dec. 2016].
The Guardian (2016). Hungary's swimming association backs coach Laszlo Kiss despite 1961 rape case. *The Guardian* [online] Available at: https://www.theguardian.com/sport/2016/apr/07/hungary-swimming-backs-coach-laszlo-kiss-despite-rape-case [Accessed 31 Dec. 2016].
Uitz, R. (2000). Does the past restrain judicial review? (reference to history and traditions in constitutional reasoning). *Acta Juridica Hungarica*, 41(1–2), pp. 47–78.
U.S. News (2016). Hungarian lawmakers have approved legal amendments restricting access to public information about the state-owned postal services and the National Bank of Hungary. *U.S. News* [online] Available at: http://www.usnews.com/news/world/articles/2016-03-01/hungary-limits-access-to-data-from-post-office-central-bank [Accessed 31 Dec. 2016].
Washington, E. (2007). Are hate crime statutes constitutional? *World Net Daily*. [online] Available at: http://www.wnd.com/2007/06/42002/ [Accessed 31 Dec. 2016].

7 Closing remarks

This book was written to document and narrate an illiberal U-turn by a once-promising new European democracy. It is a story worth telling because stories and histories tend to reappear and resurface elsewhere. Some features in this documentary may be specific to Hungary; others may point to commonalities with other states and societies. There may even be politicians and theorists who advocate exporting or transposing the Hungarian model.

Both the scope and perspective of this documentary are limited. The full picture, if conceivable at all, is necessarily more complex, nuanced and complicated. All this volume offers is a snapshot and a subjective analysis, where subjectivism also includes the areas and issues chosen for scrutiny.

***

I have made the following arguments about the development of the Hungarian illiberal democracy:

First, illiberalism is present both in "how" and "what" is being done. Criticism thus concerns the style, format and procedure of legislation and policy making as much as their substance.

Second, illiberalism (in particular the Orbán regime) is most often equated with the democratic backlash that surfaces first and foremost in the dismantling of institutional rule-of-law guarantees and weakening the system of checks and balances. This is certainly an important element, but there is more to be considered. While it needs to be stated that the systematic abuse of fundamental rights and individual freedoms has not been part of the picture, illiberalism manifests in how the new constitution fails to recognize individual autonomy as a constitutional principle and how ideological commitments and constitutionally enshrined value preferences may authorize future legislation that may restrict autonomy and freedom in all sorts of ways.

Third, I tried to show that not only was the Orbán regime's new social contract and construct unsolicited and not put up transparently for democratic pre-approval, their constitutionally framed and cemented value preferences and encroachments on intimate citizenship do not seem to be supported by Hungarians' values and lifestyle choices. Even if that is one of the important features and paradoxes (one this book could not unfold or even discuss) of the Hungarian case, the fact that Orbán was reelected in 2014 by a convincing majority, which certainly provides a political ex post (and pro futuro) legitimization of the constitutional order. (Not that a popular support for illiberal and oppressive political commitments would make them automatically legitimate: this is the very argument that makes populist illiberal democracy problematic for liberal democracies and liberal democrats.)

Fourth, even though I showed that illiberal traditions and practices have been continuous in several areas, and in many cases it was simply that law enforcement and judicial reflexes became constitutionally and legally cemented by the new regime, I emphasized that it would be a simplification to view post-2010 developments as entirely path dependent. It is sufficient to say that illiberal traditions have been used to build and solidify the new regime.

Fifth, I argued that in most of the scrutinized areas, the marginalized, abandoned, sole ethnic minority, the Roma, will continue to be the losers in the scheme.

The book does not offer an answer to the lingering question of how and why this happened to and in Hungary. A possible reply would be that Hungary's relative good fortune – moderate economic and political freedom in the last years of communism and a peaceful negotiated transition – caused its bad fate. As Kis (2012) and Tölgyessy (Lambert 2015) point out, The 1989 constitution, and maybe constitutionalism and liberal democracy, was perceived as an elite project, bringing legalism – not justice, wealth and prosperity for former communist elites or economic miracles for the ordinary people. The constitutional partnership, designed by the 1989 constitution and required a broad consensus to pass, was unfit to withstand the deliberate and lethal combat by a super-charismatic leader. This leader successfully built on the dark side of Hungarians' values and orientation: populism, pessimism and conspiracy theories that blame all of the nation's problems on hostile cooperation of foreign interests and a general disenchantment from democracy and the free market. Thus, Orbán came up with a new promise to complete the political transition in the "right way" and lead to victory.

Bibliography

Kis, J. (2012). Introduction: From the 1989 Constitution to the 2011 Fundamental Law. In: G. Tóth, ed., *Constitution for a disunited nation: On Hungary's 2011 Fundamental Law*, 1st ed. Budapest: Central European University Press, pp. 1–22.

Lambert, G. (2015). Azután egyszer csak beütött a mennykő – interjú Tölgyessy Péterrel. *Figyelő Online*. [online] Available at: http://figyelo.hu/cikkek/427454-azutan-egyszer-csak-beutott-a-mennyko---interju-tolgyessy-peterrel [Accessed 31 Dec. 2016].

Index

For Product Safety Concerns and Information please contact our EU
representative GPSR@taylorandfrancis.com
Taylor & Francis Verlag GmbH, Kaufingerstraße 24, 80331 München, Germany

www.ingramcontent.com/pod-product-compliance
Ingram Content Group UK Ltd.
Pitfield, Milton Keynes, MK11 3LW, UK
UKHW011016180926
475701UK00004B/775

* 9 7 8 0 3 6 7 3 1 2 9 7 8 *